Carol —
May all your legacy
be blessings.
— Rachael Freed
2/14

Advance Praise for
Your Legacy Matters

Rachael's Legacy work inspires me as a professional fundraiser and in the most important roles in my life, Father and Son. I urge all my peers in the 'sandwich generation' to read *Your Legacy Matters*. Then write two legacy letters as bookends for your lives. Gift a legacy letter to your children and grandchildren whose lives you seek to influence with your love and life's lessons. Then write a legacy letter to your aging parents whose lives you seek to honor for the legacies they've passed on to you....

—Bill Marsella, Director of Partner Relations
Catholic Community Foundation, St. Paul, Minnesota

Your Legacy Matters. It really matters! In 25 years of facilitating writing groups for people living with and dying from cancer, I have used Rachael's work almost exclusively. Here she has created a broad path for readers to address their universal needs to be: known, remembered, have our lives make a difference, pass on our wisdom and blessings to those we love, and celebrate life. Sit in a comfortable chair to read this book and begin writing your legacy.

—Claire Willis
Lasting Words: A Guide to Finding Meaning Toward the Close of Life

Your Legacy Matters gives us invaluable gifts. The stories woven throughout present rich insights into the meaning of life and what is most important. With a unique sensitivity the book introduces one of life's momentous realities–our mortality. The step-by-step instructions for fashioning an ethical will communicate exactly what readers need to accomplish this transformative experience.

—Larry Raphael, Senior Rabbi at Sherith Israel, San Francisco
former Director of Adult Jewish Growth, Union for Reform Judaism

There are many books about memoir and legacy writing, but few that reach so deeply. This book does more than offer techniques and exercises; it attends to the soul. Sharing her own life and values as she encourages the reader to do the same, Rachael Freed leads us toward the goal of all legacy work—the sharing of blessing and wisdom.

—**Daniel Taylor,** author, *Letters to My Children: A Father Passes on His Values* and *Creating a Spiritual Legacy: How to Share Your Stories, Values, and Wisdom*

Your Legacy Matters goes far beyond a simple guide; it inspires readers to acknowledge the power of our life experience and supports finding ways to share that treasure with those we love.

—**Toni A.H. McNaron,** Professor Emerita of English, University of Minnesota author, *I Dwell in Possibility* and *Poisoned Ivy*

A profoundly relevant book on the fundamental power of an ethical will – and how it drives lasting legacy for every person, every time.

—**Richard Leider,** author
The Power of Purpose and *Repacking Your Bags*

Through her legacy work: teaching, speaking, and writing, Rachael Freed has become an experienced guide. *Your Legacy Matters* offers wisdom for people to recognize they have a legacy worth leaving to the next generation. The letters that we write and the blessings that we offer become the treasures of another generation.

—**Brian McCaffrey**, Chaplain and Pastor, LutheranCare, Upstate NY, and Chair of the Northeast Forum on Spirituality and Aging

Your Legacy Matters

Harvesting the Love and Lessons of Your Life
A Multi-Generational Guide for Writing Your Ethical Will

Contact MinervaPress Special Markets, for information about quantity discounts for educational and fundraising purposes by organizations and institutions.

Library of Congress Control Number: 2013911329

ISBN 978-0981745053

10 9 8 7 6 5 4 3

Printed and bound by Lightning Source in the United States of America

Book and Cover Design: Christopher Kirsh

Cover Art by David Friedman, Zefat, Israel, www.kosmic-kabbalah.com

Published by MinervaPress
612-558-3331
minervapress1@gmail.com
Minneapolis, Minnesota, USA

With my gratitude, this book is dedicated

to those who have been my life teachers and mentors,

and to legacy writers throughout the world

May we continue to honor our covenant

with past and future generations

by sharing our love and our values

through our legacy writing

Acknowledgments

This book is a testament to the power of legacy writing and to the many people who trusted me with their writing process, their words, and their souls. Not all of them are represented in print here. But each and every person who picked up a pen or sat at a computer fulfilling their covenant with past and future generations have participated in a community that made and continues to make a difference in their own lives and the lives of those who will come after them. Thank you to the literally hundreds, perhaps even thousands, of legacy writers throughout the English speaking world.

I am further indebted to each generous legacy writer who allowed me to strengthen and beautify this book with their legacy blessings, thoughts, and letters: Anonymous and Martha G. Albrecht, Marianne Altschul, Ann Andrews, Carol Berger, Nancy Blanchard, George Brown, Maggie Butler, Lenny Champer, Anne Elizabeth Denny, Mike Donohue, Diane Forman, Tamar Ghidalia, Agathe Maier Glaser, Rabbi Simeon Glaser, Susan Hadlock, Janis Hall, Linda Hallen, Gracia Hegener, Carol Hill, Cammy Iverson, Sara Jaehne, Brian Juul, Tamara Kaiser, Leanne Kerchner, Rita Lafferty, Steve Levie, Bill Marsella, Evelyn Nelson, Deborah Riley, Sue Schoenbaum, Michelle Johnson Schroeder, Beth Somerville, Barbara Thompson, Susan Eastman Tilsch, Joanne Turnbull, Virginia B. Wenstrom, Claire Willis, Kathy Woods-Dobbins, Judy Young. If I have forgotten to include any of your names, I am sincerely sorry.

Thank you to those who have generously given their permission to use their copyrighted materials: Staff letter by Ben Bache-Wiig, MD, President, Abbott Northwestern Hospital, Minneapolis, ©2012; Excerpt of Message to Community Leaders of Minnesota nonprofit and community serving organizations, Ronnie Brooks, founding director of the James O. Shannon Leadership Institute, and senior staff member of the Amherst H. Wilder Foundation, St. Paul, ©2011; Excerpt from "The Death of Jacob" ©1986 Ruth Brin; Quotation from TED talk, by Candy Chang, TED Senior Fellow, artist and urban planner, creator of the urban project, "Before I Die," ©2012; Extensive quotations from *A Chorus of Stones*, Susan Griffin ©1993; "Just Old Stuff" by Diane Forman, ©2007; Excerpt from "Grace Cathedral," after walking the labyrinth, San Francisco ©Eve Hearst; "At the Crack of Dawn," Carol Hill ©2007; Letter about her grandfather, workshop for volunteer survivors at the Holocaust Museum, Washington, DC, Theodora Klayman ©2010; Primary Health Care Association retreat letters ©2008; Letter, Pastor Rebecca Mentzer, Prince of Peace Lutheran Church, Depew, NY, ©2009; Letter, Evelyn Nelson ©2013; *NY Times* interview with Lars Tornstam, "Aging's Misunderstood Virtues," Paula Span ©2010; Concepts from Mary C. Ruhr's Master's Thesis, "Objects as Emblems of Identity in Later Life," Oregon ©2009; "Post Humus" from *Ask the Dreamer Where Night Begins*, Patti L. Tana ©1986; Executive Director's Year End Reflections, Sitka Center for Art and Ecology, Oregon, Eric Chris Vines, ©2010 .

I am forever grateful to those who read my ever-changing drafts, whose editorial skills clarified and deepened the ideas, and made the book more accessible to readers: Brian McCaffrey, Joanne Turnbull, and Claire Willis. Thank you also to those who read the final draft and who wrote praise about the book.

I am honored that the book's cover is graced by David Friedman's art. I appreciate Christopher Kirsh, my cover and interior book designer, for his patience and unflappability. Special thanks to my children, Sid and Debbie—both artists—who took time from their busy lives to lend this project their smart and sophisticated eyes to help me make artistic decisions.

Contents

Forword

by the founding partners of *Your Write Mind*

Forword #1: Maggie Butler, MSW

Truth be told, I met the idea of Rachael Freed's legacy writing with resistance when my writing and business partner suggested we not only write them, but get certified to teach others to write them, as well. I was adopted; ancestors and legacies had nothing to do with me. After our first three-hour training session with Rachael, I knew my skepticism was unfounded.

I found out I didn't need to have an acknowledged or well documented past to qualify for the heart and soul of Rachael Freed's legacy work: to pass on love and wisdom to the next generation. My legacy to my children, their children, and their children's children would be to end the legacy of not knowing.

I am adopted, and for almost sixty years of my life knew almost nothing about my birth family. I am quite certainly a family secret in both of my birth parents' families. I had no history there and they had no future with me. In my adopted family I had grandparents, aunts, uncles, and cousins, who all felt like family, but those who came before them could never feel like 'mine'. Their relatives were not my history, not my ancestors; I had no place in their lives. Because most of that family has now passed on, my only sense of family comes from my daughters and granddaughter.

Legacy writing has gifted, indeed blessed me, in many ways, beginning with the importance of names. When I began to look at both my birth and adopted names within the context of legacy writing, a curious thing happened: I began to feel a sense of connection to both mothers that I'd never experienced before. It became important to me that my birth mother named me after a close family friend with whom we stayed until she placed me in an orphanage four months after my birth in Ireland.

Although I'd always known my adopted mother named me after a saint to whom she'd made several novenas hoping to receive a baby girl (my parents had already adopted a boy), I began to get a sense of this young Irish Catholic woman from South Boston who believed and trusted deep in her heart that a saint could ensure what an orphanage couldn't guarantee: a baby girl.

In writing my first legacy letter, I realized how both my names were, each in their own way, acts of gratitude, revealing the hopes and dreams of one, and heartbreak for the other. My names were a blessing to me about the importance of a close, supportive friend, and looking to God for what seems impossible (even if it's through a saint who was known to have God's ear.)

Initially, the thought of doing legacy work seemed like yet another place I didn't belong. How wrong I was. One of the goals of legacy writing is to deepen our sense of connection and belonging to our world. After committing to my own legacy writing, and now leading others on their legacy journeys, I am finding my sense of place in this world.

Throughout *Your Legacy Matters*, I hear Rachael's voice through the wonderful conversational style she uses in this gem of a book. Her compassion, humor, wisdom, experience, and sincere wish to bring more blessings into this world are all contained within these pages. I believe this book, this process, has a gift for you. May you be open to what comes, thankful for what you learn, generous with your gifts, and leave a path of love and wisdom to those who follow.

Forword #2: Joanne Turnbull, PhD

Several years ago, I served on a search committee for our new rabbi, and my task was to contact an adult learner in the Minneapolis synagogue where he was currently serving. That adult learner was Rachael Freed.

After we shared credentials (clinical social work) and at least two passions (writing and family therapy), Rachael assured me that our rabbinic candidate was indeed a winner. She supported her assertion with a story about how our soon-to-be hired rabbi had participated in one of her Life Legacy classes. That was my introduction to Life Legacy—harvesting our wisdom in order to bequeath a spiritual legacy.

I gave Rachael's book—*Women's Lives, Women's Legacies*—to Maggie Butler. Maggie is my friend and partner in *Your Write Mind*, an endeavor that creates safe spaces to enable anyone to discover their unique writing voice. After Maggie's immediate, enthusiastic response ("This is good stuff!"), we began to think about ways to integrate Life Legacies into our work in *Your Write Mind*.

The events that followed—an award that enabled us to develop legacy-writing groups, a flurry of meetings with community leaders, and most important, consultation and training with Rachael—seem a whirlwind. Maggie and I are now certified Life Legacy Facilitators and are working with several legacy-writing groups. Soon we will offer these groups to hospices, prisons, veterans' groups, and the medical community.

None of this would have been possible without the wisdom and generosity of Rachael Freed. And it is wisdom and generosity that shines in Rachael's newest book, *Your Legacy Matters: Harvesting the Love and Lessons of Your Life*. The book is a *mitzvah*.

Mitzvah is a Hebrew term that can mean several things: commandment, blessing, and good deed. *Your Legacy Matters* meets the criteria for all three. As commandments go, *Your Legacy Matters* provides a guide that celebrates parents and ancestors by preserving their stories for future generations. The book also honors the ancient tradition of the ethical will, a set of instructions usually passed from father to son. But Rachael has made an even greater contribution with this book, by transforming the patriarchal document into a contemporary practice that is accessible and relevant for everyone—men and women, irrespective of life stage and circumstance, whether secular or religious. It is this transformation that meets the other criteria of mitzvah; *Your Legacy Matters* is both a good deed and blessing.

One only has to observe a family in a restaurant—interacting with their mobile devices instead of each other—to realize how desperately we in the information age need connection. And meaningful human connection is the essence of *Your Legacy Matters*. The book, written in an engaging, conversational style, is a roadmap loaded with information on how to share not only wisdom, but more importantly, love with those who come after us.

Learning to bless those we love is a spiritual act, and *Your Legacy Matters* is, above all, a spiritual book. Esau's ancient cry to Isaac— "Father, have you no blessing for me?—resounds in our ears today. We all need to be blessed. Blessing others (and in doing so being blessed ourselves) is a universal need. Legacy writing fulfills that need.

On the day, Maggie and I began our first Legacy Groups, Rachael advised us to keep our sense of humor. "And remember," she said, "You are messengers of the Divine."

Her statement made me smile, but at the same time it bothered me. Messenger, malach in Hebrew, is a word that can also be translated as angel. Maggie and I may or may not be messengers, but angel is a term that is reserved for Rachael Freed. It is an honor to be part of her work.

Introduction

Olive Trees

In the newspaper comic "Sally Forth" created by Greg Howard we see Sally planting a tree. One of the kids says, " Mom, Dad says this tree won't be mature for 100 years."

"That's right, it's a very slow-growing tree," responds Sally. "We'll get some enjoyment out of it, but we're not just planting it for ourselves. We're planting it for the neighborhood, for the people in the future who will be here to enjoy it."

A neighbor girl asks, "How do you know there will even be a future, Mrs. Forth?"

Sally responds, "For one thing, because we're planting one."

As the girl walks away, she says, "I'm not sure that made sense, but somehow, I feel better."

> **"A society grows great when old men plant trees whose shade they know they shall never sit in." — Greek Proverb**

A similar idea is expressed in the story of Honi and the carob tree written in the Talmud almost 2,000 years ago. When I wrote *Women's Lives, Women's Legacies* I changed that story from Honi to an old woman and the carob tree to an olive. My story goes like this: "An old woman planting an olive tree was asked if she expected to benefit from its fruit or its shade. She responded that she wasn't planting for herself, but for her children and grandchildren. As my ancestors blessed me, so I bless the future by planting for the generations to come."

To me that's legacy in a nutshell: passing our blessings and love to *and values* future generations, acting in our own lives for those who'll come after and making a difference in our world.

> **"Spend your brief moment according to nature's law, and serenely greet the journey's end as an olive falls when it is ripe, blessing the branch that bore it, and giving thanks to the tree that gave it life."** — Marcus Aurelius

As moved as I am about legacy, I am also passionate about olive trees. They seem the living proof that generations are connected; imagine what a thousand year old olive tree has witnessed in its lifetime! I used the olive tree story and my logo (an olive tree with a pen as its trunk) on my bookmarks.

In 2010, just a month before the revolution, I revisited Tunisia where I'd lived for two years while serving in the Peace Corps in the mid 1960s. We reconnected with friends and students from more than forty-five years ago. Our relationships were as alive as if we'd seen each other every day, week, month, and year since 1968. We visited the oldest synagogue in Tunisia on the island of Djerba (Homer's Island of the Lotus Eaters in the *Odyssey*.) In its courtyard stands a very old and beautiful olive tree. When I had the opportunity to revise *Women's Lives, Women's Legacies* in 2012, I changed the old though beautiful cover–olive trees and poppies–to the photograph of this magnificent ancient Tunisian olive. It felt very special, honoring Tunisia and her olives, giving the tree new life in a different form on the cover of a book about linking past and future generations.

In the spring of 2013 I visited Israel. Our group studied Kabbalah with David Friedman, artist, printmaker, and kabbalist in Zefat, considered one of the most mystical places in the world. After his lecture (he taught using his artwork) we went into his studio to purchase prints. I didn't think I wanted kabbalistic works on my walls. But never wanting to miss a chance to shop, I meandered through the studio. I found a gorgeous print of an olive tree. No question that I would buy it; it hangs today, its canvas stretched proudly, in my home.

When I got to the place in *Your Legacy Matters* that I could think about a cover, I knew exactly what I wanted...that Israeli olive tree. I emailed David. He gave me permission and only asked that I acknowledge him and share his website (www.kosmic-kabbalah.com). I didn't know he had a website, but I looked it up, and searched immediately for his olive tree. There it was – almost as awesome as mine. Next to it he told a story that I share with you here. It speaks indirectly of legacy, of venerating the ancient and the value of planting for the future. You may gasp or weep as I did as you read:

"The ancient tree in this picture is at least one thousand years old. Its diameter is almost two meters wide. The insides of olive trees get hollow as they grow older, and their trunks twist in a spiral around their hollow core. I remember taking my wife and kids there when they were younger and all of us could fit inside the hollow core of this beautiful and ancient tree.

Several years ago I walked down to the small grove that contains this tree (and four or five others ...) and discovered to my horror that someone had taken a chainsaw to these ancient trees. They had been cut down almost to the ground. I cried and couldn't believe that someone would do that (it is definitely illegal). But I was glad that at least I had a photograph that showed the amazing form of this tree and was able to make this picture from it.

One of the most important symbols of Kabbalah is the Tree of Life. Life takes many forms, but Life itself is bigger than all the forms it takes. Even though it took this ancient tree at least a thousand years to obtain its form ... that form exists no more, but amazingly, the tree is still alive! It is now developing a new form, different than the twisted and old shape it had before, but it is still alive.

To me this is a beautiful metaphor for Life in general, and for the Jewish People in particular. We are an ancient People who have set down roots in various lands. We prospered in Spain until we were cut down and expelled in 1492. But we survived and eventually developed new contributions to Judaism in Zefat in the 16th Century, such as ... Lurianic Kabbalah.

We set down roots in Eastern Europe until we were viciously and cruelly cut down by the Nazis. But, amazingly, the Jewish People survives and are now making new contributions to Judaism and the world here in this new/old phenomenon - a Jewish State in our ancestral homeland, Israel."

"...the [olive] trees, the gnarly strength of them. The way they could be blasted by lightning or charred by a brushfire, and look quite dead then send forth a new green shoot out of the old wood and keep living, in spite of everything."
— Geraldine Brooks

"For there is hope of a tree if it be cut down, that it will sprout again, And that the tender branch thereof will not cease."
— Job 14:7

Welcome to All Generations

Welcome to each of you: the young and the aging, parents and empty nesters, men and women, who are planning to read this book for guidance about writing your unique legacy to those you love and future generations.

Our first question is probably "What is a legacy letter?" It may not even be a letter. Imagine a great grandmother unable to attend her great grandson's high school graduation, or her great granddaughter's wedding. Writing a blessing of congratulations and love on a card is a legacy that will be treasured for a lifetime.

A legacy letter may be one page long, expressing one idea - either hand-written or typed – that can be accomplished in fifteen minutes. Or a legacy document may be a collection of one page letters. Or it may be a lengthy document, including photos and other mementos . . . .

So if a legacy letter can be just one page, why do we need such a big book? Because we'll get less resistant to writing, learn that we have worthwhile things to express, and become heartfelt competent writers step by step as we work through the book.

We'll learn to write blessings, even the most secular of us. We'll explore legacies received from generations past to actively participate as the link that binds the generations before and after us. We'll examine who we are and what is dearest to us in our own lives. When we harvest our ancestors' values and can articulate our own, we can pass forward what really matters to the next generations.

Understanding that our families need clarity, we can write legacy letters to accompany our legal wills and our advance health directives. We can also use these letters to initiate important family conversations about our aging and dying.

But perhaps most significant is that *Your Legacy Matters* is a guide for exploring, reflecting, and writing about our lives to celebrate Life itself, and to pass forward our appreciation and awe to the generations who will follow us.

Welcome to Legacy Writers in the Final Third of Life

A special welcome to those in the final third of life: (of course that may be any of us at any age!). We are pioneers; no previous generation has been graced to live as long as we. There's a scarcity of models to show us the way. For many, this time in our lives requires adjustments and coping with losses. We may face encroaching limitations requiring us to relinquish our fierce independence. We will need to learn to ask for and accept help. Yet all of us continue to desire to live fully, with dignity, with passion and purpose.

Experts tell us that what makes people happiest as we age is giving. So we ask, in a culture that venerates youth, what have we to give at this time of our lives? The answer is bound up with legacy, where we express our love and our hard-earned wisdom. Sometimes that wisdom has been tempered by fire, but always by time. The time we've been gifted permits us to reflect on our life lessons and to translate our learning from the raw experiences of our lives.

Some assert that we have an obligation to pass on that love and wisdom; that it is our part of the bargain of aging. That we can't just sit back and accept the care we're offered even though we're entitled to it. We must give back and what we're obligated to give is our love and our learning.

That we grow in wisdom and pass it on is the essence of legacy writing, our covenant with the past and present, a gift to our selves as well as future generations.

> **"Why does anybody tell a story? It does indeed have something to do with faith, faith that the universe has meaning, that our little human lives are not irrelevant, that what we choose or say or do matters, matters cosmically."**
> **— Madeleine L'Engle**

More details as we go along, but for this moment, welcome with the promise that legacy writing will also offer ways to reflect about and express our spiritual values and experience at this season.

Welcome to Legacy Writers who are the Families of Elders

You may have bought this book to satisfy your yearning for a sense of connectedness and belonging to your historical past in this fast-moving and ever more impersonal world we live in. Or perhaps you just want to know who your parents really are as people before it's too late to ask. Or you may need guidance for your life and want to know about the values and passions that fueled your parents' lives. Or perhaps, you have a sense that there are family secrets you'd like unraveled, so they don't any longer injure you or your children. Hopefully your needs and desires about your parents will be fulfilled through *their* legacy writing. BUT THIS BOOK IS ALSO FOR YOU.

No matter your age, you have the opportunity and obligation to tell your story, impart your values, consider your life-lessons as your wisdom, and to share that with loved ones, present and future. Imagine that you are leaving for a vacation or a business trip and that you've not told your kids everything you want them to know – about you, about what matters most to you, about what you hope for them, that you love them beyond measure . . . . What if fate has it that you don't return? That's the urgency we all need to feel about writing legacy letters.

Legacy writing is both an act of service or stewardship and a way to address some of our own needs.

> **"There are four needs in all people: To live, to love, to learn, to leave a legacy. When these needs overlap, you find that internal motivation, the fire within. Starting with your own fire, you can create something that will burn brightly for many people and last a lifetime and you can empower others to live, to love, to learn, to leave a legacy."**
> **— Stephen R. Covey**

My observations differ from Covey's although I appreciate that he calls "leaving a legacy" a need. Our individual and universal needs that I see addressed as we write our legacy letters are six: to belong, to be known, to be remembered, to make a difference, to bless and be blessed, and to celebrate Life.

To nurture the spiritual flame that burns in all of us, whether we are secularists or people of faith is the result of our desire to know ourselves and be known at every season of our lives. Thus this book is spiritual in nature, though not religious. It includes content drawn from religious as well as many wisdom sources.

> **"To write is to plumb the unfathomable depths of being. Writing lies within the domain of mystery. The space between any two words is vaster than the distance between heaven and earth. To bridge it you must close your eyes and leap."** — **Elie Wiesel**

Because we can't predict or control the time or cause of our deaths, whether we're religious, spiritual, or secular, writing our legacy letters is an urgent matter.

> *My thoughts about September 11, 2001: The autumn day dawned beautiful and bright: blue sky, full sun, crisp air that made me glad to be alive. By noon our national tragedy was complete and the world was united in grief.*

> *How differently might the survivors have grieved had they received a message of love from the cell phones of those about to perish on the upper floors of the Twin Towers? How much solace those survivors left with nothing might have had over the long years ahead, had those who died that day left their families written words of love and caring? How comforting it might have been to hold personal words on paper in their hands and hearts to read and reread for the rest of their lives.*

Some commanders encourage their soldiers to write such letters before going into battle. Coal miners, expecting to die when a mine explosion traps them, scratch notes on scraps with thick pencil stubs, preserving words of love in buckets nailed high on the mine walls above the flooding.

Our reality, like victims of mine disasters, war, or unexpected attack, is that we don't know when or how our end may come. We may have the luxury of a serene, reflective elderly life in which to contemplate, reflect, and fulfill our obligation to write as do our elders with this book in hand today. But, maybe not. Amidst our full and busy days, we too have an obligation to ourselves and those we love: to express our love and values, our meaningful memories and stories, our blessings and wishes for those who come after us.

> "Many of us have prepared legal wills to distribute our belongings after we die. But few of us have considered leaving a spiritual/ethical will, a record of who we are, a document that can be offered to loved ones either while we are still alive or after we are gone. ... Our legacies are proof that we were here, that our lives mattered and made a difference. ..."
> — Claire Willis

The Book

Writing an ethical will can be as simple as a one page letter written in 15-30 minutes or it can be a longer document including all the topics in the book or anything in between. There is no one right way to write your legacy: only your way.... It's "your" legacy that matters.

This book can be used in the usual linear fashion: begin at the beginning and go methodically, page-by-page, front to back. Or open to the Table of Contents to choose a topic that piques your curiosity. Or open to the Index to search for the most relevant topic right now. Or crack open the book randomly and allow that page to direct your attention. These possibilities and suggestions and those throughout the book are meant to support your unique and universal needs.

However you decide to use *Your Legacy Matters* here are some general suggestions.

- Store all your writing in your Legacy File
- If you can, prepare a special place to write; make it beautiful and comfortable
- Write from your heart; edit later with your head
- Date every writing – musings, reflections, letters
- Limit your writing time
- Follow only the instructions that are right for you

I have also shared throughout the book from my experience in this legacy endeavor and some of my personal legacy writing (the 40th birthday letter to my daughter found in the appendix is shared in excerpted paragraphs throughout the book where they function to provide a particular example).

And then there's my hopeless addiction to quotations; they are sprinkled liberally throughout the book as inspiration. To me they indicate that we're not the inventors of these values, we're not the first to explore them, or express them. Rather we have the rich legacy of earlier thinkers, poets, and spiritual leaders, for whom these values and ideas mattered enough that they too wrote about them - from the early Greeks and Hebrews to American poet laureates of our own day.

And finally, perhaps the most inspiring part of the book is the letters that legacy writers who've preceded you shared. They've been more than generous. They've been courageous to permit strangers to read their heartfelt words, thoughts, and feelings. They offered not just to see their words in print (although that's fun), but to make a difference. They're part of a groundswell – a wave of legacy writers, people living in and beyond their own stories, committed to the generations who'll inherit the world we leave them.

May we be inspired by their words and know that our unique legacy will be treasured by future generations long after we're gone.

The Chapters

Each chapter introduces an aspect of life worth exploring for its legacy gems, and can be the body of a legacy letter. The chapters provide finite, simple steps to write legacy letters. Each chapter includes ideas, my personal experiences, suggestions for reflection, quotations, how to incorporate blessings, and sample letters by legacy writers.

Chapter 1, "The ABCs of Legacy Writing," is an overview explaining the basic principles of legacy writing. Included is a brief introduction to the ethical will and its ancient history, and how this document was transformed into a "legacy letter" in contemporary times. Included is a suggestion to create a personal Legacy File. There's also a list of appropriate subjects for legacy letters, so even as we begin, we can each be jotting notes about legacies we want to write about.

We get down to business in Chapter 2, about blessings. Titled "Blessings: The Heart of the Matter" we learn about the foundation of legacy writing: blessings. From ancient to contemporary times, needs haven't changed. All of us yearn to be blessed by our parents – we did when we were children and we do as grandparents. We'll learn why blessings are so important to legacy writing and write our first blessings.

The profound lesson of Chapter 3, "What's in a Name?" is about our very first legacy, our names, the legacy that binds us to and identifies us with our families and our people. Because we don't have family Bibles that trace the generations anymore, we may need to do some searching to recover the names of our ancestors. There's a template for recording names and their meanings that we can share with members of the family in generations before and after us. Looking for names of ancestors may be our first legacy conversation with family members.

"Linking Past and Future Generations," Chapter 4 and Chapter 5, "Digging Deeper: Legacies from our Immigrant Ancestors," help us seek the legacies we've received from earlier generations. Although we don't know everything about our relatives in this country, we know even less about the courageous pioneers who left their homelands to come to a totally unknown world. How exciting to use tools of memory and intuition to recover and discover the blessings (and sometimes curses) we received from those who came before us.

In chapter 6, "The Value of Work," we've gathered our legacies from the past and begin our exploration of who we are, our identities in the present. We'll reflect about the values we learned in our work lives. From our work shoes to theirs, we'll explore work as an aspect of our lives in which we received legacies and we can pass legacies to those who will follow us. We also directly examine the ideas of meaning and purpose as lived in daily life (inherent in all the chapters).

Chapters 7 and 8 are about the legacy of love. In "Learning about Love (Relationships I)" we reflect on the love and legacies to and from friends and mentors, the angels who lit our lives in dark times. "Me and My Family (Relationships II)" probes our relationship with our selves and our Selves. We'll consider our place in the larger world and in the cosmos. Loving in our families is probably the most complex, and we begin our exploration of those legacies in chapter 8.

"I'm Sorry," chapter 9, is about addressing our own human failings and making amends. The healing that can come from legacy letters of apology can repair relationships long given up for lost.

Chapter 10, "Cleaning Out Your Closet" focuses on two aspects of "cleaning out." The first is about cleaning out our material things, our "stuff." This includes gifting loved ones with meaningful treasures, keeping those that mean most to us to accompany us in transitions of living conditions to provide us with coherence, continuity, and comfort. The second part of the chapter is about cleaning out our psychic closets, addressing what clutters our identities and airing secrets. Deciding how and whether to tell old secrets to the younger generations in our families is a delicate matter, and a profound way to make a positive difference in the lives of those who will follow us.

The title, "About Aging," tells the content of chapter 11. In a culture in which we spend billions to avoid aging, when it's thought a compliment upon hearing a person's age, to say, "You don't look that old," it's difficult to talk about, or write about our aging. Our children are resistant to hearing that their parents are "getting old." We approach the topic gently and honestly, and conclude the chapter with preparing a specific legacy letter, one to accompany Advance Health Directives.

If you've come this far in the book, and if in fact you were interested enough to buy the book or open its first pages, you've already entertained the reality of mortality. "The Measure of Our Days," chapter 12, understands mortality as a sacred aspect of life. Legacy writers experience relief and peace of mind as they write legacy letters to their loved ones. With these letters we change the old implicit legacy of taboo, of secrecy and silence about talking about dying and grief.

Finally, the Afterword. "Wrapping Up Loose Ends" includes three subjects: first, writing a legacy letter to accompany our wills. In chapter 12 we wrote to humanize the advance health directive; here we do the same to accompany our wills. If we thought it was challenging to break the taboo about speaking about death, we'll find conversation about money, financial gifts, and inheritance at least as uncomfortable for many. Second we address the realistic questions about how, when, and where to present our legacy letters.

Third we focus on celebrating: celebrating Life itself, celebrating our success having written and given several legacy letters. Continuing to celebrate how blessed we are day by day, we'll find suggestions about establishing a practice of gratitude. The Afterword concludes with my appreciation of each of you for taking on the privilege and responsibility to write your legacies, and my blessing to you.

> **"Help me to see how the story I come from could end up with me."** — **Josh Nelson**

As you begin your legacy writing, I wish you a fertile season and an abundant harvest: From your exploration of the seeds planted long before you were born to the fruits and flowers that will blossom for many generations to come.

> **"The future belongs to those who give the next generation reason for hope."** — **Pierre Teilhard de Chardin**

Chapter 1
The ABCs of Legacy

Welcome to the fascinating journey of legacy writing, harvesting our love and learning for our loved ones. Beyond the precious treasure we leave them, our yield produces a remarkable and profound experience addressing universal needs deep within each of us.

We begin with the A, B, C's, to familiarize ourselves with basic ideas about legacy and legacy writing. Once familiar with the concepts and practice of legacy writing, you'll be ready to begin your own. Each chapter will focus on one important topic for writing legacy letters, and each chapter will guide you a step at a time.

A. What is an ethical will and how does it relate to our legacy writing?
B. What are the purposes and appropriate subjects of contemporary legacy letters?
C. Why should we write ethical wills?

What is an ethical will and how does it relate to our legacy writing?

Some of us may not have heard the words "ethical will." Legacy writing is a modern interpretation of this ancient tradition. An ethical will is a non-legal document understood today as a legacy letter.

A traditional ethical will, originating in the Biblical period, was a practice designed by the Rabbis for fathers to bless their sons and transmit ethical values to the next generation. Contemporary ethical wills are written at every age, by men and women alike, often in times of transition, personal challenge, and to commemorate family life cycle events.

Respecting the ancient patriarchal practice, I worked to make it accessible and pertinent to moderns, especially women (who often fear writing or believe they have nothing noteworthy to write). I added the word 'spiritual' to the practice of writing 'ethical' wills. For me the word "spiritual" refers to what is meaningful. I hoped to soften this rather threatening name, make it more engaging, more accessible to people of all ages in our time.

The central core of modern legacy writing transforms the often harsh instructions left by fathers to their sons, to blessings for future generations. This corresponds to the deep and often unmet need in all of us to be blessed by our parents.

The traditional ethical will was commonly transmitted in a letter format. Modern legacies utilize the letter format too. Why? Because a letter is an intimate and personal communication, and most of us feel competent to write a letter. From here on, we'll refer to ethical or spiritual-ethical wills using the more familiar words, 'legacy letters'.

Each legacy letter is unique in its content, in its purpose, and in its length. Legacy letters may take 15 minutes to write, as you'll experience with our reflections and letters in this book, or they may take many weeks and months to write. Legacy letters may be one-page long, be a series of letters addressed to different recipients at different times, or be a single lengthier document.

Legacy letters often reflect connection or belonging because their content shares history and links generations. They may focus on healing earlier issues or misunderstandings, finalizing end of life needs, or sharing wisdom with future generations.

Younger family members may choose different content, because of their season of life. But it is urgent for legacy writers of every age to write legacy letters now—to one another, other loved ones, and to future generations—given the uncertainties of life and the momentum of change in our times.

> "...death is a hungry hunter pursuing us on the highway, overtaking us in the fastest planes; Dying, there may be for us no long farewells, no blessings, and no prophecies .... while yet we live, help us to guide our children in love and wisdom, help us now to build a world of peace." — Ruth Brin

What are the purposes of contemporary legacy letters?

The main purpose of legacy writing is to communicate to family, loved ones, and future generations what matters most in a person's life. Your legacy writing may look and even feel like the telling of your life story, a memoir, or a spiritual autobiography, but it's more than that. In order to qualify as legacy writing, the intention to transmit the meaning or the lesson of the story to those who come after us is paramount.

> "We all live inside our stories."   — Salman Rushdie

Reflecting on, clarifying, and documenting a legacy is an important component of a life well lived. Its major purpose is to gather, preserve, and communicate values, wisdom, and love for future generations. Components may include family history and story, values and life-lessons, blessings and gratitude, appreciation and love. But unless the intention of making a contribution to the future is fulfilled, it does not qualify as legacy.

> "What you leave behind is not what is engraved on stone monuments, but what is woven into the lives of others."
> — Pericles

Andrew Weil, MD wrote in his 2005 book *Healthy Aging* that the ethical will is pertinent to those of us "concerned with making sense of our lives and the fact of our aging." The reasons he suggested for writing included:

- It's a way to leave something behind, to be remembered
- It's a way to document your history and stories so that others can learn from them in the future
- It can help you understand your own values and to share your ideas with future generations
- It can help you learn more about yourself
- It can help you accept mortality and create a way to 'live on' after you are gone
- It can provide an immediate sense of worthiness, completion, and accomplishment

When Dr. Weil endorsed my first legacy book, *Women's Lives, Women's Legacies: Passing Your Beliefs and Blessings to Future Generations*, he wrote, "The ethical will is a wonderful gift to leave to your family at the end of your life, but I think its main importance is what *it can give you in the midst of life*."[my italics] I believe this is true.

As I crossed this country over the past decade presenting legacy writing in a variety of settings and to diverse groups, I found that people are receptive to the concept: it touches needs deep inside, needs we can't necessarily explain, but that plead to be addressed. Psychologist Abraham Maslow developed a ladder of what it takes to become a fully actualized person. I have begun playfully to call my observations of the needs addressed by legacy writing 'Freed's needs'. These needs are to:

- Belong (feel connected)
- Be known (and heard)
- Be remembered
- Make a positive difference
- Bless and be blessed
- Celebrate Life

All of these needs are addressed as we reflect and write our legacy letters to our loved ones.

> **"Stories have to be told or they die, and when they die, we can't remember who we are or why we're here."**
> **— Sue Monk Kidd**

What are appropriate subjects for my legacy letters?

The traditional ethical will letter, instructive in tone, was circumscribed, and meant to connect the younger generation to the ethics and values of their culture. Topics of contemporary legacy letters are less dogmatic, and are as varied and unique as the writer who writes them.

Many people write legacy letters to preserve personal and family history, as well as harvest history from the seasons of their own lives. Others write personal and family stories to preserve and pass on values and traditions. Still others want to be known, understood, and respected, so their legacy letters preserve, usually through stories, life-lessons and values that matter most.

> **"Stories - and their telling - create identity, relation to self, other, and land."**
> **— Carol Ferris**

Legacy letters can also clarify values by explaining the choices and decisions we make in our wills and advance directives. These two legal documents that cry out to be humanized by personal communication, caring, and explication.

Some people, as they near the final season of their lives, write with the hope of improving family relationships, of being more intimate, honest, and forgiving than was possible in earlier seasons of their lives. Some letters function to transmit long ignored and hidden family secrets to free the next generation from the negative legacies left from earlier generations.

Some letters function to address our needs to be remembered, to bless others and to rejoice in the blessings we've experienced in our lives. Some legacy letters express understanding and learning from life experiences, translated into hard-earned wisdom to be preserved and passed on, to make an impact on others' lives. Other letters express regrets, and make amends for past deeds, something that may not be possible to do in person. Irrespective of the motivation, all of this writing shares one important characteristic: it is sacred.

> **"We cannot wish old feelings away nor do spiritual exercises for overcoming them until we have woven a healing story that transforms our previous life's experience and gives meaning to whatever pain we have endured."**
> **— Joan Borysenko**

Most people will not write about all the topics in this book. In each chapter we'll focus on a single topic that builds on what's come before and leads to the next.

Why should we write an ethical will?

I believe it both a privilege and a responsibility to record, communicate, and preserve family and community histories and values, document the legacies we've received, and the experiences we've lived that make each of us who we uniquely are. Preserving our wisdom and our love establishes a link in the chain of generations, and passes on a legacy for those of tomorrow's world. Legacy writing is one of the ways we can fulfill our individual and communal covenant with the past and the future.

I have witnessed beautiful transformations happen to legacy writers and readers as long buried, forgotten or unconscious human needs come to the surface and are written to be shared. These needs include: to belong, to be known, to be remembered, to make a difference, to bless and be blessed, and to celebrate Life.

My long-time friend and colleague, Daniel Taylor, understood the priceless treasure legacy letters are for children and the future, as well as what it meant for him to write them. In the preface of his *Letters to My Children*, he wrote:

> **"I have a terminal disease. It is called mortality .... I am concerned [my children] will little remember who their father was, what made him tick, what was important to him, what he had to say to them. What will they know of me...the one who loves them more than he will ever let himself say?**
>
> **"These letters are a partial response to this muted but persistent concern. They are, in theory, for my children, but in writing them I discovered they were for me as well. It is not just the vanity of wanting to be remembered that motivates them. For better or worse, I am the only father my children will ever have. And as their father, part of my value is to pass on the eternal truths. Never mind that many of us are less sure of the exact nature of eternal truth than before we had children."**

You may want to keep a "Legacy File," with a copy of all the legacy letters you write, including your legacy reflections. This is a good place to save your thoughts and feelings about the legacy process and your own learning. Your file may include new words and ideas learned in this book and elsewhere that inform your legacy perspective. You may also want to save particularly inspiring legacy quotations from your reading. Perhaps you'll want to keep ideas and questions that come to you as you write.

The idea of a "Legacy File," like all ideas in this book, is a suggestion. It will fit for some of you, but not others. As the wisdom of 12 step programs expresses, "Take what you like and leave the rest."

" To write is to sow and reap at the same time." — Ruth Brin

Now we're ready for chapter two where we'll explore and reflect about blessings, practice writing them, and write our first legacy letter.

Chapter 2
Writing Blessings: The Centerpiece of Our Legacy Table

Each of us has been blessed in many ways in our lives. Consequently, we may feel enormous gratitude not only for the gifts we've received, but also for the people we've become as we journey through our lives, amassing useful lessons from our relationships and experiences.

Our task as legacy writers is to determine what we value most in life, then convey those values in the form of blessings to our descendants. As we do that, we strengthen traditions within our families and communities; we honor the links between the past and the future.

The History of Writing Blessings

Sometime between the third and sixth centuries C.E. the Sages used the story of Jacob blessing his sons as he lay dying as a template to teach men to bless their children and to pass on moral and ethical instructions. (See Genesis 49.) This document came to be known as an "ethical will." (Three examples can be read in the Appendix.)

This may sound familiar to those of us aware of the instructions from our parents and ancestors to: be good, work hard, and take care of our selves and our families. We likely did not receive an ethical will (a legacy letter), and we may be unsure how we received those instructions. Maybe we ate or drank the messages; perhaps we were swaddled in the blessing, hope, or dream. It's possible that we received our ancestors' legacies by osmosis, from the hereditary ethos of the family.

Being able to receive a legacy may depend on the words and tone of the message. We're all familiar with being instructed. Even when well-meant, instructions can feel like commands, demands, even scolding. The tone may seem harsh, unfeeling, or cold.

While it may be more habitual to communicate our values as instructions, many of us are averse to telling loved ones how they ought to live. Blessing loved ones, however – with our love, our values, our hopes for their future – is a less intrusive and more loving way to share our deepest values. Transforming our instructions into blessings, we offer our wisdom and experience without attempting to control our loved ones' lives.

> When writing Women's Lives, Women's Legacies it became clear to me that instructions came from our "heads" and blessings came from our "hearts." Transforming instructions into blessings became a central component of writing legacy letters.

In their wisdom long ago the Talmudists wrote: "Words that come from the heart enter the heart," and "Even though the Sages said there are three instructions a man must give, still one must be careful to say these things gently, so that his family will accept them from him."

> I was one, who from a very young age, struggled against instruction. They felt capricious, constricting, and controlling. I wanted to do everything my own way. As a teen, I was rebellious and defiant. I was willing to live with the consequences of my own choices and mistakes, always preferable to following my parents' instructions. I wonder now how differently I might have lived my life had my parents tried blessing me rather than instructing me.

The basic human yearning in all of us to be blessed doesn't diminish with age. No one is too old or too young to receive a blessing. Blessing our children is as old as Genesis. The ethical will was modeled after Jacob blessing his sons before his death (Gen: 49). Earlier, after Jacob stole his brother's blessing, Esau approached his aging father, Isaac, to ask the question we all ask, aloud or in our hearts, no matter how old we are: "Have you no blessing for me, father?"

About Blessings

There are those who argue that although blessings feel gentle and personal – more like gifts than instructions – they may be indirect, seductive, manipulative disguises for controlling others. Some insist that blessings are reserved for clergy in houses of worship; that they don't belong to all of us.

I remember a more than awkward moment years ago when I first began teaching about legacy. I was invited to guide a group of a dozen elders in a Community Education setting for an hour-long legacy program. Beginning with the basics and history about the ethical will, I quickly moved the focus to the centrality of blessings and the importance of communicating blessings as often as possible in our world.

I provided a few tips on how to get started and invited the participants to write a blessing that we could share with each other. Noticing that the two very elderly women sitting to my left looked uncomfortable and didn't pick up their pens to write, I began the sharing part of the program with those on my right. Some people were eager to share the blessing they'd written; others passed when it was their turn, choosing to keep their blessings private.

I became more and more anxious as the attention moved around the circle. When we got to the last two women, I invited the first to share. With pursed lips she squeaked out the words, "I didn't write." Beginner that I was, I asked why. (Big mistake!) She informed me that ordinary people had no right to offer blessings. That was something reserved for priests, ministers, and rabbis. I was dumbstruck. I had no idea how to respond, how to validate the authenticity and beauty of the blessings shared by the other elders only a few minutes earlier. I said nothing, and felt relieved that our hour was over. I thanked them all for coming, wrapped-up and hurriedly left.

I thought of at least one response on my drive home. We all practice blessing each other normally when we say, "God bless you" or "Bless you" when a person sneezes. I felt badly for a long time for not being able to think of that on the spot to vindicate the hour and the blessings others had written.

> "To give someone a blessing is the most significant affirmation we can offer." — Henri Nouwen

After that excruciating moment, I prepared myself by reading about blessings. I designed an elegant handout of powerful quotations about the value of blessing and how important it is to human interaction. I still use it, no longer to persuade people that we have the right to bless, but as a way of sharing how deeply meaningful blessings are to all of us. Here's an example from David Spangler's 2001 book, Blessing: The Art and the Practice:

> "To bless—to share one's spirit with another—is a natural human act. It can be executed with all the delight, whimsy, and spontaneity of which we are capable and still be a moment in which the gift of ourselves flows to another with a depth that only spirit can provide ....We don't ever want to lose our sense of wonder, nor do we want to explain blessing in a way that we fail to recognize or appreciate the miraculous. On the other hand, we can fail to appreciate our innate power to bless if we regard blessing as a force so awesome and special, it must lie beyond our ordinary capabilities." — David Spangler

When we write blessings to celebrate a person special to us at a particular moment or on a special occasion, we are responding to the ongoing and universal need for blessing we all have. The spirits of those who offer blessings and those who receive the blessing are cherished. Blessings are special glue strengthening the bond of family, affirming caring among its members, explicitly appreciating a person and a special moment. Writing legacy blessings is a powerful way to honor our covenant with the past and the future.

> "The one who blesses becomes an agent of self-realization and fulfillment for the one who receives the blessing." — Lawrence Kushner

Everyone hungers to be blessed, and there is much to feel blessed about in every season of our lives. We'll practice writing blessings and then conclude this chapter by writing our first legacy letter (a letter with the purpose of passing on a blessing). But first let's read some blessings written by men and women of different generations. As you read them, notice what moves you. Observe how uniquely but simply people word their blessings. Be aware of the diversity of the occasions appropriate for a blessing.

This excerpt is a blessing from a letter written by a mother to her son, who will soon become a father:

"I remember when you were a small boy. When asked what you wanted to be when you grew up, you once answered, 'a daddy.' Here you are! .... I wish for you the joy of a busy, messy, loud house ... I wish for you a fridge covered in art projects and spelling tests. May you feel the pride of hearing a line in a Christmas play well-spoken.... I wish you the rich, rich texture of a family life that is uniquely yours. I wish for you, dear son, a small measure of the immense love and joy you have brought to me."

Here a grown son blesses his elderly mother as a Mothers' Day gift. Rereading it together has become part of their annual Mother's Day ritual:

"Early in life you showed me what true sacrifice is.... As I fell into the depths of drug addiction, your unconditional love never wavered and you are still my biggest fan. You have given me hope that love can conquer all things and that change is possible in even the darkest of moments.... I share this with you because I don't ever want you to wake up without knowing how much I appreciate your love and guidance."

A woman blesses her ninety-year-old friend who is returning to the family homestead for a summer vacation:

"Lorna (dear friend, almost-mother), May your summer last as long as those of your childhood. May you wake up each morning and enter a day with no clocks or structure other than that which makes you happy. May you feel the ocean on your feet, the warm sand through your fingers. May you laugh and live in each moment. May you sleep the sleep of your childhood summer nights, full and satisfied, knowing you can do it all again tomorrow."

A grandfather writes a blessing of undying love to a granddaughter, anticipating her birth:

"May you know, from the first moment of your life, how much I love you. May you know from that very first moment that there is nothing you can do in your life to make me, or

your grandma, or your mommy, or your daddy stop loving you. May you know this even as you take your first breath, and as you take your last."

Here a woman without children of her own blesses future unborn generations:

"I write to the souls who are yet to be, wondering how their lives will be touched by me...My mind grasping to understand how our lives are but a single strand woven together in mystery, connected throughout all of history - Never to be left dangling alone, but entwined together as one of God's own. May you feel our connection in this infinite Universe, striving to live a life filled with purpose. May you know you belong to an Eternal Home and that You make a difference for souls yet unknown...."

Another woman blesses future generations:

"May you reap the good lessons of those who came before you: hard work, integrity, yes, but more. May you understand that we belong to one community. May you know that everyone matters, and where any one single individual suffers, either from material want or indignity, so do we all suffer. May you recognize the insanity of war and work to create peace."

A grandfather sharing a heart overflowing with love blesses his three year-old grandson:

"May you always jump for joy at the sight of a snowstorm – May you always scream with excitement at the sound of the words 'Dairy Queen' – May you always revel at the feeling of making snow angels in the yard – May you always know how much I love you and how much you've taught me about truly 'living in the moment.'"

And finally here is the blessing I closed my daughter's 40th birthday letter with. (I'll share other parts of the letter throughout the chapters where appropriate.)

> *So, my dear peapod, it's your 40th birthday, may it be a happy one ... gather all of who you've been and what you've done, and tuck it into the pocket of your heart as you begin a new decade. I pray for you a long fulfilling life, gratitude for your blessings, intimate reciprocal relationships, meaningful work, joy in all that you do, great dignity in who you are, and awe for the miracles in and around you. I love you more deeply than I ever imagined forty years ago when I first held you, and I will hold you in my heart forever.*　**— Mom**

Writing Blessings

Now it's time to try your hand at writing blessings. Here are some simple suggestions to guide you as you begin until, with just a little practice, you'll find it natural.

1. The first blessing asks you to choose a friend or colleague whom you'd like to bless. It may be for a particular occasion or event in this person's life, or it may be that you want to express your caring just because.

2. Reflect about what you love, admire, and cherish about the person you are going to write the blessing to/for. Reflect too about the meaning of the occasion for the blessing. It may be that you've lost touch with the person, have never expressed your appreciation for their friendship and support, or that time is passing and you feel some urgency to communicate your caring.

3. For many of us, the hardest thing about writing is getting started. Here are some phrases that may help you begin: May you always...; May God (your Higher Power) bless you with...; My hope for you is...; I pray that you....

4. Draft your blessing, writing like you speak, as naturally as possible. Spend no more than five minutes writing. Set a timer before you begin.

5. Put the writing away for at least one day to provide you with perspective; when you return to it, read, edit, and finalize your blessing.

Editing Tips

These are not about spelling, punctuation, or syntax. Legacy writing is from our hearts. Our editing should support our spontaneity and our feelings. The purpose for editing in legacy writing is to assure that our words convey our message and the meaning of our blessing. Ask yourself:

- Have I really written a blessing, or disguised an instruction, a demand, or a command by beginning with the word "May"?

"A blessing, like a gift, carries a feeling of spaciousness. As a true gift, and not a transaction in disguise, it's freeing to both the giver and the receiver. It does not obligate either one." — **David Spangler**

- Have I used words that don't seem quite right or words that don't sound like me? The last thing I want is for the recipient to believe that I copied the blessing from some book!
- What is the tone of my blessing? Words of blessing should never be an opportunity to express anger. A more appropriate place for angry feelings is a personal journal. I check the intention of my blessings using the Buddhist maxim "Do no harm" and asking myself if what I'm writing is kind, true, necessary, and if it's the right time. Of course I can't control how my words will be read, how received. I can only do my best to write from my heart with the intention to "do no harm."
- Have my words clearly and adequately conveyed the message I mean to send? In the editing phase, I can use the dictionary, a thesaurus, or a synonym finder in book form or online to find the word that most clearly says what I mean, what I'm trying to express.

- Finally I can read my blessing aloud, imagining that I am receiving the blessing. If my own response is that I feel open-hearted, compassionate, and loving, and I imagine the reader feels cared for, respected, cherished, and loved, then my blessing is ready to be given.
- Keep a copy for yourself of each blessing you write, preserving a compendium of your blessings to those you love in your own Legacy File. (see page 7).

Now write two more blessings: for someone in your family, and finally write a blessing for those yet unborn. Follow the suggestions as you did for the first blessing you wrote.

One way to share a blessing is to write it on a card and give it or mail it to your loved one. If it is offered as a blessing for a special occasion: a wedding, a birth, a commencement, a birthday or a holiday, a card blank on the inside works well.

Often, however, you will find that you've written a blessing for someone because that's what's in your heart – no special day or event being celebrated. In that case, the blessing may demand some explanation, and is best expressed in what is called the "legacy letter".

 ## Legacy Letter Template

Though each of us is unique, you may want to organize your one page legacy letter using a simple four-part model, that personalizes and deepens the blessing. Here are the four components or paragraphs for this blessing letter model (See Appendix B, pages 232-233, for more detail):

- Context (gives the writer the opportunity to fill in personal, family history, and a bird's eye view of the period of time of the story and learning.)
- Story (everyone loves a good story, and connects easily and emotionally to a story. No need to be a professional storyteller; just tell it in your own words.)

- Learning (here you can be personal, imperfect, humble, vulnerable, sharing who you are beyond your public role, and it gives a deeper meaning to your story)
- Blessing (your opportunity to express your love and caring and your respect for and appreciation of the recipient)

A legacy letter using this format provides several opportunities. Recalling the context for the blessing is important not just to set the stage for your story or blessing, but to preserve a family snapshot of time and place that may not be saved anywhere else. Something you've learned from your experience in its context, the wisdom you've gleaned by telling your story follows as the center of your legacy letter.

The natural conclusion of the letter is the blessing itself, personal and unique for the recipient and from you. Not a Hallmark blessing that could come from anyone and be applied to anyone. In other words, your blessings are not generic. They are specific and one of a kind. They are expressions from your heart and your life learning, as well as your observations and reflections about the receiver.

One legacy writer explained how she understood why "this blessing" and not any other.

> **"I asked myself why I had chosen this particular blessing. I wondered what was behind my particular wish to pass this along. Then I wrote the story from my life from which this blessing had come, trying to write from my heart and not my head, integrating the wise part of myself with the personal pain, so that the blessing came from the strength of my vulnerability."** — **Claire Willis**

At this point you may feel overwhelmed and wonder how to get started. Like the tips for writing a blessing, here are some suggestions for writing legacy letters. The letter format is one we're all familiar with. Always date your legacy letters. Begin with "Dear" followed by the name of the loved one you are writing to.

Set your timer, this time for 15 minutes, and begin to write something about the context for your blessing. (Be aware that carving out a specific amount of time to write reduces your feelings of being overwhelmed, quiets your concerns about how to fit legacy into your already too busy schedule, and focuses your mind.) I think you'll be more than pleasantly surprised, perhaps amazed, by how much you can write in just fifteen minutes.

You can return to your letter for additional time on another day to add to, subtract from, and edit your letter. Refer to the editing suggestions on page 17 in this chapter. They are as appropriate for use with all legacy letters as they were for brief blessings.

Storage Tips

Any legacy letter you write that you decide not to share until some future moment: the right occasion, when you think it can best be received, or that you don't want to share while you're still alive, should be put in a special place.

Keep a copy in your personal Legacy File. (I hesitate to suggest technology because it changes so quickly, but you may opt to keep copies of your precious legacy writing on your computer, a CD, or in "the cloud" as well as on paper.) Inform at least two people where your unsent letters are so you can trust that they won't be lost. Seal a letter in an envelope; write the recipient's name and the occasion for opening it on the outside of the envelope. Tell people the letters exist and where they can be found, and put your concerns to rest.

You may want to reread quotations when you finish a chapter, and choose those with particular meaning to you to put in your Legacy File. You may also add quotations or ideas you have for future legacy letters to your personal Legacy File.

Legacy blessing letters provide us with one example of how much inner peace, how much serenity, we experience as we fulfill our covenant with the future, harvesting the love in our lives, and passing it forward with long yearned for blessings to our loved ones. Of course, blessing letters are but one type of legacy letter, although blessings may be integral to legacy letters with varied content.

Each of us is unique. We have our own stories, histories, and experiences. In the Renaissance period, neophyte artists were apprenticed and spent years copying their masters' works. Only when ready, did they go on to paint their own canvasses. That's very different than our culture, with its worries about copying, about plagiarism, about professional property rights.

In legacy writing, there is a different norm. We share our writing with others, we learn from each other and our own thoughts are enriched. Hearing or reading each other's letters provides an opportunity for us to tap into our own memories. Realizing how much courage it takes to write some legacy letters, we are empowered to take our own values seriously and become willing to write about what really matters to us.

Legacy Letters

Each chapter includes examples of legacy letters. Legacy writers who have so generously offered their work to this book believe that sharing them expands their legacy to others and to the future. Notice how each letter uniquely includes context, story, and learning, as well as blessing.

The first letter was written by a mother, concerned about her family's struggle with the economic crisis that began in 2009. The second is a brief letter, written by a mother to her son, blessing him with values and memories as he leaves home for a cross-country trip. The third is a blessing for the daughters of a mother who averted a crisis in which nine people died. In the fourth, in a time when books are so endangered, a book-loving woman writes a blessing for children of future generations. Finally, I've included a letter I wrote to my two grown children.

Dear Julie and Donald,

Life presents challenges that we often don't anticipate. Your father and I have been faced with the struggles of unemployment and the financial changes we never thought we would have to make. Moving forward is not easy, but life goes on as we transition.

We wish for you the benefit of our experience. May you have the wisdom to save for that rainy day. May you also have the knowledge that who you are is not determined just by what you do. May you take joy in each day, and understand that accomplishments can be baby steps like cleaning out a drawer, calling a friend, reading, studying, or remembering to pick up the dry cleaning.

Know that we love each other unconditionally even when times are tough, and do our best to live each day to the fullest and maintain a positive outlook. Grow from the experience and find your peace with God's help.

Mom

Dear Brian,

Your plan for cross country travel brought to mind all the camping trips I took with my Mom, Dad and Lady, the beagle. We always left before sunrise, the dog and I drifting back to sleep for the first hour or two. We had a thermos of coffee, juice and lunch packed so that we could picnic in some scenic spot.

Dad stopped the car frequently. He had a 35 mm. camera wher most people had black and white Brownies. He seemed never to miss an eagle in the sky, a deer on the roadside, a sunset, a rainbow or a scenic view. Dad had a soulful connection with nature.

Though your Grandpa never spoke about his reverence for things wild and beautiful, he demonstrated to me the importance of paying attention. He lived the values of caring for the earth, of expressing wonder, of taking the road less traveled.

May you have abundant opportunities to be spontaneous, remain curious, and be in awe of the territory you traverse.

Love, Mom

Dear Alyssa and Suzanne,

Aug 1, 2007 was a life-changing day for me. I was driving my usual route home from a work related meeting...crossing the bridge on I - 35W. The traffic was slow because of repairs being made and my car clock said 6:00. I patiently waited as traffic moved slowly on the bridge and I finally arrived home at about 6:20. My phone was ringing. A friend was calling to ask me if I was watching the news on TV. I told him that I had just gotten home and he said, "Turn it on." It was then that I realized...I had made it over the I–35W Bridge by just five minutes. As Senator Amy Klobuchar expressed, "A bridge in America just shouldn't fall down." But...one did and it collapsed in Minneapolis.

Once again I'm reminded how precious life is. So my beloved daughters, Alyssa and Suzanne, this blessing is for you – to reinforce and hope you will never forget how important today is.

Give thanks for today because we don't know what tomorrow brings. Happiness and hope can quickly turn to sorrow and loss. So please make sure to not only say thank-you, but share your inner feelings of love and values. Don't wait...seize the moment. Smile at everyone no matter where paths cross or whether friend or stranger. Your inner radiance is G-d's gift for you to share.

And make it your obligation to illuminate the sky when darkness is all around us. We don't always grasp what we have or who we are until it is almost taken from us. So please, be present...don't hurry through life forgetting to say I love you...I love life.

I love you...
Your Mom

I hope you will have a curiosity and wonder about life and the world you live in. May your exploration lead you to read great books as a source of information.

Love of reading began for me at a very early age as I sat on a davenport next to my mother, my brother on her other side. I looked forward to that time every day, listening to stories that piqued my curiosity and fantasy.

How would I see if I had three eyes?

How difficult would it be to climb a beanstalk?

What does a giant look like?

What would it be like to fight a lion barehanded in an arena?

I was very curious and encouraged to find answers by reading. Stories became vehicles for me to vicariously experience Bombay, Athens, Shanghai and other faraway cities of the world. Riding to the library on Saturday morning, my Mom pulling my brother and me in a little red wagon, was heaven for me. I was allowed to check out four books that I could keep, hold in my hand, read and re-read for a whole week.

Books are treasures; may they arouse in you a curiosity about travel, art, history, religion, and music. May you value the written word and let reading whet your appetite for life.

Dear Sid and Debbie,

In the summer of 1961,in the middle of the Civil Rights era, your Dad graduated from Officers Candidate School and began three years of service in the US Coast Guard. He was stationed at the Battery, at the south end of Manhattan. We sublet a ground-floor apartment on West 95th Street just half a block from Central Park in Spanish Harlem. My job that summer was to find a teaching position for the fall, which I did: at an all-black junior high in Montclair, New Jersey. On the first day of school, the NAACP was picketing outside the school. *Newsweek Magazine* wrote about us and with pressure, the school board closed the school the following spring. I then taught English in the integrated high school. Those 3 years were the most challenging, most satisfying, and most creative of my teaching career.

That first summer in NYC I was just 22: optimistic, ready to save the world, confident, and naively fearless. One day on my way to some exciting exploration of the city, I got on the subway. I sat down and began to read. A pregnant, homeless woman entered the car, and began to beg. I averted my eyes, buried my face in my book, and clasped my heart and my purse tightly. Silent minutes passed and suddenly the woman began to shout at the riders – crying out that it was okay if we didn't give her money, but it wasn't okay to avoid looking her in the face – that she was a human being! She picked up her bags and lurched through the door into the next train car.

I was shocked and shamed. Since then, even if I choose not to give to a person begging, I look the person in the eye. I feel more human when I acknowledge another's humanity.

So, my beloved and precious children, Sid and Debbie, I offer you this blessing: 'May you both be blessed with compassionate and wise eyes: eyes that see beyond the face of circumstance, that see the spark of the Divine deep within yourself, each other, and everyone on our planet.'

I love you,
Mom

Chapter 3
What's in a Name?

> **"The beginning of wisdom is to call things by their rightful names."** — **Chinese proverb**

When a new baby comes into the world, we eagerly ask, "What's the baby's name?" We want to know the identity of the new, precious soul. Yet most of us don't think twice about our own names, nor do we take the time to explore this essential element of our identity and legacy.

Our names connect us to our family, to our heritage. It marks the place in the world where we belong. If you were named to honor an ancestor, historical figure, or literary character, your name connects you securely to the past. Your name carries memory, legacy, and immortality, a special relationship with the person for whom you were named. Our names "brand" us to a family and endow us with a legacy of belonging. Some people believe that a name influences who a person will become.

> **"The true name of a creature is its innermost essence."** — **Marcia Prager**

In earlier times, the family Bible was handed down through the generations. Its first few pages were rich with family history written in the hand of each generation's family scribe. The Book recorded the names and family history from one generation to another. The names of ancestors, often going back many generations, included families who became related through marriage. Information about marriages and the name changes that accompanied them expanded the family. Lists of children born, birth and death dates of family members linked past family history to present and future generations.

Few of us have such a treasure today, but this information remains vital. It provides a record that binds families, especially important because we seldom live together inter-generationally today. It once was a norm of family life to spend evenings exchanging names and stories at the kitchen table: grandparents, parents, and children.

> **"... a name has its own history and its own memory. It connects beings with their origins. "**   — **Elie Wiesel**

Our children and grandchildren find work and partners far from the family farm of yesteryear. Our families are spread all over the globe, lead busy, complex lives, and may live many miles away from us. These realities make belonging and staying connected difficult and different than ever before in history.

We are often asked about grandparents and great grandparents by younger generations who are starved for their history. The young are curious about from where and from whom they came. They hunger to know what values and dreams motivated their ancestors. In this chapter we'll take the first step of recovering and preserving that history through our names.

Without a Name

Because names are the very first legacy we are entrusted with when we're born, they connect us to the generations of our history. We seldom think about our own names, or realize their significance to our sense of belonging. So let's take a moment to consider what it means to be without a name.

When names are taken or lost as a political tool of disconnection, the historical wounds affect families for generations. Think about the ramifications of name loss for African-American slaves whose family names were supplanted by the names of their 'owners.' Native South and North Americans had their tribal names replaced with 'Christian' names by explorers and colonizers. During the Holocaust, Jews' names were excised by the Nazis; they were subsequently identified by numbers carved into their forearms. More recently, *The New York Times* reported that thousands of Sunni Muslims legally change their names annually to protect themselves and their families from recognition, persecution, and possible death by the Shiites in political power in Iraq.

Not all name changes are sad or enforced. There are occasions, often related to marriage, when couples change or add to their family names. Some people have a deep sense that the name they are called is not their true name, and thus endure the legal bureaucracy to change it.

> **"There can be a certain yearning to change the name, and in so doing to signal a necessary break with the life one has led, and yet how crucial it can be that the name be recognizable, too, because it's not always clear what parts of the past will turn out to be worth saving."   — Daniel Mendelsohn**

Having just completed the chapter on blessings, I suggest that a chosen name change begs for a blessing. Here is one loosely based on tradition, but each of us can write a blessing that expresses what our name change means to us.

> **"As Abraham and Sarah's names were changed when they encountered God ... may my name change from _____ to _____ symbolize the blessing of my changed status, the different person I am becoming in relation to my partner, family, friends, and God. Just as my name has changed, so may all the harshness in my life change to kindness, may all illness change to healing, and may all sadness change to joy."**
> **— Peter Pitzele**

Most of our families were immigrants to this country. Our names function as a compass connecting us to them and to our communities and tribes over time and space. Our names are our way home.

Is it any wonder that genealogy and scrapbooking are two of the most popular and widespread hobbies among people in this country? It's not surprising to hear how many friends plan to travel back to the 'old country' to visit the homelands of their families. We hunger to belong!

> **"Every person has three names: one given by father and mother, one others call him, and one she acquires herself."**
> **— Midrash for Ecclesiastes 7:1-3**

Reflection about our Names

This reflection has three sections. It will function as a template to gather and preserve information about your names, and to consider questions related to them. Part I of the "Name Reflection" is a simple recording of your name that can emphasize and enhance your experience of belonging to a specific moment and place in time, identifying you as a part of a family with its own unique history.

You may want to use material you record in Part I of this reflection as content to write a legacy letter to someone in your family. One purpose for such a letter is for you to be better known; another is to add information for someone in a younger generation in your family who carries your name. This letter may provide new data for a family member who has taken on the role of family historian or scribe.

> **"The beginning of wisdom is calling things by their proper names."**
> **— Talmud**

Names, Part I: My Names

We all have many names; let's begin by making of list of them: My birth name (and if applicable my adopted name), my name from another country, tradition, or language, my nickname(s), my name today.

Take time to reflect and make notes about these questions: For whom am I named? What was their relationship to me? Why was I named for this person? What do I know about my namesake (facts / stories / meaning of this name)? What connection have I felt and do I feel today with my namesake? How has my namesake influenced my life? What specific legacy did I receive because I carry their name?

Does my name feel "right" to me? Have I ever changed my name? If so, why? How did I feel about my old name? How has my attitude toward my name changed at different times in my life?

Take no more than fifteen (15) minutes to remember and write stories you know about your name.

What do I want younger generations to know about my name?

Names Part II: My Ancestors' Names

Construct a list of names of your parents, grandparents, and great grand-parents. Go back as many generations as you can. When available, include dates and places of birth and death for each person on your list.

What skills do you need to do part II? Perhaps nothing out of the ordinary: curiosity and the willingness to ask others for help. Ask questions and explain why you're asking. You may need some patience. Have the expectation that you will enjoy surprises along the way. Other family members may enjoy this search, and it may bond you with relatives that you've never felt connected with before.

Ask relatives who may have information beyond or different from your own. Your request may open doors to long distant relationships.

Remember that one of your purposes for searching for this information is to offer it forward to your family: children and grandchildren, nieces and nephews, and family babies yet unborn. Without this information, future generations will be more estranged or disconnected from family. Remember, once you are gone, much valuable information is lost forever, information that can be lifesaving and life enriching for those who will follow.

> **"When someone loves you, the way they say your name is different. You just know that your name is safe in their mouth."** — anonymous 4 year old boy

Though this may be a simple exercise for many of you, it can be complex and emotional for those of you with painful pasts. Some of you may be adopted and have the dual struggle about what to pass on: information about both your adopted family and your birth family. Others may hear painful histories of emigration during, before, and after wartime. Parts of your family, and even basic information about them, may have been lost in horrific circumstances: in wars and displaced persons camps. You may be able to go back a century or more, but find that family names were changed by outsiders or by family members wanting to forget the past or protect the future.

These differences in circumstances may limit how much information is available, and how far back you can look to find data. Consider that important information too. Look for a family Bible that someone may have kept. As a source of information preserved handwritten pages is an invaluable gift for future generations.

Contemporary sources of information are available in very different forms and formats. Depending on your interest and ability, there are many genealogical sites online that can help you trace family members.

> **"A name is like the beginning of the ball of thread that will lead you through the labyrinth."** — Geraldine Brooks

Beware of the many businesses that offer to provide genealogical information. Before you go in this direction, realize that even when very successful, searches only find names and dates. This information provides limited satisfaction. Names and dates are not the same as hearing about ancestors' values that come down through the family through stories. Some professional searches may be costly and provide no guarantee of success. Be cautious. Ask lots of questions. Don't sign anything you don't understand or get seduced when you hear fanciful promises of success. Genealogical businesses may mean well, but they are businesses, and you want to be clear about what you're buying.

My personal interest in names, dates and places began long before I was introduced to the ethical will in the 1990s. I have a vivid memory of a summer evening in 1957. My fiancé and I sat on his front stoop asking his grandmother about her family's history. She loved telling us stories about her family. All had emigrated to this country as young people in the 19th century, and all but she had since died. She talked faster than I could write, and I did my best to get everyone's names – there were many siblings and cousins.

But there was a glitch. She'd said they were a family of eight, but I only had seven names. She repeated when I questioned her – yes, she said with great confidence, there were eight of them, and then she renamed just seven. I questioned her a third time, and the result was the same.

Then I noticed my fiancé signaling me with a strange look. So I stopped, thinking maybe Grandma was forgetful and he didn't want me to embarrass her.

He told me later that the family had grieved one of the sisters as if she were dead because she'd married interracially. They never said her name aloud again. It was a family secret held for three generations.

Wow!

For ancestors, include names in languages other than English, immigrant names, traditional, tribal, or religious names, nicknames, married names. Include any stories of how names were given, meaning of names in the original language, for whom your ancestor was named, and your relationship to each.

You may want to fill in your ancestors' information and pass your list to other members of the family to add information they know that you don't. When the file has made its way around the family, you can provide a finished copy for everyone.

Here's a list to start with, back three generations; some people will have more information from earlier ancestors, and others not:

1. My father's names, dates, and birthplace
2. My mother's names, dates, and birthplace
3. My paternal grandparents' names, dates, birth and death places
4. My maternal grandparents' names, dates, birth and death places
5. Names of my great grandparents, dates, birth and death places

Take time to record stories about your ancestors' names when possible. This will make them more alive as members of the family for you and those who follow. Here's where listening to relatives' memories about names, dates, and birthplaces will pay off. Stories others tell about the ancestors will make your search more interesting as well as making the ancestors real for you and younger generations.

"Naming things makes things what they are..."
— Toni McNaron

You can use the information you record in this reflective search to write a legacy letter to the generations younger than you, even the yet unborn in your family, to fill in the gaps that the old family Bible once filled.

This story suggests more than the complexity of foreign names. It's a serious reminder of how easily names can be lost.

A Russian immigrant stood in line at Ellis Island with his friend who was helping him pronounce his difficult, multi-syllable name so it could be recorded. The man reached the front of the line.

The immigration official, impatient when facing people with language difficulties, spoke loudly and clearly, "What's your name?" The new immigrant, frightened by the uniformed official, reverted to his native tongue, and responded, "shane feirgesson." (Translation: "Oh, I'm ashamed that I've have forgotten.") The official passed him through the line recording his name for that moment and forever forward as the Scottish "Shane Ferguson."

Names, Part III: My Experience Naming Others

Naming may be considered a spiritual act. In the Bible God gives Adam his first task: to name all the animals and birds that God created. This part of the reflection is an exploration about how *you* used this sacred human power.

> **"The beginning of wisdom is to call things by their rightful names."** — **Chinese proverb**

If you have children, what names did you give them?

For whom was each named?

What factors influenced your selection of names? How did you choose that name? What is the story behind the name? What was important to you about giving that particular name or names?

> **"The meaning of names often sheds light on the parents who choose the name, as well on those who receive the name. While names do not determine our destiny, they provide us with the opportunity to bring honor to the names we bear and to assure that those for whom we were named live on."** — **Bruce Kadden**

What are the relationships that were memorialized by this naming?

Write something about each of the persons whose names are carried by your offspring so they will have a substantive record to strengthen their connection to their own name, and to pass on to future generations.

Stories about how and why we were given our names add substance and significance to our names. Receiving a letter about the gift and brand of a name subtly suggests that recipients can honor their own children with similar letters to strengthen the link of family from generation to generation.

> **"The name carries the essence of the person."**
> **— Lawrence Kushner**

These unique, interesting and moving letters exemplify different ways that names are important to the named and the 'namers'.

1. Mom's letter to Leif is a superb example of sharing a mother's gift to strengthen her son's connection to family and tribe.
2. Susan's letter about her namesake gives her family a treasure and a hint about the part her family played in American history.
3. Martha's letter to her three grown children about her many name changes is an excerpt, from a longer letter about how and why each of them were named.
4. An excerpt from my letter to my granddaughter giving her the history of my names and requesting that she pass this ancestral name forward.

Dear Leif,

As your twenty-fourth birthday approaches, I am transported back to the time you were born and how you got your name.

We were expecting you to arrive on Labor Day in 1987, but you, with your independent spirit, decided to come on June 18, weighing just one pound, twelve ounces. There was no name chosen; the name-sign on the incubator said, "Baby Boy Brostrom." Your Dad and I had occasionally discussed wanting a Scandinavian name, since we are mostly Swedish and Norwegian, but we didn't have one picked out.

And here we were, watching you tubed and heated in that box, fighting for your life. Two days after you were born, they told me you were dying. You still didn't have a name – they said if we wanted last rites performed, you needed a name!

A few days earlier, when I was hospitalized and we knew you would eventually come early, your Dad had been running past Leif Erikson Park in Duluth. He came back to the hospital and said, "Leif sounds like a good name!" I didn't like it, so we didn't discuss it anymore. I liked Erik!

Then, as I sat there alone, watching you die, and your Dad was on his way and they asked me again for a name, I said, "OK, fine - name him Leif and if he's still alive in the morning, we'll change it to Erik."

Maybe it was your Viking spirit, the prayers said for you, the excellent medical intervention, your angels, but …. You did live till morning, and by then you had demonstrated for us all that you are a Leif, a persistent fighter with strength and fortitude.

My lesson in this was to listen to your soul wishing you to be named Leif and not to my personal desires.

May you continue to live your life with the compassion and love you have, in your Leif-the-Viking manner, filling us all with admiration as you create a life of unexplored territory, as Leif Erikson did.

Love,
Mom

"Fathers and mothers ... use names to identify their children's destiny." — Ellen Frankel

Dear Rochelle and Marc,

I want you to know MY history so you'll pass it on, and I want you to know from whom I received the legacy of being so outspoken, contemptuous of authority, defiant, and independent. I appreciate this legacy from Susanna and I am proud to carry her name.

This may come as a surprise but polygamy and witches are part of our family history. My name, Susan, came from past family members traced back through the precise genealogical records kept by my mother's sister, Ruth, and by my father's sister, Mary.

The name Susan can be found among the names of polygamist family members from my mother's uncle's third wife. However, the story most remembered about the origins of my name came from my father's family records, Susanna North Martin.

Susanna North Martin was born in Olney, Buckinghamshire, England on September 30, 1621. When she was young her mother died and she came to America with her father, stepmother and sister. She married George Martin, a blacksmith, on August 11, 1646, and they lived in Salisbury, Massachusetts with their eight children. Susanna was known as an outspoken woman, contemptuous of authority, and defiant if anyone attempted to ridicule her. She was hanged for practicing witchcraft on July 19, 1692, age 71, at the Salem Witch Trials.

Her problems with authority figures began 25 years before her trial. First she objected to her seat placement in a meetinghouse because it was below her station. Then she was accused of being an "imp"(another name for a witch) because during a very wet and muddy season, she appeared at a home with no mud on the bottom of her skirt or on her boots. I was always told that she was independent enough to remove her boots and lift her skirts (unheard of during Puritan times) to walk through the mud. Later she went through a lengthy trial regarding her father's estate. The courts did not agree that Susanna and her sister should receive proceeds from this estate because Susanna was "the most impudent, scurrilous, wicked creature of this world." When accused of this she said, "I have led a most virtuous and holy life."

On May 2, 1692 Susanna was arrested, along with four other women, charged with witchcraft, a capital offense. She was allowed no counsel; however, records indicate that her answers were "remarkable for independence and clarity." While awaiting trial she and the other women laughed aloud which indicated to the authorities that they were be-witched. Six weeks before her death she was given many physical exami-nations, sometimes twice in the same day, to discover if she had a 'witch's teat'. Apparently on one examination her breasts appeared to be full and on another they were slack indicating that she had suckled the devil. She was buried in a shallow grave, long since removed, but a memorial stone was placed for her in Salem, Massachusetts.

With all my love,
Mom

"The past is always present. The past is like the skin on your hands. It was there yesterday and it will be here today."
— Thrity Umrigar

Dear Carole, Bethie and Matt:

I want to tell you about my name as it was the first gift I received from my mom and dad. It has been important to me because in naming me after my grandmother they were also giving her a gift.

I was named Martha, Martha Albrecht no middle name, after my mother's mother, Martha Frost Gale. Our family called her Baba and her friends called her Mattie. Baba, my mother and I were all second daughters and in giving you, Beth, my second daughter, the name Elizabeth Frost, it was to honor my mother, Grandma Betty, and my grandmother, Martha Frost Gale. When I call you "Mattie," Matt, it started when you were a baby and you reminded me of Baba. Your name, Carole, as you know, has its own unique and precious history.

It's important to me to pass on to you who I remember my Baba to be. As a child I remember there being a heaviness to her that I had experienced as stern, but came to understand as a deep sadness in her eyes and in her bearing. She had four children, two boys and two girls. Forrest, her eighteen-month-old son died of pneumonia. Her musically gifted son, Roger, joined the Navy in his late thirties to be part of the Navy band and was killed on the USS Saratoga while he was playing, just three months before the war ended.

Only rarely did Baba mention either of her sons or perhaps I wasn't listening. I don't know. As I have grown older and have imagined her life, I feel so sad that I wasn't old enough or aware enough to have hugged her and looked her in the eyes and listened to her story. I do know how grateful I am to have the three of you and to have this opportunity to share some of my story and hers and how much I value my Martha legacy with my Baba. Each time you, my beloved grandchildren Melissa, Nick, Jessie and Carissa, call me Baba I am reminded of the continuation of that legacy and I feel connected both to her and to you.

As you well know when I married I took my husbands' names and used Albrecht as my middle name. Having been Martha Albrecht Lewis for twenty years, even though that marriage had ended, changing my name seemed like something I would get to eventually. Then one day I took my beloved dog, Benji, into his Vet's office. The receptionist said how nice it was to see little Benji Lewis. BENJI LEWIS! He had nothing to do with my ex-husband, whose name I was still using. If I didn't want Benji to have his name, what was I doing with it?!

On the inside I was still Martha Albrecht and it was time for my inside name and my outside name to match. Dad and Mom gave me a name that represented both of their families and reclaiming my father's name was no longer something I wanted, but something I needed to do. Three months later and twelve hours before my birthday my name was legally changed with the addition of Baba's last name and mom's maiden name. I will hereby and forever be known as Martha Gale Albrecht.

My wish for the three of you is that you have the wisdom to ask the questions that matter and the heart to truly listen to the stories. Sometimes the stories might even be your own.

I love you,
Mom / Baba / Martha Gale Albrecht

"On the last day that my mother spent on earth, I learned her real name, as well as that of my grandmother ... Li Bing-zi and Gu Jingmei." — Amy Tan

My dear eldest grand-daughter, Sophie,

This letter for you is about names, their power to define us, to connect us to our families and ancestors, and to our people's history and story.

I was named after my paternal grandmother, Rosa Brodsky Friedman, my father's mother, an immigrant originally from Kiev in the Ukraine. She came to Minneapolis with her first child, my Aunt Ethel, where her husband, Louis B. Friedman, a watchmaker, had settled before her. My father was born in 1907, two years after she arrived.

But there's more about her I want you to know...her name in the old country was Rachel; it was Americanized to Rosa when she immigrated. She died of heart failure on August 11, 1935, three years before I was born. I heard stories from my father, who loved her deeply ...that she smoked Tolstoy cigarettes, and was known as the local social worker because she helped immigrants, newer than she, to get settled in America. (Perhaps my becoming a social worker was a legacy from her to me too.)

When I was born, my mother, Bea...one of the women you are named for (Baiyla bat Jacob v'Minna) and father Ben (Chaim Dov ben Benjamin Lev v'Rachel bat Baiyla and Joseph) gave me her name...in Hebrew. But they told me they didn't like the name Rosa; they thought it too old-fashioned, and named me Rhoda.

When your Papa and I divorced, I wanted to change my name, which I did, and took the name Rachael as my own.

You and I have discussed that how we talk about a thing or perceive it makes it real. Well, until recently I thought about what I did as "changing my name." People understood my not wanting to be known by my former husband's family name, but why would I change my first name? I've said that I changed my name to symbolize my new life.

I had one of those "aha" moments that changed my perception, which of course changed my reality: I didn't change my name! I RECLAIMED my name, the Hebrew name given to me at birth. It's the name that connects me to my family and foremothers, not just my grandmother, but back to the Rachel of Genesis, one of our matriarchs.

Rachael had always been my name! I carry it proudly. Rachael feels like who I am from the inside out, binding me to the past, and I pray linking me to the future.

By the time you have children, there will be many people in your family to memorialize by naming. Please remember how significant your name is to you, and how powerful and meaningful an act it is to name others.

I, an elder daughter, mother of my only daughter, your mother … and you, her first daughter: Should you one day have a daughter I'd be proud if you named her Rachael. Because I am already in my seventies, and you are but eighteen, it's unclear whether I'll live to know your daughter…but whether I do or don't, I would love to know that the name that came down from your great great grandmother born in Kiev in 1882 is the name a daughter of yours carries linking the generations.

I love you, Sophie Bea,

Granny Rachael (Rachael
bat Baiyla v' Chaim Dov)

"In every conceivable manner, the family is the link to our past, the bridge to our future." — Alex Haley

We have explored our names and have been enriched by the stories that surround them. Perhaps we are defined by our names; perhaps we add layers of meaning to the names by our lives and experience. In either case, names connect us to a particular family and a specific history.

You can use the information and stories you wrote in the Name Reflection to write a legacy letter about your name or to a person you have named. You may want to include a copy of the Parts of the Name Reflection with this letter for their information (and of course a copy for your personal Legacy File). This legacy letter may fulfill the function of the family Bible of old. You may use the guidelines for writing a legacy letter found at the end of chapter two about blessing letters.

Now we're ready to harvest other legacy gifts received from our ancestors and their lives. These legacies link us to our past and as we write our legacy letters we become forever linked as well to the future.

Chapter 4

Linking Past and Future Generations

With this chapter we honor our history and begin harvesting our legacies from our ancestors. For whatever cultural or natural reasons, at a certain time in our lives we become aware of our curiosity about and a deep desire for connection with our family roots.

Some of this yearning, because we are a nation of immigrants, results in pilgrimages far from home to walk the land of our forefathers and foremothers. Others of us rely on reading, family reunions, communicating through and searching online for connections to the people in our past.

We're hungry to harvest the fruits of those relationships, especially with those who helped us grow, who nurtured and mentored us. It's harvest time, that season when we look at our values and make meaning of our lives. We've planted the seeds, watered and weeded, appreciated the power and generosity of the sun and rain to bring our lives to this season.

The Covenant Between the Generations

It's time to harvest the fruit of our lives, but there's more. Preserving and passing on those roots of our history is basic to the sacred act of legacy writing. Neither whimsy nor distraction, this is the act of becoming a responsible scribe, particularly if we are the oldest generation in the family.

It is in this context that legacy can best be understood as our covenant, our commitment: living as the conscious link between the past and the future.

> "Remember your roots, your history, and the forebear's shoulders on which you stand. And pass these roots on to your children and to other children."
> — Marian Wright Edelman

What do we give to fulfill our end of the bargain? First and foremost we take the time to reflect about and value the past and its lessons, the gifts passed on to us by our ancestors. And, then, after appreciating and integrating - perhaps for the first time - the knowledge, wisdom, and love that is our inheritance, we put our pens to paper to pass the past forward to the next generation.

> "One of the ways this reclamation takes place is through memory. This is one of the ways historians and storytellers keep us alive."
> — Lyn Cowan

What do we receive in the bargain? Realizing that the past and the future are connected, we increase our awareness of our own foundations and strengthen our identity. We experience a profound sense of belonging. We know more about who we are and where we belong. We also know the satisfaction of doing our part to strengthen family and responsibly preserve history and values for future generations. Seeing more clearly how we've been blessed by our histories, we are able to express naturally and lovingly the blessings that accompany belonging.

We hear these ideas often as our culture grays. As we age we may need to be cared for, but we shouldn't be satisfied to be merely receptors. Rather we experience fulfillment as we do our part, continue to be contributing members of the family, and fulfill our individual purpose through giving.

> **"Elders owe the family their wisdom...and they must write their letters to their grand-children."**
> — **Terry Hargrave**

So let's get personal and specific. We'll reflect to give personal form and substance to honoring our ancestors and being the link between generations past and future. At the conclusion of the chapter, we'll write legacy letters offering the next generations some of what we've learned. At the same time we can share some of the personal context of the text of our present lives.

In the fall of 2009, I worked with volunteers at the U.S. Holocaust Museum. It was a humbling opportunity. I was optimistic that these seniors could recover memories of nurturing relationships from before the war, and I was simultaneously terrified that they would feel disrespected if I did not focus on their Holocaust experiences. They had committed themselves, their very identities - some for more than forty years - to repeat their Holocaust stories so that the horror beyond understanding would not be forgotten, so the horror would never happen again.

But it's been more than sixty years since the war. I wanted their children, grandchildren, and great grandchildren, who yearned for whatever family roots were available to them, to know the treasures of family life and cultural values, not only about the horrific deaths of their ancestors.

I asked the volunteers to remember someone whom they loved before the Holocaust and to write a short story of this memorable person, and the values they'd learned from them. There was some mumbling, even grumbling, and then it got very still. I could only hear the sound of pens scratching on paper. Not more than fifteen minutes later, they were raising their hands, eager to be the first to share their precious memories with each other. Here is one of them (the introduction and blessing were added later by the author to compose a complete legacy letter):

Date _____

To my 3 dear grandchildren,

I want to reintroduce you to your maternal great great grandfather and hope you will someday tell his story to your own grandchildren. I visited him in Ludbreg, Croatia, where he lived, when I was just a little older than three. I hope you will feel as proud of him now as I did then.

Although it's almost impossible for me to remember anyone before the Holocaust, I do have a vivid memory of my grandfather—the Rabbi of Ludbreg.

In that town beggars came knocking on doors and asking for alms every Saturday and Wednesday—market days in that small town. But of course, they didn't come to our door on Saturdays, since my grandfather could not respond on that day—Shabbat. But on Wednesdays my grandfather would set up a little table in the garden when the weather was good and in the hallway in bad weather. On the table he would arrange little piles of change, and as the beggars, accustomed to this, and sometimes a Gypsy (Roma) or two came by, my grandfather would greet them and hand them each a little pile of money.

I was fascinated by all of this then—and have remembered it always as a lesson "to be kind to the less fortunate, and always be as generous as possible."

Your grandfather Dan and I grew up in very different worlds, so we were fortunate to have found each other and to have been able to share memories of family like this one. I hope that each of you, no matter what you choose to do with your lives, will never forget this simple lesson, this legacy from my grandfather: to pay attention to other people's needs and to be always as generous as you can be.

Much love from your
Grandmother Dora

Linking the Generations, Part 1: Memories of our Ancestors

1. Reflect on a time when you were very young. Remember an ancestor (a parent, a grandparent, or other relative) from before you were five years old. Remember something about that person that you want future generations to know about him or her. Here are some possibilities to rev up your memories:
    * A favorite story that keeps you connected to him or her,
    * A value of theirs that has influenced your life,
    * Something important to you about them that you want preserved and remembered,
    * Something that ancestor passed on specifically to you, with or without their awareness or yours, that you treasure today.
2. Write a paragraph to tell the story, capture the memory.
3. In a second short paragraph, write the lesson you learned from that experience, or why that memory is precious to you.
4. Before you begin your own letter, reread Dora's story and learning, and notice how the story and learning become the body of her legacy letter.
5. Reflect about someone in your family, in a generation younger than you, whom you think would value this story or who may need its lesson in their own lives. Choose this person to be the recipient of your story and letter.
6. Write a brief paragraph of context introducing the ancestor central in your story, clarifying how he or she is related to you, for the intended recipient of your letter.
7. Transform your story into a legacy letter. Start with a brief introductory paragraph setting the context. Close the letter with a blessing from you (review blessings in chapter 2), perhaps with a wish from you that they will cherish their roots and continue the legacy by preserving and one day passing these treasures to their children and grandchildren.

> **"Writing is essentially putting talk down on paper....and it creates something important to say to someone else who will be better for hearing it."** — Daniel Taylor

Now we're ready to do some editing. Remember when we edited blessings in Chapter 2? The same rule applies as we edit here: don't be overly concerned about grammar and syntax. Legacy writing is neither about perfection nor readying a manuscript for publication. Rather this editing is about finding your voice to express your authentic self, and making sure your words pass forward your love and wisdom to a future in need of both. If you are satisfied with your story as it is, make a final copy to go into an envelope for mailing. Be sure you keep a copy for your Legacy File. If you're not satisfied and want to edit your letter before you send and preserve it, consider the following as a guide.

Editing Suggestions

Set your ancestor story aside overnight or for a few days. After you and it have rested (time may offer you another perspective or more detailed memories), you can edit your story with fresh eyes.

Before you begin any rewriting, ask yourself the most important questions: Have I adequately conveyed the lesson I learned and my appreciation of my ancestor? Does the transition to the blessing express that I see the connection linking the needs of the younger person to the story honoring the relative of the past?

Limit your editing time to ten (10) minutes. If you're not finished after ten minutes, remember this is not about perfection. This is a personal letter from you, not some impersonal document. If you're enjoying the editing, continue until you're satisfied. Remember the purpose for your writing. This letter is about you being a living link transmitting your learning and love from your family's past to the next generation.

Another way to think about the precious link between us and those who came before is to consider our personal heroes and heroines, those who've impacted and influenced our lives. Below is a reflection to recall and remember with gratitude those people, some of whom exist now only in our memories, others still enriching our everyday lives.

These men and women may not be heroes or heroines in the classical sense, saving us by slaying dragons or like Superman appearing at the last second to free us from the villains of our lives. But they have witnessed for us as we wrestled with our personal dragons and demons. They have been role models, real life angels, prototypical pioneers, illustrating wisdom and love, being a living example of how best to live our lives. They supported us in dark times, had faith that we could recover and be whole, guided us in their unique ways to discover our strengths, and celebrated our successes.

> "But know this. No one has within themselves
> All the pieces to their puzzle....
> Everyone carries with them at least one and probably
> Many pieces to someone else's puzzle.
> Sometimes they know it.
> Sometimes they don't.
>
> And when you present your piece
> Which is worthless to you,
> To another whether you know it or not,
> Whether they know it or not,
> You are a messenger from the Most High."
>
> — Lawrence Kushner

The Power and Support of Heroes
and Heroines in our Lives, Part I

List 3 -7 people who fit into your personal category of: hero, role model, pioneer, exemplar. They may be people from your family, in your growing up neighborhood, schools, social or spiritual community, your work life. They may be people you knew as a child, an adolescent, or a young adult. They may be your contemporaries, younger or older than you. With each name, jot a line or two recalling why they are on your list.

Choose one person from your list, and reflect on their significance in your life, how knowing them has enriched or supported your development, growth, life or deepened the sense of who you are. Let your thoughts and your pen roam freely as you write about them...and about you and them....

Here are some suggestions to prompt your memories:

* How did you meet this person? What attracted you to this
  person? Did gender or age play a role in the attraction? How
  did your relationship develop?
* What values did you admire in this person? Were these values
  similar to or different from your parents' values? What
  influence did the person's values have on your life?
* How did this person influence who you are today—your
  relationships, career choices, attitudes and values, political
  beliefs, and community or global concerns?

Write a second paragraph reflecting on and expressing your appreciation of and gratitude for the person.

These memories and your appreciation can be simply transformed into a legacy letter. Begin with a brief introductory paragraph setting context of time and place in both your lives. Write the memories of your relationship, the influence it's had in your life, and your gratitude. Close the letter with a blessing (blessings can be reviewed in chapter 2). Perhaps you can conclude the letter with your wish that they understand and accept how important they have been to your life, that their stories and their values are now a part of your legacy to your own family and loved ones.

What you are about to read is a legacy letter written by a thoughtful and appreciative young man, executive director of the Sitka Center for Art and Ecology on the Oregon coast. He has no children of his own to pass his story and gratitude to. His letter was written to his family, the people he works with, and his friends. Respecting the link and learning from the generations before him, (homesteaders in Montana), Eric clarifies and appreciates how his immigrant Grandpa Tony influenced his values and his way of living life and death.

Notice how the context Eric sets in the opening paragraph puts him and his readers in the larger context of nature's cycles as he turns his attention to the human life cycle. We can literally feel the joy in meaningful work that Grandpa Tony has passed on to Eric.

Family, colleagues, and friends,

The end of a year, for me, brings a fair amount of reflection. I think back over the past 365 days and all the amazing things that have happened. The yearly cycles that bring the leaves and then send them fluttering. The twice daily tidal flows, the alternating rain and sunshine that helps our native grasses and spruce trees grow.... It's a breath that draws in and out in a regular cycle, refreshing and renewing.

This year I also reflect on the ones we have lost.... and both of my remaining grandparents. My grandfather passed away just this past Tuesday morning, and his death has led me to think hard about the impacts we make over a lifetime.

My grandfather was a farmer and rancher who raised cattle and wheat on the dry dusty plains of central Montana -- on the same land homesteaded by my immigrant German great grandfather in 1911. My grandfather would often say that he never worked a day in his life because he loved what he did and it didn't seem like work at all. He invented machines and fixed tractors. He built miles of fence and harvested uncountable bushels of wheat and barley used in bread, beer and food that's been shipped all around the world.

Born before electricity made it to Montana, in a time when air travel was still a curiosity, my grandfather experienced the creation of television, space flight, computers, cell phones and the internet. I remember how entranced he was with video cameras and how excited he always seemed to get with the latest model. He was a rancher who liked technology.

But what I appreciated most about my grandfather was that he was generally very cheerful. He smiled a lot, and, even in the earliest photos I have seen of him, had a jaunty pose and flyaway hair. From the beginning, he seemed ready to really enjoy his life, right to the end.

Which is what he did. When he died, my grandfather was just two months short of his 90th year, and, was only a few months before, walking his irrigated fields, helping with the cattle branding, and participating in the harvest. He loved to be in "the Chris Vines shop" welding some device or driving the combine during wheat harvest. When he couldn't work anymore, when he couldn't go out into the fields, he willed his own death, in his own bed, on his own terms, and under the gentle care of his two sons and his two daughters.

And now, as I look over the span of my grandfather's life -- all the changes he saw, the harvests he reaped, the children, grandchildren, and great grandchildren he welcomed into the world -- I realize that even with 90 whole years, our time on this earth is short indeed. That life is too short to spend doing work that doesn't feel like play, too short to not be enjoying ourselves and savoring the best parts of our lives, full and complete.

I am fortunate to be working at a place that brings me tremendous satisfaction, surrounded by people who seem bent on bringing as much joy to others as they can manage. I'll be lucky indeed if I can get to the end of my life as graciously as did my Grandpa Tony, looking back on a lifetime of accomplishments, friendships, and work that wasn't work at all. He's given me a good standard to strive for.

Eric Chris Vines

Before moving on, you may want to write legacy letters to other influential people on your list, or about someone on your list who may become a model for someone you know today. Is there anyone on your list with whom you've lost contact but would like to reconnect, in person or in writing? The legacy letter is an opportunity to share what your relationship with them means or meant to you. If you choose not to send the letter, once written, keep it in your personal Legacy File.

Personal Reflections

When you've finished with your reflections and legacy letters linking generations past and future through story, appreciation and blessing, take a few minutes to reflect, evaluate, and record your thoughts and feelings about what you've learned. Through legacy writing, you may come to see yourself and your role models differently. This private writing can be preserved in your personal Legacy File.

The purpose of our next exploration is to celebrate immigrant ancestors, to reintegrate their stories and values into this generation's family, and to learn the ways immigration has affected our families since that time, whether it happened but a few years or decades ago, or centuries long past. Eric's letter (above) connects these two chapters: about appreciating people who have influenced our lives and honoring the values of his immigrant grandfather. We're fascinated with genealogy and many of us spend years planning visits back to the "old country." Let's see what this looks like from a legacy perspective as we turn to chapter 5.

May the memories and life lessons
uncovered from your roots
strengthen your family and the identity
of your loved ones.

Chapter 5
Digging Deeper: Legacies From Our Immigrant Ancestors

In this chapter we'll explore what it means today that our roots can be traced to every continent of our planet. What's special about digging deep in our garden is that our harvest promises us surprises.

> **"One's ethnic history determines the basic formation of one's psyche."** — Lyn Cowan

Except for Native Americans, all of us have immigrants as part of our family history and our cultural identities. Like our names, we know we have immigrant ancestors, but haven't paid much attention to what that means for our lives and our legacies.

> **"I never met my maternal grandparents. Yet their lives, as much as their deaths, had a profound influence upon my brothers, myself, and multi-generations in our family.... As children, we learned about the compassion, activism, and tragic deaths of our grandparents.... Family stories of courage and survival permeated our childhood.... It instilled in me compassion for the powerless and a desire to pursue justice."** — Janos Maté

The Impact of Immigration

As we explore the impact of immigration, we expand our commitment to preserve the past for the future in relation to both time and space.

Immigration can be a catalyst strengthening families as we face the complex daily challenges of change. The inherent difficulties of immigration also have the potential to disintegrate families. Some families are torn apart, lose contact, and remain bereft of the support so needed in difficult and celebratory times. Others succeed no matter the stresses and are transformed by the challenges of the immigrant experience.

The purpose of this exploration is to celebrate our immigrant ancestors, to learn the ways immigration has affected our family since that time, and to reintegrate their stories and values into this generation's family, whether it be from as near as Canada or as far as China and a few years, decades, or centuries ago.

> **"We treasure the voices of our ancestors; we warm ourselves with the worn fragments that we have of the stories of their lives. We ourselves will be ancestors one day."**
> **— Pat Schneider**

When I began writing Women's Lives, Women's Legacies *more than a dozen years ago, one of the first things I realized was that I knew little of my grandparents, emigrants from Eastern Europe at the turn of the 20th century. I was almost sixty when I realized my loss and it was too late. I couldn't ask them my questions; they'd all passed away. My parents hadn't been very interested in their roots or so it seemed to me, but they were gone by this time too.*

Perhaps this is a wild generalization, but it seems to me that first generation Americans use most of their energy to figure out how to fit in, to assimilate, to belong. They are consumed with living in the present, and have little patience for the past, especially their old world parents, many who speak English poorly or not at all.

The immigrant generation, with a foot in two very different worlds, feels intimidated and vulnerable. They stick close to home and are most comfortable in the company of fellow immigrants. Often their experiences were difficult, painful, even horrific, and they chose not to talk about them. In that time, there was less chitchat about "the good old days" maybe because the days were thought better forgotten.

But what that meant for second generation Americans, is that our yearning for roots – our longing to know the stories and lore, to hear the music of our family and tribal history, to harvest the fruits of the seeds they sowed – was lost. Maybe we'd asked too little too late.

> **"What I do know now is this: there's so much you don't really see, preoccupied as you are with the business of living; so much you never notice, until suddenly, for whatever reason...you decide that it's important to let your children know where they came from---you need the information that people you once knew always had to give you, if only you'd asked. But by the time you think to ask, it's too late."**
> **— Daniel Mendelsohn**

It's important for us, as we commit to being the link, to seek the stories of the past if they still exist. This celebrates the older generation and preserves the stories for future generations.

I think we mistakenly understand assimilation to be that we'll all look, feel, and act the same. This not only perpetuates an unrealistic picture that America is a "melting pot," but it robs us of the harvest of diverse riches inherent in a nation of immigrants.

We need to gather and preserve the wisdom, the rituals, the music, the food, the myths, and the history of the places and cultures that immigrant Americans offer us. For those families fortunate to have immigrant elders who are still living, this respectful gathering and preserving is a way these families can know their roots, their foundation, increasing their sense of belonging as they go forward. Without traditions and history, we, and our families, and our culture are left rootless and bereft.

> **"Maybe all exiles try to re-create the place they've lost out of their fear of dying in a strange place."** — Nicole Krauss

Searching for our Ancestors' Stories

There are two main sources for searching your unique family history. One is firsthand gathering: conversing with immigrants in our family still here to share their stories. The other is second or third hand (better than no history at all): to gather stories about the immigrant generation from those who knew them or knew stories about their lives. If the latter is your source of information, be ready to hear different, sometimes radically different, versions of the immigrant's life and identity.

When I was doing research about my maternal grandmother to use in my first legacy book, most of the information I had was what I'd heard from my mother who'd had a difficult relationship with her immigrant mother.

My personal memories of her were unsubstantial: an image of a stout woman enfolding me in a grandmotherly hug; a memory of watching fascinated while she removed hairpins to loosen the long yellow-white braids she wound around her head, repeating my name lovingly, but in a strange accent.

My mother described her mother as "depressed, vain, and dysfunctional." So I accepted that was who my grandmother was. That description and perspective left me with many questions about her life before she came to America, her emigrating alone as an eighteen year old girl at the turn of the twentieth century, her marriage, and her life raising six children in this country.

I shared the story of what I found out about Gramma Minnie with my cousins and received an astonishing letter in the return mail from my older cousin Milton, who'd lived with her between 1937 and 1940.

He described Gramma as playful and loving. He shared his memories of the inviting aromas from her kitchen, of her delicious cooking and baking. He recalled her travelling alone across the country to visit them when she was in her seventies. He wrote, "No, she was not a difficult woman. She was not vain. She was a completely independent, mature person. Today her independence would not seem unusual."

Rather than compressing meaningful information into a short legacy letter, in this chapter we'll use our skills to "gather-harvest" the rich descriptions and stories often hidden deep within or available only in the memories of others.

> **"How vast is her silence in the ears of her granddaughter!"**
> — **Pat Schneider**

Some immigrants may be timid or tentative about talking about a past that reminds them of difficult or sad times. Others may believe they have nothing to tell that would interest anyone now or in the future.

Mies van der Rohe said, "God is in the details." Let's replace 'God' with 'the sacred' and 'what's memorable'. Remember the details in Dora's legacy letter, honoring her grandfather from Ludbreg before World War II? What happened in the rain, "a couple of Gypsies" among the regular beggars, and the little piles of coins on the table (page 48). Let's be sure to ask about the details: what people were thinking, feeling, and saying, not only what happened.

> **"It's always the small things. It makes it like life. The most interesting thing is always the details…."**
> — **Daniel Mendelsohn**

Our challenge is to assure them that their experiences are valuable: that their stories will strengthen the family and link the generations … and that we personally are interested and curious for our own benefit, wanting to hear all they're willing to tell in whatever form or language.

Having a structure, seeking direct answers to specific questions, will be most comfortable and efficient for some story seekers and interviewers. For others, using questions as a guide to keep things on track in more unstructured conversations works better. Each of us needs to decide what works best for the elder immigrant family member and us.

It's not surprising to find that some immigrants will share more freely in their native language rather than English. It may be easier for us to listen attentively and not take notes; we can use a recording device, provided that doesn't threaten or inhibit the storyteller. We can then transcribe, translate, and organize the material at a later time.

For conversing with those frail and easily fatigued by the effort of remembering and talking: Choose times when the immigrant is most awake and aware. Don't wear them out. Be sensitive to their energy limits, which may be very different from our own. Finally, be patient, willing to have as many conversations as it takes.

If just one person better understands the time in which the ancestor lived, if one long-estranged relationship is redeemed, if just one long held secret is released from the family's shame, if one reader experiences a family, ethnic, tribal, or historical connection, then our time and effort gathering and preserving these memories will have been worth it.

Some years ago I convened a small group of interested people to share my vision about doing legacy work with immigrants from the former Soviet Union. The project never got off the ground for a variety of reasons, but we learned a lot about the kinds of questions to ask and the difficulties to be prepared for in complex situations. We sought wisdom from people who had worked extensively with immigrants, and talked with many immigrants too.

One important thing I learned from that project was that different cultures have different understandings of words and values from my own. For example, a woman, who'd emigrated from the USSR in 1979, explained that Soviet citizens were acculturated to 1) expect that needs would be taken care of by the state and 2) that volunteerism was NOT about volunteering. Rather if you were 'invited' to volunteer, you were really being coerced. If you refused to volunteer, you could lose your job or worse. Thus Soviet immigrants distrust this word and don't have a sense of service as many others naturally do. She told me, "Be patient – wait for our children – we are a lost generation."

Another example: After planning to facilitate a conversation about "freedom" with a relatively new group of immigrants, Hmong mothers and their teen daughters, I was surprised to find out that the Hmong language does not have a comparable word for 'freedom' in their lexicon.

How to understand, born and raised in our democracy, what life means without that word, a concept so basic to our way of life?

Reading Suggestions

I've read and recommend three autobiographical memoirs and a novel that helped me understand the unique and universal issues of immigrants.

The first, *The Promised Land*, chronicles twelve-year-old Mary Antin's 1893 journey from Plotzk, Russia to Boston and describes the culture shock of her immigrant experience.

The Latehomecomer: A Hmong Family Memoir, is Kao Kalia Yang's account of her family's flight after the Vietnamese War from Laos to Thai refugee camps, where Yang was born, and finally to St. Paul, Minnesota when she was seven. "She learned to live in two worlds yet remain distinctly Hmong."

Perhaps my favorite is Eva Hoffman's *Lost in Translation: Life in a New Language*. This is the elegantly written story of a Polish girl, hiding in the Ukraine to survive the Holocaust, immigrating to Canada as a thirteen year old in 1949. Her book is divided into three sections: 1) "Paradise", about her childhood in Krakow, 2) "Exile", her voyage to and adolescent years in Vancouver, and 3) "The New World", her account of her assimilation as an American and her discovery of finally being at home in the English language.

Ole Rolvaag's *Giants in the Earth*, translated from Norwegian, is a powerful novel that suggests the wealth of human potentialities brought to America year after year by the peasant immigrants who scattered the length and breadth of the land. This is a haunting story of life on the Dakota plains in the 1800s. It highlights the dramatic contrast between Per Hansa, prototype of the pioneer who sees the promise of the wind swept plains, and his wife, Beret, child of an old civilization who hungers for the home ways and in whose heart the terror of loneliness gathers.

Reading may make your gathering of stories a more satisfying experience, useful both to you and the immigrants in your family. May you come to appreciate and take pride in their strength and sacrifice as you fill in the gaps in your history.

A Guide and Questions for Immigrant Conversations

Here are some questions and categories of questions to prompt or structure your creative conversations.

As we wrote about our names in chapter 3, we understood their importance to our identities and how names connect us to our families and history. This is a basic nonthreatening, and rich place to begin the conversation.

> "... To retrace [a name's] path is then to embark on an adventure in which the destiny of a single word becomes one with that of a community; it is to undertake a passionate and enriching quest for all those who may live in your name."   — Elie Wiesel

What was your name at birth? Has your name changed? If so, is there a story about why and when? (Possible prompts: for safety, for health, to Americanize?) What name do you prefer to be called today? Where were you born? By what name do you call the place where you were born, grew up, emigrated from? Before we leave names for another topic, we can take the opportunity to gather information about the immigrant's family's names (siblings, cousins, parents, grandparents).

Describe where you lived before you emigrated? With whom did you live? Did relatives live nearby? What do you remember about that place? Share a childhood memory. Did your family own land? How did your family feed and clothe the children? What did your parents and other family members do for work? Was your family literate, educated?

What difficulties did you and your family face in your birth country?

What do you remember about cultural and family traditions, spiritual or religious practices from your childhood? How did external circumstances affect you and your family? (Possibilities: wars, religious or racial persecution, repressive government.) Do you still have family or contacts there? How did you feel about your birth country as you were leaving it? How do you feel about it today? In the sense of 'homeland', what do you miss about it? Have you returned for a visit? Would you consider going back? Where are your ancestors buried?

How old were you when you emigrated? For how long had you planned/hoped to emigrate? Describe circumstances and procedures necessary to make it happen. What are your emigration stories (memories)? Were you alone? With others – whom? What sacrifices/losses were made and by whom for you to emigrate? Describe the physical journey of emigration with all its challenges, dangers, adventures, hopes, dreams, fears, for yourself (and those who accompanied you).

"I cannot have a future 'til I embrace my past."
— Debbie Friedman

In a 2011 sermon about this generation's responsibility to provide hope and security for future generations, my rabbi, Simeon Glaser, recounted the story of his grandmother instilling hope in her daughter (rabbi's mother) as she left Germany for America:

"In 1939 a young girl in Germany was about to depart alone for an 11,000 mile journey half way around the world to safety. She asked her mother what was going to happen when they parted. Her mother told her to have faith in God's angel that protects all children and ensures their safety.

"He said, 'I reread that part of the girl's story of my mother's book published posthumously just three weeks ago. It is a book filled with fond memories, gripping descriptions of her youth in Germany, her neighbors and family, the Nazi rise to power, her journey at age 12 alone by train through Siberia, China, Japan and finally to San Francisco.'

"There is hope on every page. ...

"He went on, 'Mom always felt that angel her mother provided accompanying her on her journey. But then at one point she realized in Kobe, Japan – the last stop before the U.S. – that her visa had expired and the officials were determining whether she could continue through or be sent back. Agata became separated from the rest of her group in a train station and she believed she had reached the end.

"She wrote, 'I walked slowly around the deck as the officials deliberated. Tears left their wet tracks on my cheeks as, finally, I cried. Oh angel at my shoulder, I thought, I can barely feel your presence. Are you there? Oh Mother, you told me the angel would be there always. Angel, will they let me go? If I fall on my knees and beg, will they let me go? Then they called me. One of them wrote something in the passport, another stamped it and handed it back to me. They all smiled and bowed. I was free to go.'

"The rabbi concluded, 'No doubt my mother was scared when she parted ways with her parents for that long journey. But her mother said: take this angel with you to remind you that you are not alone. Ever. This is not the end, but the beginning of a great adventure. Let this angel remind you that there is hope and that I have faith in your future.' "

> **"...the memory of our foremothers, whose bodies bore us and whose images are still imprinted in our souls as in rock, even though long sealed and buried under layers of soil and oppression."** — **Lyn Cowan**

More Questions

What myths about America did you have while still in your birth country? What were your first challenges and difficulties when you arrived? If you had it to do over, would you have emigrated? Why? What limitations did you (and do you) experience in America? (What doors were/are closed to you?) And what doors were open and closed to you in your birth country? What can you not yet forgive, or still have bitter feelings about, about your birth country, the United States, or both?

What are the biggest challenges you face today as an American immigrant? How do you feel/what do you think about the issues and attitudes about immigrant communities in the US political world today?

Have you become a citizen? When? What was your experience of making the decision? What did you have to do to become a citizen? Does "America" feel like "home"? How? How not? What are your views about Americans, American life and culture? Who are your friends (new or people from your birth country)? Your (social/work/spiritual) community?

What's a secret you've held about immigration that you don't want to have die with you? What (memories, attitudes, material things, feelings, spiritual or religious traditions and observances) did you bring with you, and what did you leave behind? What is your greatest disappointment? Regret? What is the greatest challenge in your life now? What are you most grateful for in your life?

If you could share with those you left behind, what would you want them to know about you, about your life in America?

What are your concerns/blessings for your family today?

If you could share the wisdom of your life experience with loved ones of the future, what would you want them to know about you, your life story, your values, your hopes and dreams for them?

Don't expect yourself to ask all those questions to any one person. They're here as a guide. Some of them will fit with one family member; others may elicit stories from another. We're each unique, and like with our unique blessings and legacy letters, we each will find our own way of encouraging and supporting, searching and conversing, harvesting and preserving.

When we've gathered the stories, histories, and values of the immigrants in our family, we'll need to make choices about how to preserve and communicate them to future generations in our families. See the Afterword, "Wrapping Up Loose Ends" beginning on page 218 for suggestions.

And finally, after all of our exploration and effort to connect earlier generations - our ancestors, to our families of today and tomorrow, there are still those who have no recollections, no living relatives to question, no written histories, no mementos, and no stories to evoke belonging.

For those legacy writers, here is a different opportunity to use our creativity to feel belonging and make connections with an ancestor. Most history is written by men and focused on men, so we'll break precedent here and focus our attention on a foremother. To build this link when we have no physical clues we'll need our imagination and our intuition, faculties beyond the fact-finding part of our brains.

> "The intuitive mind is a sacred gift and the rational mind is a faithful servant. We have created a society that honors the servant and has forgotten the gift."   — Albert Einstein

Exploring a Foremother

To begin, consider your feminine ancestors, and then choose one who you would like to know better. She may be one of your grandmothers or a great grandmother, an aunt, or another relative.

Even if you know little or nothing about her, choose a woman about whose life and experience you're curious. Or choose a woman to whom you feel particularly connected, especially if she seems mysterious. You don't have to know at this moment why you feel attracted to her. She may be a foremother you've never met, a woman whose life was lived long before you were born.

> **"Our ancestors and our ancestral wisdom live in our blood and in our bones."** — Julia Cameron

When you've made your choice, write her name at the top of a page of paper. Spend no more than five (5) minutes compiling a list of the facts you know about her. It's okay if your list is short. Consider what you know and what you don't know about her. Below your list of facts jot notes about your assumptions about her, what you believe is true about her. Here you may include stories you were told about her, or rumors whispered about her, about which you have no proof of their authenticity. Spend no more than five (5) minutes recalling and recording your conjectures.

Knowing what you know for sure and knowing what you think you know illuminates the gaps in your knowledge, the places where you have questions about her life and values, and how you are connected to her. Asking questions and remaining curious, more than focusing on the "right" answers, often yields a rich mine of meaning. When you finish writing your assumptions, record at least three questions you wish you had answers to: about her, her life, her legacy to you.

> **"Confidence...never comes from having all the answers; it comes from being open to all the questions."** — Earl Gray Stevens

> **"... have patience with everything unresolved in your heart and to try to love the questions themselves as if they were locked rooms or books written in a very foreign language. Don't search for the answers...the point is, to live everything. Live the questions now."** — Rainer Maria Rilke

You've examined the facts and your assumptions about your chosen foremother. You've asked yourself what more you want to know about her. You realize that she has given you a legacy: perhaps a positive quality, perhaps some unresolved issue from her life.

Guided imagery or visualization uses the mind but bypasses its boundaries. It integrates mind and feelings in a way that supports imagination and produces intuitive images. It is a perfect vehicle to look at a past you can't know with your rational mind alone, nor can you sense with your feelings. Here is a guided visualization to support you to recall and reclaim the legacies your foremother passed on to you.

Have a piece of paper and a pen ready. Reflect on the visualization first. You probably will have a richer experience if you ask a close friend to read it to you slowly, so you can stay inside the experience. Another possibility is to record it, then play it back to yourself writing as you listen. You can repeat these questions and the visualization with as many ancestors as you wish. Be sure to date your writing.

Visualization

See your foremother in your mind's eye. Observe everything you can about her: her age, her gestures, the way she carries and uses her body, her expressions and demeanor, what she's wearing, even how she smells. Be aware of the qualities of her character that make her unique.

Notice her physical surroundings. See how she was personally affected by her circumstances, her culture, her time in history. Be aware of her life lessons and struggles. Of what was she most proud? What were her greatest disappointments? What values, what legacies did she pass on to her children by the choices she made and the way she lived?

Imagine that you can take yourself back in time to the place where she lived . . . step into her clothes and into her shoes . . . take on her posture, gestures, mood . . . experience her feelings . . . incorporate her thoughts . . . embody the ordinary and extraordinary qualities that made her unique. Experience what it is like to be her.

Then see her sitting at a table with a pen and paper in front of her. She picks up the pen to write you a letter. This letter will include the things she wants you to know about her: her hopes and dreams . . . her struggles, satisfactions, and achievements . . . her regrets and fears . . . her loves and joys . . . her values and ethics . . . all that mattered most in her life. She concludes her letter with specific words for you . . . a special message . . . her legacy meant only for you.

Now pick up your pen and be her scribe through time and space:

"Without memories a race has no future"   — Denise Linn

Reflective Writing

Writing after a creative experience helps us to return to this moment, this place, and take stock of what happened. Writing this letter may have stimulated strong emotions, as well as new thoughts and connections. The legacy your ancestor sent you through time and space may have a significant impact on your life going forward.

Some or all of what you wrote may please you; some of it may be disturbing. Recognize the special power and gift of receiving legacies from a feminine ancestor who you may never have met. As you write about your experience, check what you trust and what feels right.

What specific legacies did your foremother leave to you? Had they been expressed before or did this exercise break a long family tradition of secrecy or silence? How has your connection to your foremother changed because of this writing? How does a relationship with her clarify or deepen your roots? How does it add to your experience of having your own special place in your family? Reflect on how receiving this legacy can affect your sense of yourself in this period of your life. Consider ways in which it may influence the legacies you want to leave your loved ones.

Although our reflective writing will probably not appear explicitly in any legacy letter, it may deepen our insights about ourselves and our ancestors, thereby contributing indirectly to our legacy communications to future generations. It may also clarify values that you want to pass forward to future generations in a legacy letter.

Excerpts of Legacy Writers' Reflections after the Visualization

I never thought to ask her questions about herself, a real regret. Now I'm thinking about approaching my mother in this fashion before I don't have the chance.

Rekindled connections with cousins in Denmark

This raises so many more questions!

Made me want to spell my name in an Icelandic way! It made me think about what brings the fullness of life.

I felt filled with insights from a wise woman of whom I had so few memories.

So much came tumbling back to my mind: The meals, the garments, the church, the cooking, the beautiful sewing. From my earliest childhood until she died, I'm ashamed that she embarrassed me when she was such an oddity.

While writing this letter I felt my grandmother talking through me. I had never heard her voice, but she had a soft voice. She wore her flowered dress covered with an apron. She smelled of sweet peas and smiled while she talked, touching my arm and sitting close. I felt loved and encouraged. It was nice to think of her caring for me.

This is the first time I've felt a powerful urge to know more about my maternal Swedish lineage.

I feel close to my paternal grandmother for the first time. And I am committed to talk with my aunts who knew her to get the stories they can tell about her.

I realize how hard her life must have been. I learned doing this exercise that family is important to remember. Why else would we care about our legacy if we didn't value our roots?

Her shoes are too tight, the laces tickle, and her stays are poking. Time to go!

Grandma felt very present to me, and I to her. I want to continue this conversation.

Important place to be to realize she did the best she could.

This was eerie and I feel how much J___ does live on in me – physically, on a cellular level. She found order in a very hard set of circumstances, and so have I…. I recognize her legacy to me and can bring in the joy.

For me the process of writing facts, assumptions, and questions was more useful than the letter.

I realized how lonely, how overwhelmed and terrified she must have been as an immigrant woman.

I saw my grandmother as so one dimensional before this.

Writing it down seems to be magic! I experienced the actions of my grandma and verbally heard her ideas and beliefs

This was a very deep experience that gave me a whole new respect for my grandma. I wish I'd have taken the time to learn more about her when she was alive and told her how much she was loved and appreciated.

It felt as though the 'message' just flowed and came easily for me to write coming from my heart. I even thought my handwriting started to look different from my own and when I started to 'think' I felt I was 'leaving' and started to analyze too much.

I feel touched by her – she knows about me.

Enjoyed visualizing her. Expanded on limited information about her and possible unfair portrayal of her.

I feel like my head is a jumble of memories – a warm, familiar sort of longing to be together again.

I feel like I'm writing about a small part of who she really was.

I felt like she spoke through me and often guides me in my life – mostly without me being aware of it.

I loved thinking about my grandma but it is also more emotional than I thought it would be.

I felt a lot of compassion for a woman that had to leave her country and marry a man that was related to her.

This visit will remain in my heart forever.

We change the future as we heal from the past in the present. I thought this writing was about forgiving my mom. I now think it's about forgiving myself. I forgive myself for covering up my mother's secrets.

This opened the door to my past that I had never thought of exploring.

I was pretty young when my grandmother died and I only had one mental image of her. This gave me an opportunity to think differently about her.

From Facts to Reflections:
An Adopted Legacy Writer's Experience

Here is a moving exploration and letter from an unknown ancestor, the birth mother of a woman who was adopted very early in life. Note the poignancy and yearning in her questions, and the power of healing in her reflections after she scribed her mother's letter to her.

My Foremother: My Birth Mother

Facts:
1. She lived in New York City and had me there on April 24, 1945.
2. She was of legal age.
3. She was a tall, statuesque blond.
4. She gave me up for adoption.
5. Her whereabouts are unknown to me.
6. She gave her name as _____, also known as _____.
7. She named me _____

Assumptions:
1. She wasn't married to my birth father.
2. She was scared.
3. She wanted to keep me, but couldn't.
4. She was determined to move ahead with her life.
5. She thought about me often.

My Questions About Her:
1. What circumstances resulted in you giving me up for adoption?
2. Did you ever marry and have other children?
3. Did you ever try to search for me?
4. Are you still alive?

Her Letter to Me:

My Dearest Daughter,

I have so many dreams for you. I hope that you will be adopted by people who I would have chosen to be your parents if I had been able to pick them. I hope that they are well-educated, and that you have the opportunity to learn, to read, and to travel. I hope that you have inherited my love of music and the arts.

I wish for you good health, close friendships, and a life with someone who loves you for yourself, and who cherishes you. If you choose to have them, may your children respect and adore you. May your grandchildren have special memories of wonderful times with you.

I wish you a life of purpose; a life lived to its fullest; a life with no regrets. The only regret I have is that I will not be the one who will be at your side to teach and guide you.

I will always love you.

Post-Writing Reflections:

"I have something important to say. Writing is a comfortable way for me to convey my feelings. Writing made me feel validated. Writing this letter from her was a very emotional experience for me, even after all these years."

Making the Secular Sacred

If we accept the premise that all life is sacred, then our lives and the lives of our ancestors are sacred too. From a legacy perspective this means that we're writing these sacred stories as part of our legacies.

Here's where the Hebrew word and concept "midrash" clarifies our legacy writing. Midrash literally refers to interpretation of sacred text. Though midrash is technically concerned with studying Bible, I believe it describes our legacy writing for ourselves and our ancestors. My logic follows: Our lives are sacred. Our stories are our interpretations of our lives. Our legacy writing is then a personal, family, and cultural sacred text.

> **"As we tell our own stories we often discover the divinity that is present in our lives. And if we listen carefully, we hear our stories as part of the cosmic story."**
> **— Rabbi Laura Geller**

Before we shift our attention from decades and centuries past, from oceans and continents away, to an exploration of who we are here and now, our work and our relationships, let's enjoy the details and midrash of a legacy writer's experience with her grandmothers when she attended a legacy writing program we did at Vina de Lestonnac, a Catholic Retreat Center in Temecula, California.

At the Crack of Dawn ...

"The Grandmothers" arrive in my room early this morning. "We heard something about you writing our stories," they say softly, sitting on the sides of my bed. "Is it true...?" asks Rosa Wagner Erb, my Bavarian grandmother, her brown eyes glowing. Although it is not yet light, I can see her smiling at me...her black and silver hair folded into lacquer combs atop her head. "I have so many stories to tell you," she says with that girlish excitement I remember from sitting at her farm kitchen table 60 years ago.

"This is a good idea, Carol," my Norwegian grandmother says, speaking her own mind. I have not heard her speak my name before; she died when I was three. But this morning...Christine Berg Hesla is very much alive. So much so, I can smell faintly the cow's milk and the coffee on her cotton apron edged with lace. "Ah, so many stories, and not enough time," she says sadly, this grandmother I never knew. "You will do us a kindness to pass our stories forward. And if you take the time to listen, we shall tell them to you. In fact, you will remember them as if you had been there." Christina Berg Hesla smoothed her pale apron, as if she had said enough. Her blue silver eyes are gemstones in the half light...reflections from the fjords of Norway.

So here I lie in a convent-retreat bed, wrapped in my own mother's shawl with two departed centenarians inviting me to write their life stories. It is 5:30 AM on February 19, 2007, and I myself am 62 years old. My grandmother then has spoken the truth—"so many stories, and not enough time."

My rational mind defies all the quiet chattering around my bed. But after an hour, I can no longer dismiss it. At this ungodly hour there are 3 of them gathered on my bed. Christina Berg Hesla on my left side. Rosa Wagner Erb on my right. And sitting at the end of my bed, with her legs crossed is – "Midrash." How she ever got here I'll never know, but the Grandmothers are anxious to speak.

"You are resistant to writing this down, aren't you?" Christina says. I nod. "Well, let me tell you, Carol, that we are more eager to write this story than you are. Moreover, you must understand that we are as alive as you." I see Midrash in the early morning shadows. "Do you think we ever stopped loving you because we are here, and you are there? That is impossible. Just touch your own heart, and feel that surging river of love you have for all your granddaughters – and you will know we speak the truth."

"You must trust us. There are still people alive who can fill in the details, the datelines of our lives. As they say, 'God is in the details.' And believe me, She will be! But there is so much more than details that we can tell you," she continues. "We both know the hardships of surviving bitter cold. And yes, we both know much about being in love. The needs of one are the errands of the other. As for Midrash ... She serves the truth, always. She serves the Spirit. She has both a light touch and a heavy hand. But it is because of Her, that we are able to have our voices again. Your part is to wake up. Oh please wake up..."

Finally I am alone in my room and it is quiet. How bizarre this is, I think. That these two women, one from Bavaria and one from Norway ... came to Saskatchewan as pioneer wives in 1905. They homesteaded 47 miles from one another. Their son and daughter married each other. And they never ever once met.

Chapter 6
The Value of Work

In chapters four and five we harvested legacies we received from ancestors, from the family homestead as well as from centuries and continents away. Not only did we fulfill our yearning to capture and preserve our ancestors' history for the future, but we also addressed one of our own most important needs: to belong, to know our roots in our history, to revitalize the foundation of our being.

Now we connect the past to the present. From the experience of putting down roots we grow empowered to develop our own unique selves. None of us exists in a vacuum. We each have growth experiences in our families, with our friends, in our life work, in communal experiences, in our own country, and the world in our generation.

> **"Don't judge each day by the harvest you reap, but by the seeds you plant."** — **Robert Louis Stevenson**

This chapter begins an examination of who we've been since our births, and what we've made of our lives so far. This exploration will help us begin to recognize and articulate our values, and verbalize what means most to us. When we've harvested our values, learning and love, we'll be prepared to share our legacies with future generations.

Reflection

Shake free of thoughts about ancestors; Put on your musing cap and return to the present. What would you want someone of a younger generation to know about who you are: about your rootedness, your identity: Something you want to be remembered for, something in your life you feel joy or gratitude about, something that you find precious, something you love to do, or love about your life? When you've finished, store your writing in your Legacy File so you can use these important thoughts in a future legacy letter.

Here's an example of a grandmother sharing aspects of her identity with her granddaughter. She connects her qualities to a blessing for the five-year-old girl. Put in a Legacy File, this writing is clearly the body of a legacy letter special for Charlotte when she's a few years older:

To my smart, beautiful granddaughter, Charlotte,

I wish we lived closer and could share our lives more. We are both Aries. Last week, your mother told me that she and your grandfather were watching you at your nursery school graduation ceremony, and your grandfather remarked, "I thinks she's (you, Charlotte) inherited your mother's competitive spirit.

Your grandfather said this kindly, and it is my hope that no one ever makes you feel bad about being a leader. My feistiness has served me well in the life challenges I've faced, now face, and will face in the future. Two weeks ago, a friend was presenting me with an award, and said that I had an indomitable spirit and a brilliant mind. I don't know about that last part; I'm still ashamed that I flunked Algebra in the ninth grade.

Everyone faces challenges. At this stage of my life, I accept my feistiness; it is a disposition that allows me to focus on the positive—what I have, rather that what I do not. I am grateful that I am able to be grateful. And so, a positive, feisty spirit, intelligence, and generosity are things I hope for you, my beautiful first granddaughter. I pray that you love yourself and are valued by others for who you are and not what you do.

Working on Work

Who are we as working people in this arena where we spend more than thirty per cent of our lives?

Our work—whether in factories, at corporate desks, on the land, in schools, in healthcare, at our computers, as homemakers for our children and others', or as volunteers in the non-profit world—is worthy of exploration and reflection. Many of us have experience working in unique combinations of these very different worlds over our lifetimes.

For many of us work has only been a means to an end, but for others, work whether as a volunteer or for money is and was where our life purpose manifested and the setting where meaningful relationships flourished. We can clarify our values and pass forward our ethics, ethics learned from our own work experience and the generations who came before us.

Perhaps our unique life purpose can be distilled from observing how we spend and have spent our work-days, although some of us may find that our life's purpose has little or nothing to do with our daily work.

Maybe work and purpose are a matter of perspective. Here's a story that illustrates what I mean: A man walking by a construction site asked three stone masons what they were doing. The first man grumbled, "Can't you see I'm cutting stone?" The second laborer groaned and sighed, saying, "I'm building a wall." The third mason responded with a radiant smile, "I'm building a cathedral to glorify God for centuries to come."

> **"At birth our divine potential is folded up in us like a tent. It is life's purpose to unfold that tent." — Hildegard of Bingen**

Purpose

Before we roll up our sleeves to get to work on work, some thoughts about purpose.

There are those who suggest that we are born to this earth for our own soul's learning and evolution. There are others who submit that we are placed here to help make the world a better place. Still others say all that is hogwash and we're here just because; it doesn't matter what we do or don't do; we just live out our years and then we die.

> **"The purpose of life is to live a life of purpose."**
> **— Richard Leider**

In my days of doubt about the existence of a Force greater than myself, youthful and sure I knew everything, I declared myself an atheist. Yet always something nagged at me to abandon that position because it opposed what I could see: a world filled with beauty, inexplicable variety, and amazing complexity.

My naive perspective didn't allow for purpose, meaning, or gratitude. Today I deeply believe that all of us have some purpose for being here and that as we make our journeys through life, we eventually discover by living, not by thinking or reading, what our purpose is.

I was particularly fascinated in my late thirties when Rachel Naomi Remen and I, working with an Institute in San Francisco, interviewed patients recuperating from near-death at San Francisco General Hospital. Though their words differed, their stories were similar. They described traveling a long tunnel toward light (like the birth canal) and were told by a 'being' that it was not yet their time to die – that they had more to do on earth. They were turned back to their lives. And here's where the stories were uncannily alike. They weren't told specifics, but they were advised that they had more loving and learning to do.

Loving and learning is one definition of purpose that we can use as a prism to measure who we are, to examine our beliefs and values, and understand what we are charged to pass forward to next generations.

> **"If you judge people, you have no time to love them."**
> **— Mother Teresa**

Legacy writers often ask, "What if I'm not a good lover or a good learner? What if I feel angry, afraid, resentful, neither grateful nor joyful, wise nor loving?"

As you write your reflections, express both the negative and positive you uncover and experience. Putting feelings on paper may have a healing effect, reducing some of their hold on the critical story you've been telling yourself. (You may find the material powerful enough that you will seek outside help – a counselor, coach, or spiritual advisor – to help you with those feelings and experiences.) Once processed, those reflections are best shredded or burned.

Consider fifty or one hundred years from today – when you're gone and your great grandchildren are reading the legacy letters you've left them. You won't want to be remembered because you passed forward the old pain and negativity you experienced. Future generations don't need more anger, fear, or hate. Our world and theirs need more honest love. Future generations deserve to be blessed, supported, cared for and about.

Remember the editing suggestion in chapter 2, page 17, suggesting to assess how you'd feel if you received the letter you'd written. Remember the principle attributed to Buddha from the East, and in the West to the Greeks of antiquity, "Do no harm."

Reflection and Writing: Who Am I as a Working Person?

Write about any of the questions that pique your curiosity about who you are and have been as a working person. These questions are meant to stimulate, not constrict, our consideration of the meaning of work in our lives, what we've learned from our work, what we value about work, and what we want to share about ourselves and our work with someone of a younger generation.

Personal reflection

Begin with a history of your work life. What was your first job? How did you get your job? What was it like to earn money for the first time and what did you do with your earnings? What problems did you encounter? What did you learn from that first job?

What family values did you inherit that defined your perspective about work? According to your family's expectations, what work was acceptable, useful, meaningful, important, to do? What are *your* attitudes and expectations about work today?

What do the words *job*, *career*, *profession*, and *retirement* bring up in you?

For some men and women, "doing" and "achieving" make them feel worthy. If this is true for you, describe your experience—your work, time spent working, your workplace, and how work has influenced who you are.

What skills and gifts has work given you that you use in other parts of your life? What price have you paid for your achievements? Has your success or failure in the workplace defined you as a worthwhile person?

What have you learned about yourself from the workplace? Did you try to fit yourself into a structure antithetical to your basic nature? If yes, what's been the effect on who you are? How do you think that structure changed the direction or purpose of your life journey?

> **"The pitcher cries for water to carry,**
> **And a person for work that is real."**   — Marge Piercy

Has your work been a source of meaning and identity in your life? What do you appreciate and feel grateful for about your work? What values and traits have you been able to express in your work life? What have been your greatest challenges in your work life?

Has work distracted you from finding and knowing who you really are and what you value? Has work been a source of difficulty as you balanced other needs, desires, and responsibilities?

> **"I long to accomplish a great and noble task, but it is my chief duty to accomplish small tasks as if they were great and noble."** — Helen Keller

How do you define domestic work? Has domestic work defined you? What was your attitude toward domestic work? What is your present attitude about domestic work? Has your attitude changed over your lifetime? How does/did domestic work define your value and worth in others' eyes? Was your domestic work supported and appreciated or demeaned or ignored by family, friends, your community?

Are there specific domestic work activities that were significant in your development as a person, transferable to other areas of your life, or helped you express something uniquely you?

If you are a part of the generations of stay-at-home moms and housewives, how do you value your work? How has domestic work been an opportunity to make a positive contribution, make a positive difference in your world?

If you are a woman with a natural inclination to care for the home, how have you integrated your desire or the need to work outside the home? In retrospect, are you clear about how your work and other aspects of your identity define who you are?

I remember complaining to my therapist Lenore more than 35 years ago. I was so bored with homemaking. Making peanut butter and jelly sandwiches every day for years was driving me crazy.

Her response went something like this: it didn't matter what I was doing. What mattered was the attitude with which I did it. This abstract "being/doing" lesson was about my having a choice about the energy I brought to the task of making peanut butter sandwiches for the kids' school lunches. I could choose to fill those sandwiches with boredom and resentment or I could fill them with love.

At the height of my "doing" before I was forty, I wanted to be successful, seen and admired for how smart and hardworking I was. Her words made absolutely no sense to me then. It took me many years to begin to understand It. Even today when I feel bored and resentful about repetitious tasks, I still am far from mastering the idea of finding purpose in everything.

What is your vision of positive and authentic work in your future, whether you are or not yet officially retired? How can work continue to be a source of your development, your ability to repair our broken world, and to express yourself and your values?

Using a Journal as a Work Tool

Reflection: One practical use of journaling is to grow our power to observe and reflect about what we do. Writing can take us beyond the places we think we already know! A method for building awareness, journaling can also help us make thoughtful, informed choices. This tool/practice can be replicated about many topics and used with many work groups, for example your work team or your Board.

This reflection is specifically about "the preciousness of time." Its purpose is to increase your ability to observe within and without, and to use your observations ... for any or all of the following:

1. impart "what you do"
2. separate what you do from what you think/believe/feel - define identity/mission/purpose
3. prioritize your precious time
4. make informed decisions especially about transitions and changes (letting go and beginning anew)
5. articulate your values and your wisdom
6. build a foundation for a written legacy for those who will follow you

The Preciousness of Time: purpose/process/practice

With this reflective journaling process you may decide what you want to preserve and impart about the functions, the process, the vision and purpose that informs your work.

Commitment: 15 minutes a day, 5 days: to observe and explore how you use your time at work Monday – Friday.

Spend the first day exploring Monday

What to write? Just 2 things:

1. What you do on Mondays...can be a list of things—no need for full sentences or prioritizing—just get the functions recorded
2. Choose one of those functions/activities/tasks and explore its dimensions ... how you do it; why you do it; what's its value to you and/or others in the context of your daily work? How does it fit into the larger container of "your work"? Is this task solo or relational? How do you "feel" about the task ... from pure joy to dislike/resent/detest. Stop short of judging the activity or your performance or your feelings; your single goal is to increase your power to observe and be aware, later perhaps to communicate and preserve.

In day 2, write about Tuesdays; in day 3, write about Wednesdays, in day 4, write about Thursdays, and in day 5, write about Fridays.

When the 5 days are over, you may choose an additional 2 days – to explore your "leisure," non-working, weekend days.

After the five (or seven) days of 15 minute journal writing, you'll be prepared to choose a next step – here are some possible ones:

1. Burn the journal and continue your life as it is
2. Reread what you wrote to extrapolate your priorities and values
3. Differentiate *what* you do from the *value* of what you do
4. Prepare a legacy document for those who will follow you in your job in the future
5. Share what you've learned where it could be useful: with your fellow workers, your boss, your Board, the person who will follow you in your position

Use the learning, not so much as legacy for the future, but as a foundation to make new choices about the way you use your precious time each and every work day.

> **"The ethical will is a wonderful gift to leave to your family at the end of your life, but I think its main importance is what it can give you in the midst of life."** — Andrew Weil, MD

Sharing Your Perspective

Here are questions to turn the kaleidoscope from your reflections about work to share your thoughts with others:

If you could do your work life over, knowing what you know about yourself and your world today, what would you change, why? If you are nearing retirement (or have retired) is there a legacy (work that you initiated or were committed to) you want to share with those who are continuing that work?

The context seems always to be shifting: Our grandparents were part of a long gone agricultural society; our parents belonged to an industrialized society; and we are part of the transition from an industrial to a technological way of life. Each of these transitions signaled losses of familiar ways of life and work, including joblessness and retraining.

If you have children, what do you hope to teach them about work, and what of your work experience do you want to share with them?

Write a legacy letter to someone of a younger generation to share about some aspect of your work life and its context. If you could be an angel sitting on the shoulder of your successor, whether you're 75, 55, or 35, what work wisdom from your experience would you whisper in their ears? Perhaps you enjoyed some special work talent that you don't want lost. Or your letter may simply answer the question, "what did my Dad or Mom 'do' with their days?"

About Work and Making a Difference

> "In this life we cannot do great things. We can only do small things with great love." — **Mother Teresa**

One of the needs we all have is to make a positive difference in the world before we leave it. Here is an opportunity to do just that, in writing, that can be referred to long after you've left the store, the assembly line, the office, the early childhood center, the warehouse, the factory, the hospital, the nursing facility, the boardroom.

This is different from a job description of all that you've done for those who will fill your shoes though that might be useful. No, this is about assessing the value and meaning of your work, giving your voice and your respect to that work as a gift to those still on the job: giving them something useful, even inspirational as your departing gift.

This legacy letter by a leader expresses with good humor his love of his work and his fellow workers. It also offers the lessons and values the leader hopes to solidify, simultaneously respecting his team, trusting their ability to carry on after his departure:

Dear Guys,

This is a letter I have thought often about writing because it is about my departure, about how to explain moving on to other things and about trying to convince you what a good thing this is. Never doubt that I am well aware that many of you will not need convincing.

All of us should look upon this day as a reason to celebrate . . . to celebrate our accomplishments, to forgive our failures, to predict victories not yet won. If life here hadn't been all about change during the many years of my tenure, I might feel I hadn't prepared you for this day. If from the beginning I hadn't tried to convince you all that each of us is replaceable, including me, I would expect you to be apprehensive, skeptical, or even sad.

But our work life together has been all about looking ahead, mostly about looking to a better future. So today we have arrived at that better place.

In our tradition, whenever we arrive at where we are going, I let you know what is next and that usually means what *you do* next. At this stop, it means you remember for me a time we laughed, a time we found something so funny or preposterous we laughed uncontrollably or until we cried.

In parting, as you always have, I don't doubt that you will remember a moment or two when amid everything else, we shared some fun.

Picture for example what it would mean to you to receive a legacy letter from a president of your board, or a leader of the company where you work, when they were leaving.

Imagine the gift you could give by writing a legacy letter expressing what you'd valued, what your passion and purpose were as you did your job, and what you hope your organization will accomplish as someone else puts on the mantle of your position. Imagine that you could express your appreciation to people with whom you've lived "on the job" as you retire.

You can envision the support the person inheriting your job would experience knowing what mattered to you, what you tried to accomplish, what values drove you.

This letter, from a pioneer/founder of a state community health center, was written to his successor at the time of his retirement. The legacy letter served to ease the transition, reduce apprehension about "filling the retiree's shoes" and encouraged and supported the successor's adjustment to her new position. Though concise and constrained, we can feel the man's love for his work, the appreciation for him to have made a difference in people's lives, and perhaps even sense his sadness as he lets go.

Dear Successor,

There have been so many anxious moments in my work life that did not need to be. As strong as my wish for you to avoid those moments, I know you won't.

It is my hope, the blessing of your predecessor, for confidence in your ability, trust in your team, and that you don't/won't ever need to know it all. That will help you avoid some anxious moments.

You have one of those once in a life time moments on the stage of service to mankind. Don't be intimidated. Be energized and enjoy the contribution you have been blessed to have the opportunity to make.

God's speed and best wishes for success.

Your predecessor

Though few of us are presidents, executive leaders, board members, none of us worked in total isolation, and often our fellow workers have been the most supportive, the most fun, the most like-minded people in our lives. Especially if you're approaching retirement, or if you're transitioning to another position or company, you have the opportunity to gift your colleagues with your blessings.

This letter, written by a middle school teacher is a thank you to her faculty friends. They'd said their goodbyes to her with a baby shower at the end of the school year.

Dear Faculty friends,

I can't thank you enough for the beautiful baby gifts. I learned so much in these four years from your encouragement and generous coaching especially during my first year at JFK Middle School. I wish I could put all of you on my shoulder to whisper your wisdom in my ear as I begin my new career of mothering. Your most useful advice was to have a sense of humor, especially about myself when I was so serious and intense, never wanting to make a mistake.

I was embarrassed to tell you this story when it happened, but will now: Near the end of my formal schooling, some young teachers came to a class to give us practical tips from the field. We were eager to get something "live" to reduce the terror about being in a real classroom alone. One fellow said that something that'd worked for him when a kid wouldn't stop talking was to say, "Maybe you'd like to come up and lead the class."

Months later I had the perfect opportunity to use his tip with an adorable, smart, and very talkative boy who sat in the back of my 7th grade English classroom. When I said, "John, perhaps you'd like to come up and lead the class," he readily came to the front of the room, hopped up on the table (I often sat on), pretended to smooth a skirt over his knees, leaned forward and said, "Class dismissed."

Lucky for me the kids didn't dismiss, but they howled in delight. I had to laugh too, and at that moment something shifted for the good.

Thank you for reminding me often about having a sense of humor – seeing myself mirrored by a twelve-year-old boy was humbling, but in truth, also funny. I learned to stop fearing the kids and to treat them as little people – with dignity, and usually they treated me similarly. I always held high expectations for them, and they usually responded with creativity and good will, both qualities they'd be able to use beyond the classroom.

Thank you again for our years as colleagues and friends. I'll treasure our years together always,

Fondly, Ramona

This year-end letter to caregivers from the president of a hospital expresses his commitment to and appreciation for their compassionate care for patients. Ben's letter exemplifies using power to inspire others in the workplace.

Good morning--

One of the joys of being president at Abbott Northwestern is the opportunity to host the employee recognition luncheon. At the luncheon, we honor employees who have been nominated by a co-worker, patient or visitor for exceptional performance. At the most recent event--the first that I have hosted--each of the employees received their nomination for an act that demonstrated compassion. For some, the compassion was directed toward a patient, for others a visitor or a fellow employee, but all evidenced critical quality. From the days when our advertising slogan was "The loving arms of Abbott Northwestern," it is clear that putting our hearts into the care we provide has been one of our staff's core values.

I decided on a career in medicine after a formative episode in my life. As a young adolescent, I was a math nerd (hard to believe, I know, but it's true) who thought about engineering as a career choice. That changed after my brother, John, five years my junior and the athlete of our family, developed headaches that were diagnosed as a rhabdomyosarcoma of his jaw. This rare tumor was treated with surgery and radiation, and when those failed, chemotherapy. Unfortunately, the treatments available in the 1970s were not sufficient to save John, and he succumbed to the cancer after a six-month ordeal.

The experience was devastating for my family, and I attribute our ability to keep going to the compassionate care we received. The physicians and nurses who cared for my brother took us into their hearts and helped relieve our immeasurable suffering. I was profoundly affected by my brother's illness and realized that, as great as math and engineering were, I needed to be a caregiver to pay back the great gift the physicians and nurses who cared for my brother had given me and my family. I became more focused on my studies with a steadfast goal of getting into medical school. In my practice, I often thought of my brother as I tried to go the extra mile for my patients. I took a particular interest in hospice care as I knew that patients and families experiencing their final days together often feel deserted and need our support.

For me, compassion is at the heart of who I am, and I am thrilled to be part of a hospital that shares this value. I believe that compassion is a key driver of patient experience. When patients come to our hospital and feel cared for in a heartfelt manner, they will feel good about their experience. Although the other elements of an experience can't be neglected, we need to focus our efforts on supporting compassionate care. For most caregivers, working with patients is something they feel called to do, so they will naturally provide care that is compassionate. I see my role as removing obstacles to providing this care, supporting those who provide it, and celebrating outstanding examples of exceptional care when they occur. I appreciate the passion and compassion you bring to your work. It distinguishes Abbott Northwestern as a place where high-tech and high-touch care come together. You inspire me.

Sincerely yours,
Ben

Creator of the James P. Shannon Leadership Institute at the Amherst H. Wilder Foundation, Ronnie Brooks' letter to new leaders exemplifies the power of a person retiring to make a positive difference in people's lives. Here's an excerpt from her letter about choice making:

Dear Future Leaders,

I am thrilled to be ... at this point in my life and to have the opportunity to speak to the future...And what I wish for the future is that you—and many, many more people like you and not like you—can and will provide leadership that is effective, satisfying, and therefore sustainable....

Making this happen requires choice making based on clarity of purpose, reflecting deeply held values, and exercised with care and discipline, the kind of discipline that creates and respects limits....

I have a small garden for edibles—mainly tomatoes and basil—and am a generally frugal person, so when I was given a package of carrot seeds, I took the seeds home, dug a row, and planted them that very afternoon.

They soon sprouted; every one bright green and full of promise. I loved them and nurtured them and they grew steadily. A few weeks later a colleague and master gardener came over. When she saw the crowded carrot sprouts she told me I needed to thin them out. There were too many carrots in the row. Unless I thinned them, she warned, none would get adequate nourishment to grow.....

A few days later I returned to the patch and confronted my dilemma: How to choose which ones to pluck? All were green, all looked healthy, all had the potential to be a delicious, nutritious vegetable. I felt blessed by all the life. I deferred plucking action.

Weeks later it was harvest time and I went out to pull up my carrots. They were tangled, gnarled, intertwined, and stubby. Uncleanable, unpeelable. Not one made it into a soup much less a salad. Not one had been given the space, attention, nourishment it needed to achieve its potential because I had not done the thinning, not made the required choices. I had no system for making them. I lacked the confidence or the courage and perhaps the belief that I had to act. I had no system for selection; and without a system

the choosing is random, unthinking, painful. With a system it is not necessarily easy, but it can be purposeful, understandable, and satisfying. This is
not a difficult lesson to understand, but it is a hard one to apply....

I ... leave you with the intention to think more deeply—on your own
and with your colleagues—about the real purpose of your work and the
core values that guide your work now and in the difficult years ahead. The
work you are doing is important, demanding, diverse, and difficult. And
there is often too much of it—like the carrots....

Even if the work you do you consider boring or drudgery, and you fail
to find any value inherent in it, it's possible to find satisfaction in the relationships you establish at work, whether over the neighbor's fence, the
factory cafeteria, or the board-room. It is to relationships, perhaps the
most meaningful aspect of our lives, that we now turn in Chapter 7.

Chapter 7
Learning About Love (Relationships I)

Our work, our focus in chapter 6, does not define us wholly. In order to be known by future generations, we need to know who we are and what we value most. What better way to answer those questions than to examine our relationships with others.

As blessings are central in writing legacy letters, so relationships are central to our identities. Relationships give us a different view about who we are and what we value. Values are basic to legacy writing, yet they're hard to explore directly. We recognize them more easily as we explore our relationships. Who we are, how we relate, and what we aspire to in our relationships is what our lives are all about .

> "Two of the most valuable things we have are time and our relationships with other people. In our age of increasing distractions, it's more important than ever to find ways to maintain perspective and remember that life is brief and tender." — Candy Chang

Relationships with our "Angels"

We'll begin by exploring joyous, inspiring, and magical relationships in our lives: our relationship with our angels. What I mean by angels can best be described by sharing my story about three angels who brought me to this work.

> People often ask me how I got into this unconventional work with legacies. Before I can tell you the story, I must share my belief that we all have angels: people who come in and out of our lives to give us something we need. Neither of us may recognize that they are messengers bringing sacred gifts, but that's not what my story's about.

> I was deeply committed to my work with families of cardiac patients, supporting their emotional and spiritual recovery. My rabbi had introduced a group of women to the concept of the ethical will, blessing our children and passing on our values as a legacy. The idea kept dancing around in my head and wouldn't go away. It seemed that daily there was something in the news, in a film, in a novel I was reading - everywhere in my life I saw and heard LEGACY.

> I noticed my frame of reference shifting as I was seeing through the prism of legacy. I labeled a file folder in a drawer of my desk and began to collect legacy ideas, thoughts, quotations, poems, not knowing why or what I would ever do with the legacy stuff I was saving.

> In the spring of 1997, a woman came to our Bible study group to invite us to a gathering – five days on the University of Wisconsin campus in Beloit to study, eat, schmooze (converse informally), sing, and worship. It sounded like Eden to me: mostly the "s" words – singing, studying, and schmoozing – and eating sounded pretty good too.

> I signed up for a class about the ethical will. It sounded fascinating, but I didn't have a clue about why. The next summer I went to the camp, and signed up again for the ethical will class. When I arrived at the classroom, the rabbi remembered me, and said, "Rachael, you already took this class." I responded, "I know Rabbi, but you're a year different as am I, and the participants will be different…." With a hug, he agreed, "All right, come in."

> You know the next line, year three. When I arrived, Rabbi Raphael gave me a big welcome hug and I sat down in a room with him and six people. Rabbi was reading a poem to us when the strangest thing happened.

I've never heard voices in my head before or since that afternoon, but the words were clear and commanding, "Turn this into a healing tool for women." I sat a moment, stunned, listening for explanation. But no other words arrived. I looked around, saw no one, and raised my hand to tell the Rabbi what I'd heard. He smiled benignly, pointed his finger at me and said, "Do it; it's an important niche."

How could I say no to a voice ringing in my head and a rabbi's finger pointing at my heart? Thus began my life's work that has transformed the lives of many, and has transformed me as well. Today, I know that three angels: the woman who appeared to tell us about the camp in 1997, the Rabbi and the Voice, changed my life. Today I think of myself as one of God's stenographers. I remain passionate about being a modern messenger of an ancient tradition made new.

Reflections and Legacy Letters to Our Angels

To begin: make a list of the angels who have appeared in your life. As you rediscover your angels, you may feel gratitude, surprise, even regret that you've not expressed your feelings of appreciation. But here is your opportunity. Snuggle into your favorite chair, pour yourself a cup of tea or coffee, have your pen and paper ready as you reflect about who your angels were and are, and how your relationships with them have impacted your life. Not to worry, you need not write to all the angels on your list, though you may find over time that you choose to.

> **"Sometimes our light goes out but is blown into flame by another human being. Each of us owes deepest thanks to those who have rekindled this light."**
> **— Albert Schweitzer**

Angel Guide

Search for the angels in each period of your life so far: in your childhood, adolescence, young adulthood, middle age, and years beyond the middle. You may find it efficient to discover them decade by decade. When you remember an angel, write his or her name followed by a brief and specific phrase about the gift that person gave you. In the days following this reflection, as you think about angels and your gratitude, more names may enter your awareness. Be sure to add them and their gifts to your list.

> **"Love and compassion are necessities, not luxuries. Without them, humanity cannot survive."** — Dalai Lama

Remember back in chapter 2 (on page 21) we explored copying as a way that apprentices learned at the time of the Renaissance. We can think of ourselves as apprentices to legacy writers who've preceded us. What others have written can spark your memories, and facilitate your feelings and thoughts, enriching and expanding what you might choose to write. Because each of us is unique, no one's personal legacy letter would be exactly like another's. Yet we benefit by reading how others have expressed their thoughts and wishes to their loved ones.

Before you write your own letters to your angels, here are some that other legacy writers have written to theirs: The first is the letter I recently wrote to Rabbi Raphael. Though you know the content, it's worth a moment of your time to see an example about how a memory can be transformed into a letter.

Dear Rabbi Larry,

This letter is a long time in coming, but its topic is as vivid to me today as the day it happened in August of 1999 at Beloit where I studied the ethical will with you for the third time.

The afternoon was hazy and warm; the college classroom cooler and darker. Six of us sat listening to you reading a poem, the name and content now long forgotten. I may have had my eyes closed to avoid distraction. I thought I was listening intently when I heard a clear Voice in my head. I was more than a little shocked; I'd never before heard that voice (nor since). What I heard and promptly shared aloud was, "Turn this [the ethical will] into a healing tool for women."

You responded without hesitation, not a moment of doubt, giving credence to the reality and rightness of the Voice. You pointed your finger directly at me and said calmly, but with all the rabbinic power of your practice and your Biblical predecessors, "Do it! It's an important niche."

As you know, from that day forward my work has been to fill that niche. I've seen women of diverse circumstances healing. I've had the privilege of attending to women as they find their voices, clarify their values, and express their love.

In that moment, you were like the radiant Moses standing down from the mountain with the Commandments in hand ... and I was changed and found. You were the angel who confirmed the sacred message I'd heard.

I'd respected you before that moment, as a kind and gentle man, sensitive and caring. I respected you after, but in that moment, I experienced awe and felt wholly seen.

Thank you for being a rabbi – a teacher, my teacher. Thank you for hearing my words and confirming their value. That moment of transformation is etched in my heart forever, and I am eternally grateful to you for blessing me with this work.

Thank you for your blessing. Thank you for being my guide in this sacred work. I pray that you too be blessed by angels and teachers who confirm you and your sacred experiences.

With love,
Rachael

This letter is to an angel who transformed the career of the legacy writer as she witnessed the angel's work:

Dear Gail,

About 25 years ago I was working at the Cancer Center with hospice. Although I was very invested in bereavement and grief work, I was not very experienced. My manager suggested that we ask you to mentor me through my first grief group with children.

At first I was intimidated by your expertise – performance anxiety – but you assured me I could do this. Your comfort with the kids amazed me because, for heaven's sake, one of their parents or beloved grandparents had just died!

Next came a demonstration of pure compassion in that group. You spoke with a boy of 7 or 8 using hand puppets. This boy had not yet spoken until, through his puppet voice, he told you his story and spoke his grief. It was pure magic yet it was so simple. That night changed my life and my career. I began to trust that I could do this work. It was not hard to receive the blessing of another's story.

Thank you, my angel mentor. You guided my grief work, you inspired my career, you answered many questions through the years and you continue to model a balanced life of work and play. You have a secure and dedicated place in my heart.

With deep appreciation,
Judy

"I've learned that people will forget what you said, people will forget what you did, but people will never forget how you made them feel." — Maya Angelou

In this letter a mother blesses her child with her wisdom and her appreciation of an angel appearing in an unusual way to teach her an important lesson.

Dear Zoe,

I'm writing this letter to you from the lovely wilds of Oregon, where the trees sway to the heavens and the moon lights the night's ground with a pale glow. I've come to this place to continue my legacy writing, to tell you who I am and what my wishes are for you and your children.

You and I went to the co-op one day, many years ago. Just a regular visit for ingredients for dinner. On our way through the store, we were delayed several times by the same woman. By the third or fourth run-in, I was angry, and when we got to the checkout counter—the only one open— there she stood, the same woman who had blocked my path several times. She made me wait again, as she cheerfully carried her unmarked coffee to the rear of the store for a price check. In those moments that I waited, furious being held up against my will, I blindly grabbed a magazine from the rack and threw it into my cart.

Days later I drove to a sacred place above the St. Croix River to do some writing. I looked through my bag of readings that I'd brought along and pulled out a magazine. I stared at the cover, for there, smiling at me with utter kindness, was the Dalai Lama. His loving face was so beautiful that all I could do was stare for several minutes. Where had this magazine come from, I wondered? And then I remembered; I'd bought it that day at the co-op, the day that I'd been furious with some woman who held me up in line. I had cursed her that day, knowing that you would hear me, but unable to contain my rage. Her actions had forced me to stop, if only for a moment. And in that moment, I had picked up the magazine that I held in my hands.

I opened to the first story and read the words: One cannot feel compassion for others until one feels it for oneself.

That sentence put me on a new path: Buddhism studies, al-anon, and above all—compassion for myself. In the years since I learned the lesson taught to me by the Angel in the Co-op, I have continued to forgive myself for my flaws and in so doing, learned to forgive others for theirs. It is a path with heart that I walk to this day.

My beautiful child, you carry within you the earth and stars: May you feel compassion for yourself.

Love forever,
Mom

The beneficiary of this angel letter is deceased. Because she could not send it to her angel, the legacy writer decided to send it to her daughter, who she'd blessed with the middle name of Juliette. (Remember the power of names that we explored in chapter 3.)

Dear Juliette,

It is a little funny to write to you in English since you and I spoke French to each other...

You were this dramatic, little and strong woman with a big voice and huge emotions: how many times did you start crying at the piano when I sang Schubert's "German Lieder"? You forced me to learn German so I would understand the essence of what I was singing. Silly me! I thought that, with Latin, French, English, Italian, Spanish and Hebrew, I was pretty set with languages, but you obviously thought differently!

You and I used to sit and talk about the composer, the text of the song, my interpretation, your interpretation, and you made me sing lying on the floor, so that I would project my voice correctly.

You were so happy when I was pregnant because you decided that my voice found "its pedal" and never sounded better. You were kind and resourceful: you told me what you did to not cry while peeling onions (It did not work for me).

You met my parents and fell in love with them. Of course, they already worshipped you because I stopped smoking, thanks to you! You and your husband Mitu invited them to dinner at your home and I remember my parents telling me what brave efforts they made to eat, since you cooked all dairy dishes and they did not eat dairy (I guess it is the difference between growing up in Tunisia versus Algeria).

You supported me in my decisions when I got married and when I got divorced, and attended both of my weddings. When you heard her laugh at five months, you told me that my first daughter, Tafat, would have a lovely voice because her laugh was like little pearls. You were right!

You were not present when my second daughter, Avital, was born, because you had died of pancreatic cancer in 1986. I could not have been more sad.

To show my love and gratitude for all you were to me, I gave Avital your name, Juliette, as her middle name. Your husband Mitu was at the baby naming and gave Avital Juliette her first Star of David. I said that I hoped my daughter would be as strong, brave, and wonderful as you.

With love always, Tamar

> "Each one of us has the possibility, probability and privilege to be a rainbow in someone's cloud."　　— Maya Angelou

Before we move on to the next section, choose someone from your angel list, and try your hand at writing an angel legacy letter.

Friendships

Though you may consider your friends to be your angels, let's distinguish between the two so we can refocus on knowing ourselves more clearly through our friendships.

Our friendships define us and sustain us. Often they feel like the best family; they cheer us on when we're doing well and support us in challenging times. They cry and laugh with us. They provide us with a lovingly different perspective when we share our problems. Of course like family and lovers, friends also disappoint us at times when we find our expectations unmet.

> "A friend, as it were, a second self."　　— Cicero

Friendships, some short and some lifelong, help us learn trust, how to listen, how to give and receive support, caring, and love. The nature of each friendship is unique; some friends we play with; some we learn from and others we teach. Others are available when we need a shoulder to cry on.

> **"I have gifts that you don't have, so I am unique. You have gifts that I don't have, so you are unique. We need each other. We are made for the delicate network of interdependence."**
> **— Archbishop Demond Tutu**

Friendships include challenges: building and maintaining a relationship with a new friend, changing your relationship with an old friend, admitting when you have betrayed a friend, forgiving friends when they disappoint you, and letting go of a friend.

> **"Deep down there was understanding, not of the facts of our lives so much as of our essential natures."**   **— May Sarton**

What is your experience when you are met in your "essential nature"? This is the dual essence of friendship: to know better who you are at your core and to grow in your understanding of others.

> **"To have a friend takes time."**   **— Georgia O'Keeffe**

Reflections about Friendship

Here are some suggestions for thinking and writing about you and your friendships:

How has the nature of your friendships changed over time because of internal or external circumstances? Some of your friends have moved away, now care for aged parents, or have moved to warmer climes. How do you replace friends who don't share the history of your old friends? How have you maintained your friendship with someone who lives far away, or when there have been changes in circumstances, values, and life decisions? Remember the old Girl Scout song that begins:

> **"Make new friends, but keep the old. One is silver, the other gold"**
> **— Anonymous**

Consider your "best friend:" What is the essence of that relationship and what makes it so? What do you value most about this friendship and your other friendships? What are the gifts of your friendship? Describe the sacred experience when you "meet" in the space of your essential natures? When we've experienced the pain of losing a dear friend, do we agree with Alfred, Lord Tennyson's famous words? "Tis better to have loved and lost than never to have loved at all."

Are there values or actions you won't tolerate in your friends or in yourself as a friend? How have friends disappointed you? How have you betrayed your friends? How do you or have you forgiven one another for these lapses? What changes would you like to make in your friendships now in your life? What specifically is it you most value about your friendships?

Legacy Letters to Friends

It is said that we are rich if we can count a handful of friends ... how many do you count? List their names. (The list may include some who are no longer alive.)

As preparation reflect about and write about the qualities you value in a relationship, and what specifically you value in your friends.

Choose one friend from your list to write a legacy letter to that celebrates them and your relationship. Consider the history of the relationship, adventures you've shared, and what you're most grateful for about them. Be sure to describe what you know about yourself through your friendship with them. Your letter can include description of memories, stories, an expression of your appreciation for this miraculous relationship, and a blessing.

Share your letter as a gift to celebrate the relationship or share it at a special moment in time, like a birthday or reunion.

As a part of your ongoing legacy writing, you may want to write a legacy letter to someone of a younger generation about how much you value friendship. You may also want to write letters to others you count as friends.

These sample letters, one from a specific chapter in a woman's life and the other about a long and intimate relationship, express gratitude and learning.

Dear Loretta,

When my husband Bill died unexpectedly in 1999, I was working at the Minnesota International Center. We had been married for 35 years and we had two children – Christopher the oldest, had just become a father himself six months earlier, and Jessica, who was in college. I was lost. Christopher lived in Kentucky with his family. Jessica lived on campus and was completely preoccupied with her own life, devastated by her father's death and in her own world about that.

My boss told me about a grief support group that met at her church on Wednesday evenings. I started attending and one night you walked in. I think we kind of sized each other up and said to ourselves, "I like her, and I want her to be my friend." In addition to attending the meetings, we used to meet weekly at a bookstore or a coffee shop, or a mall – to do our retail therapy. That was in the midst of the first big recession and President Bush was exhorting Americans to save the economy by shopping. We did our part and assuaged any guilt feelings by saying it was for the good of the country.

But really we didn't care about anything – we had lost our husbands and we knew that everything else paled before those facts. We learned what was important in life as our priorities shifted radically.

Week by week, month by month, year by year, we became stronger. Our lives changed. We needed to see each other less often. We became grandmothers, we retired, we asked ourselves what do we do next with our lives and we shared and laughed together at our outlandish solutions.

One night we went on Match.com to see what it was like. We both agreed, not for us, yet we continue to search for that companion – that loved one who would make our lives complete. So far our score is zero. But we have learned that there are so many ways to give and to receive love. Our lives have been blessed with friends, family and good relationships.

Loretta, dear friend, may you continue to find love – in every interaction you have with others. May you know that it is already abundant in your life, within you, that you bless us with it whenever we meet you.

Your loving friend, Barbara

Dear Harriet,

All of our jokes about our idiosyncrasies and foibles aside, I write you today to share my love and appreciation of you and us in relationship over these many long years.

My first appreciation goes back to 1972, the days of us having young children and being family – camping, both as parents and as adults in the Boundary Waters – cross-country skiing, canoeing, spending Saturday nights together as couples, finding your cabin – teasing you about "mousy."

But when I was lost, maybe not for the first time, but the first I was aware of, when my mother died, you were there supporting me, even long after I thought I was done grieving. I will never forget you appearing with some lame excuse like shopping nearby, an excuse to come sit with me – just sitting, listening, drinking coffee together, while I repeated stories about my mother that you'd heard the last time you just "stopped in."

You've been there for me often – even when I didn't know I needed support, in the crisis of divorce and other changes that have been trans-formative. Your support has been so grounding and important to me as I maneuvered the sometimes dangerous curves my path has taken me. And I am so grateful that you stuck by me through it all, even when you neither understood nor approved of my choices.

You're always concerned about my wellbeing, financial and otherwise. And you have been so generous to me, sharing the cabin and your winter place as though we were sisters – thank you for that too. I was so touched when you told me that you and Steven would be there for my rehab if I chose shoulder surgery, again loving me like family. And you're always inter-ested, pleased, and proud of my kids as if they were your own, never forget-ting to tell me when someone says something nice about them.

And beyond all the seriousness we have fun together whenever we have that opportunity. You are a trustworthy, compassionate, and gener-ous friend, and I am grateful for your loyal friendship. I hope in some small measure, I give you a portion of all you have given and give me.

Thank you for being my friend. I love you. Leah

Chapter 8
You and Your Family (Relationships II)

After exploring our relationships with our friends and angels, we'll continue our exploration of our relationships with ourselves and with our families. We best see ourselves not by looking in the mirror, but through what we do and have done with our days and in our relationships.

> **"For now we see through a glass, darkly; but then face to face."** — **St. Paul, I Corinthians, 12:13**

No matter our distorted views of ourselves, we want to see ourselves and how we fit into the larger scheme of things. Examining our relationships can help us clean the glass to see more clearly.

A commitment to writing legacies assumes that no matter how difficult our lives have been, no matter how low our self esteem has fallen, we all yearn to be whole, to be free and to know that beneath it all, we have the capacity to love others and that we are lovable.

It is this longing that gives us the courage to want to know who we really are and to look at our family relationships—whether easy and loving, or fraught with challenge and difficulty—and to write legacy letters to those we care about, those to whom we owe appreciation and amends, and those whom we are glad and proud to know.

Legacy letters are traditionally written to younger generations. But recipients of our letters may be members of our family in generations before and after us. Legacy letters may be written to relatives who are alive or dead, to family members who have touched us briefly or with whom we've had long and intimate relationships.

Writing is a way of seeing ourselves through the lens of our relationships that gives us the opportunity to complete the unfinished, come to terms with reality and our dreams, finish neglected emotional family business, and express our appreciation and love of others.

> **"No one has loved exactly the people and places you have loved. Who will tell that part of the earth's story, if you do not?"**
> — **Pat Schneider**

Our Relationships with Our Selves

Note: This examination of who we are in relation to our Selves is not about religious belief unless we choose to define it in religious terms. It is rather an opportunity to assess how a higher meaning infuses our lives, perhaps with gratitude, in spiritual study, meditation, or by spiritual practices and traditions. However we define it, most of us have had experiences that touch a different level of meaning in our lives than in our routine, habitual, daily lives. Though difficult to describe, these experiences define an important aspect of who we are.

Spiritual Relationships

Some of us experience that transcendent relationship with and in Nature; others of us with a personal God of our understanding, and still others within an organized religious structure. What's most important is, no matter how we define or experience it, that we realize the miracle of Life and have a way to understand and express it. For many of us, especially as we age, this becomes the most significant relationship we have.

Grand poet of nature, Mary Oliver, dazzles us with her honest guidance about our search and the importance of authentic companions along the way:

> "Let me keep my distance, always, from those who think they have the answers. Let me keep company always with those who say "Look!" and laugh in astonishment, and bow their heads."
> — Mary Oliver

Given our individual uniqueness, each of us experiences our spiritual relationship differently. Perhaps focusing on purpose is a way to tap in to the spiritual. In Richard Leider's book, *Something to Live For: Finding Your Way in the Second Half of Life*, he puts words to the eternal question we ask: "Is life a meaningless movement from one moment to the next or is there a grander purpose for living?" This question becomes more essential in the second half of life. Leider suggests that our search for meaning and purpose lead us to profound spiritual experiences.

Eastern spiritual leaders teach the value of silence, mindfulness, meditation, centering, and "staying in the present." These are doors that open some of us to a deeper spiritual relationship. Doors may also open when we are involved in daily, habitual tasks, tending to household details, that we consider mundane or without value. Jean Shinoda Bolen, MD, contemporary author of *The Millionth Circle,* suggests that "tending to household details is a centering activity, a means through which a woman puts her house and herself in order. . . . As she sorts and folds laundry, irons or cleans up clutter, picks and arranges flowers, prepares dinner, or puts her closet in order, she is totally in the present moment."

Our spiritual relationship may not be intellectual or even verbal. Awe, gratitude, and thanksgiving open us to relationship with the Source of All. Holy moments, witnessing (and experiencing) birth and the loss of a loved one, though painful can also be vivid and awe-inspiring. They are difficult to describe in language.

When we can find words, they are simple, authentic, and surprisingly, often poetic. Here is Elizabeth Alexander, the 2009 Inauguration Day poet about the value of poetry:

> "... human beings have always made song. Communities, tribes, peoples have always told each other the story of who they are in song. And I use the word song to be roughly analogous with poetry because it's not just words on the page.... poetry has always existed and always in a communal context .... part of what people get from that is the story of who I am and who we are."   — Elizabeth Alexander

Read Eve Hearst's poetic legacy after walking the labyrinth at Grace Cathedral in San Francisco,

> "Looking back on my life I wonder why
> I did so many foolish things.
> How could I have been so careless
> to ignore the warning signs,
> turns that would lead me to disaster?
> Recklessly I plunged into danger.
>
> "In retrospect
> maybe those turns were needed
> to get me where I am today.
> Now I have reached the center
> the place of wholeness and enlightenment.
> But only for a moment can I stay.
> Then back again into the turns and twists
> of unexpected detours.
> The maze of life will lead to new surprises."

Maybe author Margaret Atwood was inspired by Mahatma Gandhi's wise words, "To forget how to dig the earth and tend the soil is to forget ourselves" when she wrote simply and lovingly celebrating her spiritual relationship with the Earth:

> "Gardening is not a rational act. What matters is the immersion of the hands in the earth, that ancient ceremony.... In the spring, at the end of the day, you should smell like dirt."
>   — Margaret Atwood

Reflections about Our Spiritual Relationships

Take some time to reflect about your relationship with Spirit. It is likely very different today than when you worshipped God as a child. Many people relate best to God outdoors in nature; others are moved by music, and still others find that solitude or its opposite, joyous family events, bring them closer to God. For those who meditate through writing, explore with your paper and pen. Others of you may want to sift through the questions below or form your own to think about how your spiritual relationship permeates and influences your life. Reflect in your favorite solitary space with or without music or walk at the ocean shore, climb in the mountains, or stroll in the woods.

Who are you at this time in your life? What questions do you find yourself pondering? What matters most to you now? In what ways and situations do beauty, awe, and gratitude inform and enrich your life?

Consider exploring your life with a time line separated into seven year segments: 0-7 years of age; 8-15, and continuing through your life so far. After you compose your time line, fill in spiritual experiences from each period. You may find interesting blank spaces and other periods full to overflowing.

When you're ready, write a legacy letter about your spiritual relationship with Life, tell someone of a younger generation something they don't know about what really matters to you, what is most precious to you. The letter may be that "angelic message" needed now or later for them, and it will also let your reader know who you really are. Remember, the more specific you can be, the more understandable such a personal and sacred subject will be to your reader.

You might try writing a poem, or a series of poems that express your spiritual relationship in the poetic way such moments are experienced. It's okay to keep your poems for yourself in your Legacy File, or share them with someone who will appreciate them.

Here are four very different letters written by legacy writers: the first is about being called by God; the second is explained by its title "A Housewife's Letter to God;" the third is about listening to the "still small voice" within; the last expresses a father's pain as he struggles to stand with his God and express love for his son.

Dear Colleen,

It has been a while since we last spoke, but I want you to know how close you always remain to my heart and how I watch from afar with great hope for the woman you are becoming.

It has not always been easy for me to be the strong, faithful, fearless woman I hoped and still hope to be. Coming to a place where I can be at peace with who I am and where God is calling me has felt impossible at times. Even when I entered seminary, I held back. I was afraid to go to unknown places ... afraid to change, afraid to let go.

And for a while I let that fear rule me. I postponed going on an internship, explored other calls, cried endlessly to Paul, and even looked for other jobs or careers.

But then one day I found myself opening a letter from a man who had been my advisor in college. Who had invited me into his life more deeply than any other person I admire, when he got sick with cancer. We would spend hours talking about life and death and hope together. And now, here was this letter that had been left unopened after his death.

I don't remember much of what it said except the last line where he wrote: "I want you to know I would have been honored to have you as my pastor."

In that moment when I read that line, my fear fled my heart, my ears opened, and for the first time I listened without fear to where God was calling me.

And so my dear Colleen I offer this prayer and blessing to you.

May you always be free to be you. May your heart be fearless in the face of life. May your ears always be open to hear what God is whispering to you. And may you, like me, be blessed to encounter those people who can say to you, "peace, be still, do not be afraid." I pray that you are able to hold onto the hope they offer.

Love, Rebecca

Dear God …

I come to this beautiful summer Island and I see pine cones to be picked up … cobwebs to be swept, and laundry to be done in my one-speed washing machine. I see gourmet meals to be prepared for my cancer-survivor husband, drooping flowers that request a small drink … a cat I cannot find. And this morning I am so tired I can't hold my pen.

Please help me to let go of my obsessive Kitchen Behaviors before I become the "Mad Woman of Kipling Island." Please give me Your eyes today … to see the profound architecture in the pine cones under my feet … and keep me from stooping to collect them. Keep me standing tall. Let me hear the Spider's spinning song … and feel Your Breath whisper … "Do not disturb … spiders at play."

Help me to know that there are more ways to reach a man's heart than through his stomach. Keep my hands from cooking lentils all day, when I could be building crooked sandcastles with my grandchildren. As for the flowers, Lord … a little rain would help me out. But there are others here with me, who love the daisy-faces as much as I do. Prompt me to ask them to grab the green hose … and spray diamond coloured water with childlike swoops.

And now that I think of it, God, maybe the old washing machine is my best teacher. Could You be saying, "Just slow it down. One gentle cycle at a time is OK. One day at a time, lived well … is walking in Heaven. One breath at a time … is being with You."

Carol Hill

Dear Carol and Emma:

On May 17, 2004 the Gay Marriage Act in Massachusetts (Goodrich vs. the Massachusetts Department of Public health) was passed allowing gays and lesbians to marry and have some of the benefits of heterosexual couples on a state level. It was for the gay lesbian community an enormously liberating law that gave us rights that had previously been denied. It's all too easy to forget the battles that were fought to facilitate the passage of this monumental bill.

When Dad and my marriage ended, I made a commitment to myself to never marry again. I did not want any law to dictate the economic terms of my personal life So not being able to marry as one who subsequently came out as a lesbian, I was not aware of the rights that I did not have.

With the passage of that 2004 bill, I felt an exhilaration that surprised me. While Karen and I had been living together for 15 years, the passage of this bill made me aware of the level of oppression to which I had accommodated. I suddenly wanted to be married. It seemed like an important political act and a validation of our relationship, albeit with a heavy dose of ambivalence on my part. When I would bring up my ambivalence, it created enormous upset with Karen. Not wanting to act in a way that was hurtful for her, I suppressed my own voice and accommodated her deep desire to be married.

On the morning of our wedding, with a tent in the backyard, the caterer preparing our dinner and the florist arranging flowers, I woke up having dreamt that the walls were caving in. Water was pouring into the house. When I called the contractor, he said that there was nothing he could do. Seventy-five people were expected that afternoon, and the ceremony at the church that was a few hours away.

Ignoring my needs in favor of another is a deep disservice both to myself and to others. What is but a "still small voice" is often the early tendrils of an authentic and profound message. Another lesson that emerged from this was to watch carefully the balance between accommodating to another and simultaneously holding my own needs without relinquishing my sense of self. In this particular instance, I erred on the side of relinquishing myself to accommodate Karen's wishes.

May you both come to know the wisdom of hearing your own still small voice with open eyes and an accepting heart and not consider any of your actions as "mistakes." Try to trust that you will create the crises and conditions in your life that will take you to the next level of your own healing. May you hold this with love and acceptance for yourself.

My love, Mom

The mystery and beauty of spiritual guidance and spiritual questions are tested when we meet everyday life situations and trials. In this letter a father stands with his God expressing love for his son. After reading Bill's letter we'll reflect about the legacy letters we want to write to our own family members.

Dear Joe:

I know we'll both never forget the day we spent together at the Mayo Clinic and you were diagnosed as having an inoperable brain tumor—a Stage 2 cancer. I remember how proud I was of you that day—taking the news with courage, asking the doctors all the questions that needed to be answered, and accepting the treatment plan they laid out for you.

What I haven't shared with you was what happened to me on the long ride home I took alone from Rochester that day. I vividly remember how utterly hopeless I felt and how scared I was for you. With tears running down my face I silently prayed to God to help me....help you get through the long ordeal you were about to endure.

When I got home that evening I went straight to my computer and wrote you a letter that I've never given you. I remember telling you in the letter that God did not give you this cancer, but that He did give you a rare gift...the gift of 'time,' the 'present'. I admonished you in the letter not to worry about whether you would be alive to walk your two daughters down the aisle but to dance with them today. When I finished the letter I shared it with your mother and my spiritual director, an old Benedictine nun I was seeing at the time. Both of them had the same reaction to my letter. They told me to put the letter in the drawer, that it would unnecessarily frighten you before we even knew how the treatment would go, what the long-term prognosis would be. I remember saying to my Spiritual Director, 'But Sister, you don't understand; this letter came to me as I was praying to God in my car on the way home.' She responded, 'Bill, God did hear your prayer that day, this letter wasn't for your son Joe, this letter was for … you.'

I learned a special lesson that day, son---that I want to pass on to you. God does answer your prayers---even in ways you may not understand at the time. And so my blessing for you, Joe, is that you always know how much God loves you and that God will always answer your prayers if you have the faith and courage to ask for His grace.

Love, Dad

Family Relationships

Many of us have more than one family; we may include friends as family, and have a spiritual family as well. This section is about two other families: the one we grew up in, and the one we created with a partner. The last can be subdivided too: for those of us who have been divorced or widowed, we may have more than one family in which we are considered a parent.

Families, like friends, see us differently and make a profound difference in our lives; they impact who we were and who we have become.

> **"Family knowledge can be useful in making abstract history concrete."**
> — **Eva Hoffman**

Our relationships with family members are at once the most complicated and nuanced. Whether we had or have intimate and valued relationships within the family, the complications of family secrets, sibling rivalry, competition for our parents' blessing, remain a part of our every day lives and follow us into our twilight years. None of us is perfect, and the limitations we face in our present day relationships have roots in our growing up families.

We learned how to treat family and those different from us. We learned how to cope with sickness and dying. We learned how to protect ourselves from the fallout from alcoholism, unfaithfulness, and rage we didn't understand. No matter how terrifying or terrible our family situation was, it was and is our family. As innocent and vulnerable children, we relied on family for our very lives, and in most cases, though we didn't understand why the situation was as it was, we loved family anyway.

Today we are neither as innocent nor vulnerable. We can attempt to see more clearly, not get stuck in our old stories, nor expect the impossible. We can honor them as family, and make our way in the world.

That said, if your family relationships were and are good, your letters will be full of appreciation and fond memories. If your relationships were more entangled and difficult, now is the time to forgive yourself and other members of the family, to accept the reality of what was, realizing the wisdom of Twelve Step Programs teaching: "You neither caused the situations, you can't control them, and you can't cure them." What you can do is reflect on and respect your own story and go beyond it, doing your best to make peace for your well-being and for the generations that will follow you.

This excerpt from my daughter's 40th birthday legacy letter concentrates on the transitions we've shared and how those changes have also marked the evolution of our relationship.

> *That transition in both our lives - you becoming a woman, a writer and professional, a wife and mother, over these past 15 years, and me becoming too - building a new life for myself post-marriage, and always feeling supported by you. Our intimacy keeps evolving - from mother-child, to mother-mother, companion and friend. I appreciate that in your busy life you carve out time for us to be together. It's a weekly highlight for me. And I think I've finally learned what you tried to teach me in college - that you know what to do, you'll ask for my advice when you want it, but that you want me to listen to you. And you listen to me too. What a gift both hearing you and being heard is. Thank you for that. I so treasure our relationship as it has been, as it is, and who knows what it will yet become.*
>
> *Sweet daughter, who teaches me today and supports me today in equal measure as I teach and support you; I feel so blessed, and know that we've worked hard on our relationship for a long time, and we're harvesting the benefits of our effort.*

> "She was just talking the way mothers will, not realizing that each word is a rock that daughters carry around ever after: a rock to build a fortress, a rock to throw at someone else, a rock to stand on while crossing rivers." — Ann Roiphe

Reflective Questions about Families

Consider the following questions to ascertain who and about what you want to write, or simply trust your intuition to explore different facets of your relationship with members of your family:

Which family members have had the strongest positive or negative influence in your life? What is the defining story of your family? How have family holiday rituals or spiritual activities changed over the years? Which traditions have you maintained?

How does your family cope with illness? How have responses changed over time? How does your family express concern, approval, humor, disappointment? What topics are taboo to talk about in your family?

Are there family secrets best left untold? Are these secrets doing harm to those who only sense that there is something hidden in the family history? Will these secrets continue to profoundly affect younger and yet unborn family members? (See further discussion of secrets in Chapter 10.)

> "A grandmother's name is erased. A mother decides to pretend her son does not drink too much....wherever there is a secret there is a rumor....For deep in the mind we know everything. And wish to have everything be told, to have our images and our words reflect the truth." — Susan Griffin

Which family relationships have been or are the easiest, the most intimate, the most challenging? Do you have words (in the form of a letter) that may begin to melt the tension and be a beginning for healing in your most difficult family relationships?

You may want to put your musings about family members into your personal Legacy File to be saved until it's the right time to write a letter to them, or to store completed letters until you find the appropriate time to share them.

I received a telephone call from an anxious legacy writer who'd written a birthday blessing letter commemorating her oldest daughter's fiftieth birthday. It was well received; both mother and daughter experienced increased intimacy and gratitude each for the other.

So why was the mother anxious? She has three younger daughters, and she was concerned that she might be unable to write for each of them as their fiftieth birthdays approached. Worse, what if she died before they each celebrated their fiftieth birthday?

I asked her what prevented her from sitting down now, while she was well and full-witted, to write a letter to each of them for that important moment in their lives. She could put the letters in her Legacy File until they were needed (informing her loved ones that she has a Legacy File and its location). Since it was likely that she would still be around and have her wits about her, she could edit and adapt each letter as appropriate at the time of each 50th birthday.

I could feel the legacy writer's relief, her purpose renewed; she thanked me briefly, said good-bye, energized to write the other three letters.

These legacy letters express love from widely different frames of reference and occasions. As you write legacy letters to your friends, angels, to the God of your understanding, to your family, and to younger generations, may you be courageous, honest, and generous.

"What comes from the heart reaches the heart." — Talmud

Appreciating a grandfather who died over fifty years ago exemplifies the power of a legacy of love and its influence on a woman who is now a loving grandmother herself.

Dear Grandpa,

You were a prominent person in my life from the moment I was born. Because Daddy was in the Navy, serving on an aircraft carrier, Mommy and I lived with you and Grandma for several months after my birth. Although I have no specific memories of that time, I do know you were a constant from the beginning of my life. You were always there, as much as my own parents were…. Until I graduated from high school, you were a welcome daily presence in my life.

I spent a great deal of time with you and Grandma. Your home was, for me, a haven of laughter, love, and acceptance. I could be who I was without correction or even discipline!

My fondest memory is attending elementary school just across the street from your office in the county courthouse. Looking out the window of my classroom toward your first floor office, my anxious fears about school…the fear of failing or not doing everything right or being rejected… were calmed. Knowing that someone who believed in me so much was just a few yards away gave me security and peace.

Many days, at lunchtime or after school, I walked the few steps to your office. No matter what you were doing, you always looked up with such joy and pride on your face. "Hi, Honey Girl," you'd say. And then you would walk with me to the offices of your co-workers to introduce me and I think to show me off!

Often after these unannounced visits of mine, I would go home with you, and you would call to Grandma when we walked in the door, "Look who I found!"

I don't remember you ever telling me, "I love you." But unlike some relationships in which the lack of verbal affirmation is a huge stumbling block, I never expected you to declare your love for me in effusive terms. You didn't have to. Your face told me all I needed to know…that I was loved and adored…and even amazing!

You and Grandma never bought extravagant gifts for us or planned fantastic adventures. But you did give me the intangible and lasting gift of love, freely given and joyously exhibited. That is what has lasting value and it is what remains. Even fifty years after your death, you remain with me as a constant presence, gone from my sight, yes, but never from my heart.

Grandpa, may you rest in the knowledge that you graced my life from the moment of my birth. Your love stays with me in blessed remembrance. Until the end of my days on earth, I will bless your name.

"Honey Girl"

Sisters have a special relationship, often complicated and intense. This letter is especially poignant because it reveals the writer's vulnerability. Trusting her sister with her personal pain and learning, Beth's letter has resulted in a deepening of their relationship.

Dear Diane,

When I was growing up I wanted to belong so badly. I often felt different from others. I was afraid they would reject me. Yet, I was also getting the message to be myself. I was encouraged to explore my dreams; mom and dad told me I could be anyone I wanted – do whatever I wanted.

This created a terrible tension. I wanted to live my soul's purpose, to reach for my dreams. Yet, I was afraid that doing so would make me a freak; push people away; leave me alone and lonesome.

I began to choose only the safe dreams, the fulfillment of which would equal success. Telling these dreams didn't make others uncomfortable; I could point to my resumé proudly. I ignored the deeper, more longed for dreams. They rested in my shadow. I created a false self. I wore a mask. I was discontented in my life, my work, with my friends. But, I wouldn't let go – until I had to. When Carl ended our marriage, it seemed to be the most painful thing ever. Yet, it forced me to take a closer look. It pushed me to see clearly where I was and what I really wanted. It gave me the opportunity to start anew and learn to live my real dreams.

I am still learning. I'm still uncovering who I am and how to live my soul's purpose. The journey now, however, is full of excitement and curiosity – I love it!

My wish for you is that you know how strong you really are. May you live open-heartedly in that strength, seeing the world and your soul's purpose clearly. May any troubles you face simply be stepping-stones to greater knowledge and ultimately deep contentment.

Your sister, Beth

"All history is taken in by stones.... perhaps we are like stones; our own history and the history of the world embedded in us; we hold a sorrow deep within and cannot weep until that history is sung." — Susan Griffin

A grandmother makes sense of her history as a privileged white woman. This letter passes her learning to her three grandchildren with her hope that the 21st century will bring change, change in which there will be less fear and more love for those different from themselves.

Dear Jessie, Nick and Melissa:

You were alive, though very young, to witness the most historically important event of my lifetime. I want to give you some background about the miracle of Barack Obama's swearing in ceremony as he became the President of the United States of America.

In 1952 when I was 10 years old, my dad and mom drove our family to Florida. It was my first time driving through the South and the first time I remember seeing 'Negroes.' Their dilapidated houses, which we called shanties, lined the sides of the roads, sometimes had only three walls, some had boards missing on the roofs. My nose was pressed to the window and I felt pity and curiosity and confusion and fear. I didn't know about life beyond suburban Minneapolis. We stopped to get something to eat and I wouldn't eat the food from their stores, accepting only a coke because it was in a bottle.

In the 50's and 60's my eyes were further opened by protests and civil rights workers killed and the assassinations of Martin Luther King, Jr. and Bobby Kennedy, and race riots as the struggle for equal rights played itself out. What an awful truth knowing that our country was wrong, when I had been raised to believe we were close to perfect, as I comprehended some of the 'truth' of the lives of African Americans. The knowledge that life is horribly unfair and my blessed life was an accident of birth was humbling and in some way shameful.

During the fall of 2004 I was invited to attend a gathering to meet a young black man running for the Illinois senate seat. He had spoken at the Democratic Convention and I was impressed by his vision for America. When he arrived on the lawn of a local mansion there was an aura around him. I didn't have to see him to know where he was. I don't remember what he said, only that he excited and inspired all of us. This young charismatic man, who happened to be black, shared his belief with grace and passion that we could become a better nation. Finally, I had found someone I wanted to support, this man who filled me with hope: that he and we could bring about change. He believed in the greatness of our people.

When Obama decided to run for president I feared that our people were still asleep and wouldn't hear his message, but he won the Iowa caucus and the impossible no longer was. Everywhere men and women of all backgrounds were listening and starting to believe that we could be THE United States of America, that honesty and openness, caring for those who are vulnerable and leading by example, were values worth fighting for. This man, Barack Hussein Obama, who happened to be black, brilliant and articulate, compassionate and idealistic, shared his ideas and he was heard.

Martin Luther King, Jr. asked that we not be judged by the color of our skin but rather by the content of our character and that day, November 4, 2008, arrived in my lifetime. The enormity of the emotions of that night and the days that followed cannot be expressed in words. We celebrated, we cheered, we laughed, we hugged each other and many of us wept because the joy was too deep, the significance too great, and the price too heavy, and we continue to weep and to rejoice.

The lesson witnessed is that ANYTHING is possible and dreams can come true.

My prayer for you, dear loves of my life, is that you pay attention to the world around you and not just your world. That you see others through eyes of love and not fear, that you are quick to see the similarities and slow to see the differences. I pray that you are open to the miracles all around you and the divine in all you meet.

Melissa, Nick and Jessie, each of you is a miracle and each divine.

I love you, Baba

Celebrating seasons in our family's lives provides us the opportunity to express our personal love and appreciation. These legacy letters will be saved and treasured beyond our days. Remember exploring blessings in chapter 2 where we learned how all of us yearned to be blessed by our parents? Well, it goes the other way as well. Here are excerpts of a grown man writing to honor his father's eightieth birthday.

Dear Dad:

If you're like most fathers you must have wondered if your children, while they were growing up, knew you loved them. As your oldest child I would like to use this letter to answer that question for me. You're probably thinking that I'm going to mention the 'big' things in a little boy's life...like the time you took me and Bob to Disneyland when it first opened in 1955! ....

Actually those were great times Dad, but not what I remember today almost 60 years later. What I remember today are the smaller, more simple, mundane things ... like hearing in my mind's ear like it was yesterday, the way you used to sing 'Silent Night' to me when I was in my crib at night ... it always put me to sleep ... like the Saturday mornings when you let me go with you in the big red pick-up garbage truck to the 'dump' ... sitting with you on that front leather seat and grabbing that gear shift knob to help you shift was a big deal to me ... even though I'm sure my presence doubled the amount of time it took you to get that job done.... or when I was 11 and although I was voted to the Little League all-star team, I couldn't play because I had broken my thumb ... somehow your arm around my shoulder and your words of consolation helped take away the hurt and disappointment I felt ... or when Mom insisted on us kids doing chores around the house on a sunny summer day. You told her to relax and let us play with our friends: "Lorraine, they have their whole lives to earn a living, let them play while they're young," you'd said ... or when you wrote an inspirational poem to mark the birth of my first son, your first grandchild.

Dad, I'm at that age when I can't remember what I had for breakfast yesterday, let alone where I just parked my car, but somehow these memories have stood the test of time because they've been etched on my heart by the hand of a loving father who in spite of all the demands on his young adulthood always found time for his son. The lesson I've taken from this has also been 60 years in the making: that your loving attention wasn't just an accident. It happened because you also found time to be with someone else, your loving Father, our Lord, which is the last memory I want to share with you ... those rare occasions when you weren't home on a weekend. You returned on Sunday and told me that you were someplace with other men and you couldn't talk! I now know you were on a religious retreat and did that often ... not to escape the demands of being a father ... but to replenish your soul so you could be an even better Dad.....

Yes Dad, I knew I was loved by you as a boy growing up, as a young man raising his own family, and now as an older man looking forward to his own golden years. My blessing for you Dad on this, your 80th birthday, is that you know how much I have loved and love you. I know the best way to convey that love is not by putting words on paper, but on living the values you've taught me with my children and my children's children. It's a wonderful legacy, Dad ... one that I hope you take great pride in.

Love, Bill

Legacy writing has the purpose of passing forward our love and our learning. This does not mean that your letters should be sugar coated or dishonest. In chapters nine and ten the material of our legacy letters is about apologizing and breaking the taboo of silence veiling generational secrets. There we'll see that not all legacy letters are light and happy, though hope for the future seems universally present. The commitment to express the truths of our experiences and our learning from them, suggests discernment rather than judgment, and accepting – not necessarily liking – reality. This too is love.

When you're ready, we'll move on to Chapter 9, "I'm Sorry" with these inspiring words:

> **"I personally believe whenever one member of a family heals, that healing goes back and forward through time and space, uplifting the whole line. A ritual of honoring our ancestors helps bring us into a more conscious relationship with our family story that promotes a healing of everyone who has ever been, or will be born into, our family."**
> **— Joan Borysenko**

Chapter 9
I'm Sorry

As the title suggests, this chapter is about forgiving and apologizing. The words, "I'm sorry" are simple enough to think about, but not so easy to say, especially with sincerity. The power of this chapter is that writing letters of apology has the potential to heal relationships. As important, we the writers harvest a legacy of inner peace and acceptance.

> **"Everyone says forgiveness is a wonderful idea until they have something to forgive."**   **— C.S. Lewis**

We're going to take on the task even though it's not easy, because the outcomes will free us, and perhaps free the recipients to whom we'll write.

We all have regrets about things we've done and not done: about dreams we feared to live or that weren't realized (remember Rebecca's and Beth's letters on pages 116 and 125). As parents we made choices we regretted or that had unexpected consequences. We have regrets too about how we treated our parents, friends, family members, lovers, and the earth, purposely or inadvertently.

Not long ago I led a blessing workshop at the home of a dear friend in Boca Raton. The female participants ranged in age from age forty to eighty. My friend's thirteen-year-old daughter came downstairs as we were setting up, announced that she was ill and didn't want to go to school.

After her mother agreed that she could stay home, I invited her to join us for the workshop. She was delighted, listened attentively, and partici-pated throughout the day. The last blessing the women wrote was for fu-ture generations (you wrote that blessing in chapter 2).

When everyone had set down their pens, I asked for volunteers to share. The girl raised her hand, and solemnly read her blessing. Its essence was an apology for the way her generation and those before her had mistreated the planet, misused its resources and took its beauty for granted. She concluded with a blessing of love for the earth and all its inhabitants. The women were stunned by her maturity, her passion, and her compassion.

The list of topics appropriate for legacy writing is expansive enough to hold regret, vulnerability, apologies, amends, and forgiveness. In a leg-acy letter we can acknowledge and take responsibility for wrongs we've done and ask forgiveness, make amends. This is an opportunity to use the present moment to forgive the past and express love to the future.

We'll focus our legacy letters on expressing those regrets, being car-ing and compassionate with ourselves for our human failings, taking re-sponsibility for our actions, and making amends where appropriate. Be-fore we begin writing, let's explore some ideas about regrets and forgiveness, and read some samples by legacy writers.

No one wants to pass on a legacy of hurt, disappointment or pain, yet many of us live wounded with painful legacies from those who came before us. We seem unable to get free ourselves in order that we not pass forward the betrayal to those we love.

Caveat: Writing a legacy letter of apology does not guarantee that we will never hurt that person again. Nor does it guarantee that the re-cipient will accept our offering. But an expression of love by honestly and transparently admitting what we've done or said, and expressing our sorrow and regret because we believe we've acted or spoken hurtfully, can go a long way toward healing a relationship or melting old pain.

A gift of a legacy letter of regret and apology that can be read and reread is not easily forgotten. It is one of the most satisfying and fulfilling for both the writer and receiver of all legacy letters, long cherished, and healing for the writer and the reader.

On the other hand, writing does not necessarily require sending/ sharing what we write. It is our choice whether to send the letter now or later, to save it in our Legacy File, or to destroy it in a ritual act.

Betrayal and Forgiveness

James Hillman, a widely respected Jungian writer, wrote about betrayal. He suggests that betrayal is inevitable in human relationships: broken promises, family secrets, refusal to help, deception in love. The betrayed person ultimately betrays himself by failing to be him or her self.

We get stuck in the stories we tell ourselves about how and why we were betrayed. With each repetition, the story gains power over us. To protect ourselves from further hurt, we craft protections: denial, cynicism, revenge, paranoia. But, Hillman says, there is a way out: forgiveness.

> **"Just as trust had within it the seed of betrayal, so betrayal has within it the seed of forgiveness."** — James Hillman

My mother, betrayed by her immigrant mother, told herself a story that she believed all her life. She never forgave her mother for being emotionally abandoned. The estrangement between my mother and hers deprived my sister and me of a relationship with our grandmother. Perhaps more significant was that our mother, so wounded and so stuck in her story, unwittingly passed on a legacy of distrust, bitterness, unexpressed rage, and disappointment to my sister and me.

> " ...memories in themselves are not a problem....It is only when memories...take you over completely that they turn into a burden, turn problematic, and become part of your sense of self....almost everyone carries in his or her energy field an accumulation of old emotional pain, which I call 'the pain-body'." — Eckhart Tolle

After reading James Hillman and then Eckhart Tolle's A New Earth *about carrying the emotional "pain-body" of our parents, I had an unexpected internal experience of lightness. My mother's pain was not my pain! Wounding me was inevitable, but not intentional nor purposeful. For the first time, though I'd long ago forgiven her intellectually, (she died in 1972) I experienced a powerful wave of compassion and forgiveness for her, almost immediately followed by a sense of new freedom to be me.*

Legacy letters are never limited to living recipients. Our parents and grandparents may be deceased, but our relationships with them live as long as we live. The benefits of writing letters to them are often profound. (Remember Carol's experience with The Grandmothers and Midrash on page 77.) Here is an example of the unanticipated ways legacy writing can promote our healing.

In Memphis some years ago, I facilitated a program focused on writing a legacy letter of apology. Afterwards a woman in her early thirties rushed over to me, declaring anxiously, "I think I did it wrong." I interpreted her words as an invitation to ask her what she'd written and to whom. She responded that she had written her letter of apology to her father.

I thought she believed the letter's recipient had to be someone from a younger generation, so I assured her that writing to a parent or ancestor can be a legacy letter too. She responded, "But he's dead!" I continued, "Our relationships don't end at death; they live on whether we inhabit the same space or not." She first appeared surprised by my words, then visibly relieved. She looked pensive, and then thanked me, saying, "I could never have told him while he was alive."

> "To forgive is to abandon your right to pay back the perpetrator in his own coin, but it is a loss that liberates the victim."
> — Archbishop Desmond Tutu

Parenting and Regrets

Parenting is a good place to begin exploring our regrets. I've never met a parent who doesn't have some regret, most have many: some tiny and specific, others long-lived and significant. Taking responsibility for them lightens the load of unfinished business we carry around as part of our personal baggage. It can release us from guilt. It may make us more compassionate toward others as well. Read what this mother wrote, hoping to clean the slate as her daughter was leaving home for college:

> **"I have no way to lessen for you the pain you suffered in having been an acutely sensitive child in the hands of a strong and assertive mother. But I will tell you that always, always, I gave you the best that I had available to give. And sometimes my best was simply not good enough. I'm sorry for that."** — Sharon Strassfeld

In my letter celebrating my daughter on her fortieth birthday this brief paragraph is how I once again took responsibility for betraying her when she needed me most. This amend is one more step that deepens and heals our relationship today even though my apology is about my actions over thirty years ago.

> *"Looking back, I know that those young years were particularly painful in your life and mine. Often I focused not on you or my parenting, but on things outside family, like work, where I was respected and felt appreciated and accomplished. I have often told you how sorry I am for having neglected you. I know you've forgiven me as much as you can, and for that I'm grateful. I so regret that I wasn't available to you in the ways you needed then. I know I can't change the past or its hurts, but I do my best to be present to you in your life today."*

A legacy letter can be read and reread, is not easily forgotten. For the writer it is a most satisfying and fulfilling redemptive act. A verbal apology may more easily slip away. For both the writer and receiver, written words can heal and will be long cherished. Writing sincerely from an open heart, we become more compassionate with ourselves about our failings. Inner acceptance and peace follows whether the receiver acknowledges or accepts our amend or not. Hopefully our written regrets and apologies will be understood as acts of love and will be appreciated now and long after we're gone.

We live in turbulent and dangerous times, which make us more aware of our mortality than ever. None of us knows how long we'll live. This uncertainty encourages us to ask forgiveness now for the harm we've caused ... and to consider forgiving those who have harmed us.

> **"New beginnings are often disguised as painful endings."**
> **— Lao Tzu**

This letter of love for her children expresses a mother's understanding of the cause of the hurts she's responsible for, followed by an apology, an expression of love, and a commitment to behave differently.

Dear Daughter and Son,

Several months ago, I heard someone say that in her family she had learned how to love and how to worry, but not how to trust. I immediately recognized that I had learned the same lessons. I understood her to mean trusting God to help me and those I love — however we might define that force that is both in us and greater than us. Trust, to me, means profoundly accepting what is—not what I wish it was or think it should be—and knowing that we are all ok in the deepest sense of what that means. Instead of trusting, I felt alone, as if it were totally up to me to make everything work out.

Because of my lack of trust, I often try to fix things—primarily others' feelings and behaviors—both are outside of my control. I worry that if I don't, things will not be ok either for them or for me, or for our relationship. I've also tried too hard to fix, rather than accept, myself. In the past year or so, my level of trust has increased rather dramatically and, as a result, my internal sense of peace and confidence has grown and my behavior has changed. But, of course, it's a process that is not consistent and far from perfect.

Today, I want to apologize for having hurt you—perhaps by teaching you to approach the world in the same manner and certainly by trying to control you or others in relation to you. Son, you recently referred to your tendency to fight other people's battles. I too have done that because of my lack of trust .... if you and I were upset with each other, I've worked too hard to make it ok by processing and explaining too much, and trying too hard to get you to explain yourselves. I know I can be intense, partly because it's my nature and partly because of fear. This intensity has been hard on both of you, perhaps especially on you, Daughter.

I love you both enormously and am sorry for the difficulty that I've caused you. I am committed to continuing to strengthen my own boundaries, to be clear about what I feel and think, what I want and where I stand, to remember that I am responsible only for my own behaviors and attitudes, that the rest is out of my control, and that divine wisdom will help us all.

Love always,
Mom

This letter is a poignant expression of love by a grandfather to his grandson, who is working, going to school, and has responsibility for his own newborn son. Included is the grandfather's thoughtful reflection about his own life and his regret about a lack of close connection with his son.

Dear Tom,

As your grandfather, I wanted to write you a personal letter as a blessing. Perhaps you will keep this and reread it when times get tough.

When your Dad was growing up, I was heavily involved in my graduate studies and establishing a teaching career. I often put him off when I was busy. As a consequence, I missed out on many of the joys and pains of being a father as he was growing up.

Then when major crises came, I was not prepared to deal with them and I was overwhelmed with the problems he was facing. I think it would have been much easier for him and for me if I had established a closer relationship with him while he was growing up. We did, however, get much closer after he became an adult.

Now you have this opportunity to enjoy the involvement with your new son, Jack, in all his joys and sorrows. It is my hope that you will be blessed with the joy of his laughter, the tears of his disappointments, and the closeness of holding him tight. These are the things that make being a parent so special.

Tom, you are very special in my eyes. I am so proud of the way you are trying to get your education and at the same time meeting your responsibilities as a father. I am sure there are times when the road seems long and rough. I have every confidence that you will prevail. I want you to know that no matter what happens, Grandma and I will always love you. I once told your Dad, there is nothing he can do that will take that love away. I have the same promise for you. May God bless you as you continue your journey into adulthood and beyond.

With love,
Grandpa

Forgiveness

A legacy writer friend, Caroline, shared how a lifelong resentment melted away in time for her to make peace with her elderly aunt. When she was eight, she heard her aunt and mother fighting and as she neared, she saw her aunt kicking her mother. Neither woman saw her. From that moment she held hate in her heart for her aunt. Not a surprising reaction for a seven-year-old girl.

Some 60 years passed. Caroline went to visit her aunt in hospice before her passing. As she stood in the waiting room, a middle aged Asian man came out of her aunt's room. With tears in his eyes, he asked Caroline if she was related to the dying woman. Caroline said, "Yes, I'm her niece." The man took both Caroline's hands, and said, "Your aunt was my angel. She voluntarily taught me English when I immigrated as a child. She helped me adjust to this country during my very difficult youth."

How amazing. Caroline had believed her Aunt was the devil, and in this man's life she was an angel. It was a sacred moment for Caroline. Her aunt was human. Caroline could go into her room with compassion and forgiveness in her heart to say her last goodbye.

After holding on to this powerful resentment for sixty years, Caroline let go in little more than an instant. That's not how it always happens. We must respect our own as well as the timetable of those from whom we ask forgiveness. Sometimes the timetable is beyond human understanding. The slogan from Twelve Step programs, "Progress, not Perfection" can help us combat our impatience over the snail-slow pace of forgiveness.

> **"Forgiving can take time. It takes as long as it takes, and it's important to have patience with yourself and your internal process."**   **— Denise Linn**

Courage and Healing

When legacy writers gather for a day or a longer retreat to write our legacy letters, we sit in a circle. After writing, I invite writers to share, always reminding the listeners that we are neither in a therapy group where we might analyze each other's writing, nor in a writing group per se, where we critique what each wrote and shared.

This caution makes the circle safe for everyone, those who share and those who choose not to. Having the choice about whether to share frees each writer to write deeply from the heart, knowing that they are not in a competition to be the "best" writer or to try through their writing to impress others. Legacy writers write from their hearts to others' hearts.

This honest and unflinchingly courageous letter was written and shared from one participant to another at such a retreat. It followed a conversation that went on outside the circle, and the original writer's expression of anger when we returned to the circle.

Dear _____,

In this beautiful place, where we women have gathered to sustain one another as we write our legacy letters, I, in my arrogance, my conceit, wearing my self-anointed wise crone crown — I have hurt you deeply. "Too much hurt was done to each other that cannot yet be forgiven."

In my lifetime, I have struggled daily for self-confidence. It comes slowly, needs constant reinforcement. Yesterday I must have showered in hubris — and when I listened to you read of your struggle about your dream of land ... I wanted somehow to help, to play the adviser, counselor, and perhaps — I don't know — offer a different point of view. Was this about me playing some egotistical role?

As soon as I heard myself babbling, overstepping, making obvious suggestions — and then — Ouch — it hurts to revisit — "Maybe it's something else . . ." or whatever my foolish words — I wanted to bite my tongue. You had wrestled with your demon and you knew yourself. Who was I, a stranger, to tell you what you "might consider"?

My blessing to you is one of gratitude — you have taught me a difficult lesson as you told me how angry you were with my advice. We had been guided to listen as a sacred gift to each other, to listen without response — and I have listened to you.

Today I am chastened, humbled, embarrassed, ashamed, and I am grateful for your honesty, your directness. May you be blessed always with your clear-sighted honesty with yourself and continue to share it with others. You have taught me a lesson more valuable than gold, the gift of awareness and humility.

With great respect, _____

"The weak can never forgive. Forgiveness is the attribute of the strong." — Mahatma Gandhi

This courageous and tender letter from a daughter to her mother combines regrets, yearning, amends, and hope for healing their relationship. Here is an excerpt:

Dear Mom,

It was great talking to you on my birthday and thinking about what the future holds for us. I was happy to hear your idea for parking a trailer on a half-acre in Sonoma, where I hope to soon live.

The idea of living so close to you after all these years has made me think about the "lost years" of our relationship. It's been a long time since we've lived together, or even in the same state. For a long time, I was happy to be so far away, but the older I get, the more I long to be with family. And California will always be my home.

I'm sorry that I didn't make more of an effort to get Zoe out to see you while she was growing up ....

I am sad that we haven't had a closer relationship over these many years. I'm more like you than any daughter cares to admit, and I share your strong desire for space by myself. That can be to the exclusion of people I love at times, and I have drifted away from you.

I always thought it was a parent's job to keep in touch with their kids. That it was up to the parent to give it up for their children and free them to move on with their lives. Now that I'm a mom, I realize how difficult it is to name my own flaws and make amends for the many, many mistakes I have made. But that is what I have done. It took having a child to make me see how stuck I was in my own way of being, and I made a conscious effort to apologize to her and tell her what she means to me. And yes, it was one of the hardest things I've ever done.

I wish that you and I could have had such a breakthrough, and maybe we will, one of these days. Not so that you can feel bad about what happened, but so that we could be closer, and I can begin to understand why it happened the way it did, and how you felt and feel about it now. We've never talked about such things, and my heart yearns to hear from yours ....

Now I want to be closer to those I love, and that includes you, Mom. We've never really had a chance to be close since I left home at a much too young age. I'm a little scared by the thought, because I'm not really sure who we are together anymore. But my heart is open and I'm willing to try. I love you.

Mom

"You will know that forgiveness has begun when you recall those who hurt you and feel the power to wish them well."
— Lewis B. Smedes

Reflection and Writing

We've reflected about regrets and amends, apologies and forgiveness. We've had the honor of reading others' legacy letters, imagining what a precious gift they are for their readers, and sensing how they set the writers free. Now it's our turn. Let's pick up our pens to express ourselves to those we love. Feel free to begin writing now, or follow these suggestions that have helped other legacy writers.

Begin by listing three (or more) people to whom you want to offer amends or ask forgiveness. (Remember, they do not have to be living.) Putting a person on your list does not mean you're committed to either write them a letter or send it to them.

Add for each person on your list a brief notation indicating why they're there. (You want to share a regret, you want to make amends for something you did or didn't do, you want to tell them you've forgiven them, or you intend to ask them to forgive you.)

Choose one person from your list (it may be a good idea to begin with the least threatening, the easiest person for you to write to). In your journal or on your legacy pad, write notes about your reasons for seeking resolution. Note if there is a specific memory to refer to; remember we learn best from stories.

Set your timer; write (for just 15 minutes) to your valued person a letter that describes your regret, or the harm you did and your amend.

Put the letter away at least overnight. When you reread it, you can edit it (remember editing tips from chapter 2). You may want to add a blessing or some words of appreciation, hope or love at the end of the letter. As you reread it, you can decide whether and when you will send it. If you decide "not now", put the letter in your personal Legacy File. Bring it out regularly to reconsider your decision.

Repeat this practice with the other two or more people on your list. You can add as many people to your list as you think of as time passes and you can return to the list anytime.

We'll close this chapter with a blessing for forgiveness, written by my colleague and friend, Claire Willis, a legacy writer whose work is to support cancer patients to write their own legacy letters:

May I forgive myself for the harm I have done to others, knowingly and unknowingly

May I forgive others the harm done to me, knowingly or unknowingly

May I forgive myself for the harm I have done to myself, knowingly and unknowingly

May I forgive myself for what I am yet unable to forgive.

Chapter 10
Cleaning Out Your Closet

It's always challenging to try to figure out what a chapter title means and how it relates to legacy. In this chapter, we'll explore two different closets. First, we'll assess the legacy value of the material things we have in our physical "closets." That's the stuff that we've been given, that we've gathered and collected, and haven't given, recycled, or thrown away. Then we'll look inward to see which of our feelings and thoughts need to be cleaned out and which would be valuable to share with those we love.

Physical "Stuff"

We're used to hearing that *our stuff* has no value, and that we can't take our possessions with us. I disagree. Let's look through the lens of the value of our stuff, beyond the material value (although we spend lots of money on stuff, and on homes to house our stuff).

What about the *things* we've inherited, that help us stay connected with loved ones who are now gone? What about mementos from important trips, and that we've received as gifts from a beloved? These objects are infused with personal and familial meaning. They stand as symbols of our identity, our values, our relationships. But there's other stuff...

Letting Go

Riv Lynch, the creator of sacredspaceshome.com, suggests that we create an ideal vision of our authentic space and let go or minimize the *excess stuff* that clutters our space. Tops on her list of stuff that "procreates uncontrollably" are greeting cards, magazines more than three months old, our kids' art work, cords for electronics, and packaging for things we buy "just in case." Here's an action tip: OHIO: "Only Handle Items Once."

> "To change skins, evolve into new cycles, I feel one has to learn to discard. If one changes internally, one should not continue to live with the same objects. They reflect one's mind and the psyche of yesterday. I throw away what has no dynamic, living use." — Anais Nin

Imagine the value of letting go. Reflect and journal about your experience and learning as you consider simplifying. Keep your reflections in your Legacy File as inspiration for what can be a lengthy process. Everyone's timing for becoming able to let go is different. There is no right or wrong way or timetable; there is only *your* way! Make a commitment to whatever level of de-cluttering fits for you and make it happen - let go!

Respecting your personal timetable, there is another consideration: an urgent reason not to procrastinate. The hard reality is that we could lose all our stuff in a heartbeat. Many of us know people who've lost everything: in a fire, a tornado, or a flood. Letting go as a regular exercise helps us to be prepared emotionally when *stuff* or the loss of it is beyond our control for any reason. Letting go is a task for all of us at every season of our lives.

In my letter celebrating my daughter on her fortieth birthday this paragraph recalls her learning to organize her stuff. You may find it instructive.

> *"You were always on the go, like a whirlwind and then I'd find you fast asleep in a doll bed, on the living room floor, or in your tiger toy box. One day when you were about four I sent you to clean up your room and a half hour later I found*

you there, sitting in the midst of the mess, paralyzed and in tears. You said you didn't know what to do; it was just too much. I sat down with you, and we made four piles: one to throw away, one to give away, one to keep, and one to decide about later. Soon we were done; you were all smiles again and ready to play. We could see your bright yellow carpet, and you had room to cartwheel again. Today you are a superb organizer, whether the challenge is a closet, a house, or a corporation, and you do it with that "cartwheeling" spirit with which you face all the challenges in your life."

The last time I de-cluttered I'd sold my house and opted for life in a condominium. Although I'm not moving anywhere now, I owe it to myself to lighten my load, to let go of the too much that I have. I've begun to frame my commitment to purge stuff as a holy task. Getting rid of what I don't need and what distracts me from my purpose is in itself a holy act. The emptier I can be of what I neither need nor value, the more space to live lighter, more spaciously inside, and to focus on what really matters. As a bonus, the stuff left to my children to make decisions about: what to keep, what to recycle, what to give to others, what to trash, will be simpler.

"Have nothing in your houses that you do not know to be useful or believe to be beautiful." — **William Morris**

What is our responsibility to de-clutter as we age, respecting the next generation who will have to clean up our stuff after we're gone?

I've imagined dying suddenly, and watching from somewhere as my two children wander through the morass of my things: paper, books, pictures, collections, and accumulated mementos. Not only is it an unfair burden to leave them, but my stuff makes a statement about me.

I ask myself, "How will they know the junk from the stuff with meaning? What might they conclude about their mother who holds on too long and too much?" I imagine their resentment being left to go through my things because I didn't take the responsibility to leave life expressing what I 'say' I value, including simplicity, order, and beauty.

How Do We Decide What to Let Go Of?

There are two more things to consider about stuff and legacy. First, what criteria should we use to make decisions about the stuff to be passed forward as inheritance to future generations? Then, what things do we want to accompany us should we need to make a transitional move from the physical space we inhabit today?

> **"Letting go leaves space for more to come......Cleaning house—both literally and as a metaphor for life—is a great way to hit the Refresh button. When you look at your relationship to things—and the energy they contain—ask yourself if they promote joy, beauty, and usefulness, or are they burdensome?"** — Oprah

Several years ago I did a Minneapolis radio interview about my first legacy book. While driving to the interview, I turned on the station to get the feel of the interviewer. Kevyn Burger was preparing her listeners.

As I remember, she said, "I'm so excited for this next half hour. I'll be interviewing Rachael Freed who's written a book about legacy. One part of her book reminded me of when my grandmother died. My sisters and I got to go to Grandma's house and pick out something to remember her by. I'm the oldest, so I got to choose first. I picked my grandmother's olive dish. It wasn't fancy; probably she'd bought it at the dime store for 89 cents. But I loved it. It reminded me of going to her house for supper. Always that dish, filled with pickles and olives, awaited us at the table. Now when I see that dish, I'm reminded of how much I loved my grandma." I knew as I drove and listened to Kevyn that the interview would be fun. She "got it."

We need to stay current, realizing that young people are not very interested in having "inherited stuff." More often they value our blessings and love in a legacy letter. Knowing that, how do we make decisions about gifting our material treasures? What criteria do we use to decide which objects go to which loved ones? When is the right time to give them? How will our loved ones know which *stuff* is their memento?

Instead of thinking I knew what of my stuff, if any, my grandchildren would want, I asked them. When they came for a "sleep-over" I asked them if there was any of my stuff they would want after I'm gone. Not wanting to scare them, I assured them I was not (actively) dying and ex-

pected to be here with them for a long time. I wrote their choices on my clipboard as we moved from room to room. Selections they made were very different from what I thought they'd choose, and it was fun for me and for them to look around to discover their favorite things.

I recorded their choices and put the list in my Legacy File. I plan to annotate each of their choices, explain the items' history and meaning, electronically store pictures of the things with their written history and label them so their future ownership will be clear. Tip: These photos (and others of your valuables) would be useful to your property insurance company for replacement should your "stuff" be lost.

Physical Transitions and Stuff

Gerontological wisdom suggests that the *things* elders choose to take with them in the complex transition of surrendering private, independent homes for communal housing, are powerful aids to maintain coherence and continuity of identity. This stuff is emblematic of belonging, kinship, and relationship, all basic and universal human needs throughout life. They are reminders of life history, achievements, and life roles. Precious objects support security and the dignity of each individual's life. Even when memory fades, this special stuff can provide comfort.

> **"The power of everyday things carry both ideas and passions... emotional and intellectual companions that anchor memory [and] sustain relationship...."** — **Sherry Turkle**

Coherence and Continuity

Mary Ruhr, a legacy writer wrote her Master's thesis with the hypothesis that our *stuff* functions to enhance continuity and coherence, especially in a transition as complex as leaving our more spacious homes for a life with limited private space and impersonal public dining and recreation space. Her field-study included living in a nursing home for a month, becoming friends with residents, and being invited to their rooms to share stories about the things they'd brought with them when they'd left their homes.

We hear about people leaving a hospital or rehabilitation center not for home, but for strange new permanent quarters. Following hospitalization and with no warning, the mother of my friend was transferred directly to a nursing home. There'd been no time to gather her things. As she sat in the bleak room – lost in her new "home," staring into the distance, she said to her daughter, "I feel like a refugee." How unprepared they were for this heartbreaking transition.

An artist friend of mine intuitively understood how disarming and difficult this move might be for his partner after hip surgery. He brought her favorite paintings and part of her miniature collection of porcelain and pottery animals to the rehabilitation center, her temporary home after leaving the hospital. Beauty and familiar objects helped her to regain her psychic balance after surgery, anesthesia, and pain medications. That *stuff* and more went to their new apartment because she could no longer negotiate the stairs in their previous home of many years.

> **"...even though you're far away from home, you start to feel okay, because after all, you do have some of your stuff with you."** — George Carlin

We don't know when a fall or sudden onset of an illness will change our reality. Thus I advise legacy writers to spend some time journaling about favorite objects and their meaning. Sharing this information in a legacy letter to a close relative or friend (and identifying/marking the special *stuff*) helps insure that should circumstances cause you to make an unexpected move, those things that mean something to you will accompany or follow you. This information can inform professionals hired to pack up and dispose of the household in a transition, if your loved ones are unavailable or live far away from you.

> **"To us, our house was not unsentient matter - it had a heart, and a soul, and eyes to see us with; and approvals and solicitudes and deep sympathies; it was of us, and we were in its confidence, and lived in its grace and in the peace of its benediction."** — Mark Twain

Younger generations need to encourage their elders to choose things to accompany them before the transition becomes a reality. Even the most compassionate professional caregivers or movers can't know the history or the meaning of personal objects of a lifetime. We can consciously strive to diminish our elders' vulnerability and enhance their sense of dignity and empowerment as they confront the inevitable passage of illness or aging.

Reflections and Legacy Practice

Now it's time to begin your legacy reflection and writing about *your stuff*. Here are suggestions to guide you, should the task seem overwhelming or something to put off until perhaps it's too late. Do any or all of these. Some reflections belong in your Legacy File; others are subjects for legacy letters to those you want to inform and gift with your words and material things.

1. Make a list of 5-20 of your favorite objects that you would want with you should it become necessary to move from your home. Write about why you chose the things you did ... their value to you. (You may want to use the criteria of coherence, continuity and comfort – the objects that fit like "an old shoe".) Make copies to include with your communications about aging, advance health planning and end of life wishes (see chapter 11). Make sure at least one person in your family knows where this information is.

2. Take de-cluttering seriously. Begin exploring ways your life is complicated by clutter: Go through each room in your home to compile a list of items or categories of things you determine to be clutter - those things you can let go of. Reflect and journal your thoughts and feelings about your clutter. Consider possible motives for holding onto things beyond their Usefulness or Beauty: company, comfort, distraction, sloth.

3. Invite your beloveds (children, grandchildren, friends and family) to name objects of yours that have special meaning to them. (Don't be surprised if their lists are quite different from yours.) You may decide to give away some things sooner rather than later! If later, be sure to put

the information with your legacy materials – or in your Legacy File until you're ready and will enjoy letting go.

4. Choose one object from all your valuable stuff to write a legacy letter about. Here are some prompts to help you describe why the object is special to you. (What is its history, biography? What is its story? How did it come to you? What makes it meaningful to you? What does the object symbolize to you? What do you appreciate about it?) You may decide to send this letter to a loved one because the writing illumines some aspect of your identity that no one knows about. Why have you chosen the person you did to receive it? And consider gifting that person with the object you've written about.

5. Have fun!

From an aunt in her nineties this simple and moving legacy letter to her niece about a diamond ring expresses history, caring, and the value of a family heirloom imbued with meaning.

My dear Sue Caroline,

You are such a dear and I want you to know how much I love you. You were such a help to your mother during her last years and choosing to live so close to her made it possible for you to be right there when she needed you.

Now you have become a supportive presence for me, and what a joy you were to your Grandma B_____. She was a dear, sweet lady and she welcomed all her grandchildren into the family with love and her time and great patience.

I have something of hers in my possession - something that I believe she would want you to have. It is the ring she wore for over 50 years and I have been wearing since her death. It contains the wedding diamond from Grandpa on whose birthday you were born and you were given Grandma's name as part of your name.

So, dear Suzy, I believe you are the one who should have the ring to enjoy - hopefully for 50 years or more, to cherish and eventually to pass on to Ruth or Jeanine.

I love you, my dear. May my blessings surround you with love and may God's grace, mercy, and peace be with you always.

Aunt Ginny

Just Old Stuff

Wait! Don't toss it out
Because you think it is just old stuff.
It is – but then it isn't.
These are bits and pieces I recall
From times of my life,
People I held and hold dear,
Places I loved and love,
Histories hidden but soaked
Into the fabric of paper, cloth, wood.

How will you know
The treasures from the surfeit,
The meaningful, significant parts,
Those meant to survive beyond me
Imbued with precious spirit,
Tender memories, passed down,
Now passed along?

Wait! Let me tell you
About some of my stuff.
Read the stories, consider, and then decide
What is Mom
And what is just old stuff.

- Diane Forman

An Aside About Beauty

Beauty is an important legacy to live and leave. We appreciate beauty as nature dressed in the finery of her seasons. We feel awe in the presence of a magnificent flower, a perfect pinecone, a majestic mountain, an ancient tree, a unique sunrise or sunset painted on our sky.

Remembering we are all created in the image of God, we have the possibility and the ability to add to natural beauty using our creative natures. A simple example: when we de-clutter our homes we create a harmonious and more graceful atmosphere for living. Human-made beauty lifts us and generations to come: music, dance, all the arts, including crafts, graphic, architectural, and industrial design, and more.

From whom did my legacy of beauty come? My mother expressed her love of beauty domestically as she set a table, decorated her home, by her personal grooming, and her style in dress. Her love of flowers, colors, textures, fabrics, furniture, and shoes was a legacy she gave me. Though she died 40 years ago, I remember her when experiencing beauty that momentarily takes my breath away, awakens me from the sightlessness of habit. I often think how much she would have treasured the gorgeous colors and rich textures of today's yarns, beads, fabrics, and wall coverings.

I remember my sister and I going through my mother's things after she died, choosing beautiful bags and gloves to give to her many friends to remember her by - each beautiful and all her exquisite taste and eye for the unusual, the delicate, the elegant. People tell me even today they still wear her gloves, carry her bags for special occasions.

Leaving a legacy of beauty for future generations means cultivating beauty wherever we can.

> **"Flowers... are a proud assertion that a ray of beauty out-values all the utilities of the world."**
> — **Ralph Waldo Emerson**

Psychic "Stuff"

Cleaning out our physical closets is challenging for most of us. Harvesting peace and serenity as a reward for having accomplished it is well worth the effort. We face one more legacy challenge about stuff; that is the stuff within. Most of us don't have or take the time or, like my daughter at age four, don't know how to look within to see what the clutter is. We may have carried the stuff within for a long time, and some of us have carried family stuff – secrets – passed to us as invisible legacies from generations ago.

Let's think of this stuff as secrets. We keep secrets from ourselves as well as from and for others. So let's begin by investigating the idea of secrets and the effects that secrets have as they live from generation to generation. Once we've reflected, we can decide whether or not to share the secrets that have affected us, that are a part of our identity.

Many secrets in our psychic closet are born of shame, a sense that we are bad, ugly, cold, selfish, cruel, unloving. We may believe we have a quality that makes us "other," unfit for inclusion in the human community. We've pushed these feelings so deep into the back of our closet that we don't even know or feel them to be true. Unaware of them, we have no idea how those feelings may affect our daily lives, our relationships, and families.

Then there are the secrets we inherit. We may have a sense that something in the family history is wrong, something has long been hidden, and it's too terrible for anyone to talk about. (Remember my fiancé's grandmother's story about having eight siblings, but she would only name seven, on page 33.)

> **"It's become gospel that silence is not golden but toxic in family relationships and marriages."** — Anna Quindlen

Whatever is not spoken of is a secret for all time. We only have an inkling that something happened once back then. The good thing is that we live in a time now when our culture has evolved so what was once taboo can now be shared. Examples abound in every family: alcoholism, extramarital affairs, interracial marriage, homosexuality, abortion, children born out of wedlock and more. These "shameful" skeletons kept deep in the closet can now be spoken in some families, and in turn free future generations from the harmful effects of unknowingly carrying the secret.

As preparation for writing legacy letters about inner stuff (emotional clutter, secrets) one legacy writing circle focused on personal secrets we'd kept. When we began, we had no idea what the content of our writing would be, how we would feel about what we found inside, or whether we would choose to share our secrets with loved ones. Here is one writer's writing experience followed by her thoughts about the experience.

I had finished my first year of college in a nursing program known for its holistic care—back in the 60's. I applied to be a nursing assistant for summer employment at our small, local hospital and was hired to work on two separate med-surg. units. One unit had a pediatric area where small children were admitted for pneumonia, flu, and other short-term illness episodes.

One evening I worked the 3-11 shift and the census on the unit was low. We had one child in 'peds' … a baby under a year who had been admitted with pneumonia a couple of days prior to my working on the unit. The head nurse was a grumpy older woman—short and chubby with hair growing out of a wart on her chin. Her answers to questions were usually short and clipped so she was rarely approached unless something major occurred.

Dinner was at 4:30 for staff and because the census was low, the head nurse decided to go to dinner leaving me in charge of the unit for ½ hour. I stepped into the peds unit to gather what was needed to feed the baby. I remember pulling the high chair over to the counter. I was nervous about feeding this baby. I'd never babysat one this young when I was in high school. This new experience had me asking myself: Do I feed the food first or the bottle? Do I use a small spoon or a larger spoon? Where is the bib? How does the high chair work?

I waved to the meal servers as they passed trays to the small number of patients. They would return in 45 minutes to retrieve the trays. The high chair posed a problem: I couldn't quite get the tray figured out. I placed the baby in the chair and maneuvered the tray in place. I remember hearing the click on one side and assumed it had clicked on the other side. It hadn't. I turned around to get the bib and fastened it on the baby. I stepped away to pick up the applesauce and jello and turning around, I saw the baby falling from the high chair onto the floor. Oh, how she cried and how frightened I was. I checked her: no bumps, no bruises. I just held her and walked her until she stopped crying. I looked around outside the peds area. No patients. No nurses. No kitchen personnel. No visitors. I was safe!

The baby would not eat from my arms and I didn't trust myself with the high chair so I put her back in the crib with her blanket, and she quieted. I was frightened to death. Questions raced through my mind: Would she be all right? Would she have bumps and bruises that would show up tomorrow? Should I say something to the head nurse? What if I had to fill out an accident report? Would the parents be angry? Would the head nurse be angry? Would my folks be angry? Guilt ate at me.

I put the high chair back in the corner. I walked out of the area into the quiet of med-surg. Patients were eating their meals; the head nurse was walking down the hall and asked how everything had gone. I said, "Fine." I lied and told her the baby had taken a couple of ounces of milk—no solids. She said she would check on her later. Routines were done for the evening, and when I left the unit the baby was sleeping comfortably.

I did not sleep comfortably that night or the next night or for the remaining weeks of summer. When I returned to the unit two days later, I was relieved to hear the baby was discharged and the pneumonia had cleared. Of course, I was relieved. But I had lied and kept this from my superior, my co-workers, my parents. What if something major had happened—death for instance? The guilt was more than I could bear. I told my mother what had happened and she, too, was relieved that all was well. I mentioned filing a report and she didn't understand "why." I did nothing more.

I still wonder about that baby who is now in her 40's if living. I picture every space in that hospital. Details jump out at me from the peds room. I have dreamed many dreams of catching her mid-air. The guilt still haunts me. I vowed to tell the truth from then on—to be humble—to be responsible—to admit my failures. This image-filled experience haunts me often reminding me to live with integrity and the challenges that provokes.

Reflections after Writing

Remember, reflective notes after legacy writing are an opportunity to consider your experience of writing. Writing may stimulate strong emotions, even tears, as well as new thoughts and connections. These notes may or may not be included in what appears in your finished legacy document, but they can clarify your values and deepen your insights, thereby contributing implicitly to your legacy communication. Here are the legacy writer's notes about cleaning out her psychic closet that had held her secret for forty years. She expresses what it was like for her to let light shine on what had lived so long in the dark.

"So many things went through my mind as I wrote this. I caught myself trying to fib, trying to make it less serious than it was, crossing out sentences and then reassuring myself that it was okay to reveal what had happened. This was painful, as I had already done much self-recrimination, putting myself down for what I did and did not do. Forgiving myself is so hard. I felt such shame and thought if I ever admitted what I did, I would be ostracized by family, friends, co-workers. Time often tones down the vastness of the sin that I felt and thought this was. That did not happen to me. I wasn't losing sleep any longer, but I could conjure up the images quickly when faced with children and high chairs. I felt grateful for being able to write this, to walk through it and be gentle with myself. God's loving grace held me in the process. And when I decided to read this in the legacy writing circle, I felt a trust with fellow sojourners who held my words with loving respect and were grateful for opening a door for them to do the same."

Concerns about Telling Secrets

Fear is a powerful factor to consider before deciding to share a secret you may have found within. This is particularly prevalent among those who have been abused: they often believe, perhaps accurately, that silence will protect them.

While exploring the secrets within, many of us discover that we've been abused verbally, emotionally, physically, or sexually – secrets we've kept even from ourselves. Writing down these secrets may be dangerous to us or our children. In other cases this fear may be left over from a time when we were young and vulnerable.

Remember, you have more power now than you did then. You alone will determine how or whether to write your secrets (in code, private shorthand, or traditional narrative form) and what you will do with the writing when you're finished (save it, shred it, burn it, or share it). Make sure you have a safe and private place to store your writing until you complete this exploration.

The act of writing can liberate us from the burden of our secrets. Moving a secret from heart to paper may help resolve old fear or shame. Some secrets we carry may not even be ours. They may be family secrets from generations before we were born, though they have undoubtedly continued to affect lives to this day.

> **"To be human is to become visible while carrying what is hidden as a gift to others."** — **David Whyte**

On the other hand, consider long and hard before you decide to tell a secret. There's an ancient story about a man who told rumors about another man. Realizing he shouldn't have spoken, he went to the local monk for help. The monk told him to go home, cut open a pillow and watch its feathers fly away. Once they'd scattered, the monk advised the man to pick them all up and refill the pillow. You know the lesson: it was impossible, as are rescinding words once spoken.

A grandmother legacy writer had such a decision to make. She chose to write a legacy letter expressing her support and love to her grand-daughter, who was troubled with drugs. She tempered her words, believing that exposing the secrets of others could add to the "conflict" in the girl's home. She shared her own secret about her father, the girl's great-grandfather, hoping to receive the girl's trust, which she ultimately did:

".... I worry about you – my heart aches wishing I could protect you. I know that I can't. I can be there for you if you will let me. I understand a great deal of your pain. I am aware of the conflict in your home. I am aware of situations you are faced with, situations that no child should ever have to deal with.

I want you to know I had a father who was an alcoholic and I suffered much of the same hurt and pain you are experiencing...."

In *Sacred Legacies*, Denise Linn writes candidly about the effects of secrets on our lives:

> "Secrets can take on a life of their own. They can create 'territories of the unspoken,' where there are tacit rules that those subjects can never be discussed. Often there will be some family members who know the secret and some who do not. This division creates covert alliances to keep the secret. Those who don't consciously know of the secret are still deeply affected by its negative influence on their psyches .... Children know and feel the unspoken; they have an inner radar for the forbidden, dark secrets of a family ...."
> — Denise Linn

When we dig the secret out of the closet for good purpose, especially when the topic is taboo, we offer hope, support, and inspiration to family members who are isolated in their situations. Writing about the mistakes in your life and the family secrets, which everyone knows and no one speaks about, can be healing for you and can offer understanding for those who follow you.

We can consider sharing these secrets with younger generations in our family at an appropriate time, so they won't have to carry them and pass them forward to their children and grandchildren.

This aunt's brave letter speaks openly of the disease of alcoholism, and the consequences to the lives of all her family members. She closes her letter with love and hopeful direction.

My Beloved Nieces and Nephews,

I want you to know what is important to me, and I leave you this legacy:

Each of you has added a rich and beautiful texture to my life since the day of your birth! I have forever watched over you, hoped the best for you and shared many family adventures with you.

For four generations, my eyes have also watched our family struggle with alcoholism - grandparents, parents, my siblings and now some of you, the youngest among us. Alcoholism robs the family of joy, trust, hope and enthusiasm – even if you are not the alcoholic. Some of the harshest pain that I have ever known was watching my Dad's suffering with addiction for over thirty years and Mom's umbilical dance with this devil we call alcoholism.

Yet somehow, early on, I was inspired to step away from home and try to change the nature of my engagement with Life. Rather than follow the familial paths that I'd known, I've worked hard to foster my own wellbeing, joy and wonder for Life. At the same time, I have always been willing to step back into the fray of family struggles in hopes that I could hold up different paths and choices for you to see.

I pray that, if you would honor me and accept one small gift, then let it be this thought: Let true joy be the only addiction in your life! If joy eludes you, then change the nature of your engagement with this wondrous world. Simply try something different! Hope, inspiration and wonder are far more worthy companions than alcohol. Trust this, and God will guide you to your joy!

All my love, Aunt Darcy

This mother's letter blesses her children by telling them of her loss of faith and her learning from her painful experience:

Dear Children,

When I was in my third year at McGill University, I experienced a crisis of faith. I lost my way.

I was born into a Jewish home, filled with tradition and I received an orthodox education at the Hamilton Hebrew Academy from kindergarten to eighth grade. I was a happy child who felt surrounded by love, acceptance and faith.

However, while studying at McGill, I began to learn about the heartache, tragedy and pain in the world. Through my social work education and practicum, I no longer saw the world through rose colored glasses. In fact, the glasses that I wore caused me to see the world as confusing, disillusioning and concerning. It was difficult for me to navigate with my new "perspective"; however, I now realize that this crisis was the impetus for enormous growth, change and personal development.

The reason I am writing to you about this "crisis" in my life is to share an important lesson that I have learned. It is through our difficult times (not our joyful times) that we transform into the person that we are becoming. Our pain and sorrow are gateways into seeing the world (and ourselves) through a new lens. Never be afraid and always know that you will avoid suffering by seeing the world in this way.

May you be blessed to embrace your moments of crisis and see their aftermath of pain as a gateway into an entirely new (and wonderful) perspective.

I love you forever,
Mom

"The dead take their secrets with them, or so they say. But it isn't really true, is it? The secrets of the dead have a viral quality, and find a way to keep themselves alive in another host. No, I was guilty of nothing more than advancing the inevitable."
— Nicole Krauss

In a 2012 interview the great American author, Toni Morrison, linked the personal and public secrets that we need to clean out of our closets: "I guess every nation does it, but there's an effort to clean up everything. It's like a human life— 'I want to think well of myself!' But that's only possible when you recognize failings and the injuries that you've either caused or that have been caused to you. Then you can think well of yourself because you survived them, confronted them, dealt with them, whatever. But you can't just leap into self-esteem. Every nation teaches its children to love the nation. I understand that. But that doesn't mean you can gloss over facts."

A grandmother shares her very personal thoughts with her grandson in a loving blessing letter:

Dear Drew,

Living so far away from each other, I've never had the chance to spend much time with you, but I want you to know your grit and bravery following your surgery when you were eight years old have been instructive to me. Before each MRI you were asked: "Do you want valium or can you hunker down?" You always chose to hunker down. I'm sure you have had to hunker down many times as you worked your way through graduate school and learned to navigate with sight in only one eye. As I age, I find new challenges and thinking of your courage gives me strength.

Now, as you approach marriage, I want to share with you a regret: your grandpa and I never talked about our dreams or our annoyances with each other. As a result, we grew apart. Unshared dreams and unshared annoyances breed resentment and emotional distance.

May you be blessed with courage and grit to always share your dreams and annoyances with your wife and may your marriage be blessed with the closeness that comes from accepting each other's differences.

With love, Gram

The powerful thinker and writer, Susan Griffin, illuminates further the relationship between private secrets and public tragedy in her 1992 book, *A Chorus of Stones*:

> "What a multitude of decisions, made by others, in other times, must shape our lives now.... A nation refuses to permit Jewish immigrants to pass its borders, knowing, and yet pretending not to know, that this will mean certain death. The decision is made to bomb a civilian population. The decision is made to keep the number of the dead and the manner of their death a secret. But wherever there is a secret there is a rumor.... For deep in the mind we know everything. And wish to have everything be told, to have our images and our words reflect the truth."　— Susan Griffin

Griffin's words, dense and difficult to take in, may be clarified as we read this mother's lionhearted legacy letter to her daughter upon returning from a 2013 trip to Europe:

Dear _____,

Dad and I recently took a trip to Europe and like most journeys, I learned things about myself that I could not have foreseen.

We walked the streets of southern Germany and I found that Germans saw me in a different way than I viewed myself. They saw me as a Jew.

I've struggled with that part of my genetic identity for a long time, and in America I've been able to disappear, be invisible for all these years. When people asked, I told them I was Italian, as that's how I grew up.

My experience in Germany – being looked at in a hostile way – made me realize that I cannot hide who I am. I am a Jewish woman and although I don't completely understand all that entails yet, I am beginning to learn what a rich and beautiful tradition Judaism is.

My grandfather's name was Henry Reingold and when I was in Vienna I saw a sign for a jeweler of that last name. Perhaps my family was from Vienna – there is no way to know.

But the odds are that I lost family members in the Holocaust and that may explain my desire to go to Germany in the first place. Something has always called me to the experience of seeing Europe myself – going to a concentration camp and walking in the places where so many drew their final breath. But even if I were not Jewish, I would feel the need to experience such a place, as I believe we honor the dead by opening our eyes and seeing things as they were.

I have carried my mother's secret and shame for many years now, too afraid to claim my own identity – unsure of exactly where I fit in the world. This latest breakthrough is a powerful one for me and I am only beginning to embrace and understand that part of who I am.

I am ready to drop the shame carried by my grandmother, then my mother, and myself. I am ready to proclaim with pride, Juden! Perhaps letting go of the secret will finally allow me to feel I fit somewhere, belong to a tribe.

You, my daughter, carry my legacy. May you feel the blessings of being part of a rich and ancient tradition.

I love you,
Mom

Suggestions for exploring secrets

Now it's time for you to explore *your* secrets. Here are suggestions to guide your reflections and decisions about whether and with whom to share what you learn. Some reflections belong in your private Legacy File only. Others you'll harvest to use in legacy letters for those you love and want to inform and liberate from harmful secrets.

Make a list of your important secrets, the psychic clutter that you're aware of. Begin by inventorying the secrets housed within your own family. They may be about immigration, marriages, births, divorces, diseases, abuses, alcoholism, job losses, crimes, deaths.

Then expand your list to world events that have impacted your life. These may have been hidden from you and others innocently or purposefully. Consider civil and human rights, industrialization, scientific and technological development, abuses of our environment and the planet, poverty, restricted education, elections, revolutions, wars, recessions and depressions ... you get the idea. Decide which secrets you want to explore more deeply.

Here are some suggestions that may clarify these secrets and their effects on your life.

What was your life like before you received and held this secret? How long have you known about the secret, and when, where, and why did it begin?

In what ways has your life changed because of this secret? (Sometimes what feels like a curse turns out to be a blessing.) How has the secret affected your relationships, the lives of your family or community?

If applicable, note the intertwined relationship between public events and private lives. Reflect and write about how secreted world events have influenced *your* life and *your* values.

Do you think there is a way to resolve the secret today? In the future? What are the potential advantages in confiding your secret to others? What are the potential risks or unintended consequences if you expose the secret to family members or friends? What will become of the secret once you've told it? And what might become of you and your relationships?

Note the nuances between keeping a secret and guarding your privacy. Compare the isolation, hopelessness, and loneliness of secrets with the quiet, restorative, inspirational benefits of privacy. Consider possible motives for holding onto things.

> **"Write to record how you saw and felt before you were silenced."** — **Natalie Goldberg**

Writing about Secrets

Write a legacy letter or several, about the clutter of secrets that has affected you and your relationships, and that you see affecting those you love. Share your insights and vignettes of your life path's twists and turns. Write through your legacy lens, with the goal of improving your life and those who will come after you who can be freed from old secrets.

Editing Tip

After writing your letter(s), ask yourself: has what I've written accurately conveyed how my personal understanding and the larger human story blend and affect individuals and families? Have I communicated my truth and my deep yearning for belonging and integrity, as well as how we are each related to the fate of others?

> "The Patriarch said, 'Think neither good nor evil. At this very moment, what is the original self of the monk Myo?' At these words, Myo was directly illuminated. His whole body was covered with sweat. He wept and bowed, saying, ' Is there anything deeper still than secret words and secret meaning you have just revealed to me?'
>
> "The Patriarch said, 'What I have told you is no secret at all. When you look into your own true self, whatever is deeper is found right there.' "
> — Katsuk Sekida

This Zen story by Katsuk Sekida about secrets and the wisdom to look at our own true selves leads us to chapter 11 where we'll consider the deep wisdom awaiting us as we age.

Chapter 11
About Aging

Because we live in a culture that venerates youth, we've learned to keep the realities of aging in the closet. Do we fear aging? Of course we do, because we fear the unknown, what we don't understand, and we can't control. We seldom reflect on the changes that are happening to us, and even more rarely speak of them; we certainly do not document them. The proof of our fear is made obvious by the billions of hours and dollars we use and spend every year to camouflage our aging from ourselves as much as others. Either Maurice Chevalier or comedian George Burns who lived past one hundred gets credit for this quip "Aging is better than the alternative." We laugh, but more self-consciously than whole-heartedly.

> **"When we have passed a certain age, the soul of the child we were and the souls of the dead from whom we have sprung come to lavish on us their riches and their spells...."**
> **— Marcel Proust**

In our youth-adoring and speed-worshipping culture, older people can't help but believe that worth declines with age. As we have less control over our own lives, we feel fearful and isolated. Our issues are not unique, though we seldom talk with others about them. We're fearful of suffering as we become more physically frail and subject to life-threatening illness. We fear being a burden on those who are younger whom we love, and we fear, perhaps most of all, a meaningless life.

> "Those of whatever age who have been near death tell us that life, when they returned to it, was never the same. I think that that same intensity, that constant awareness of newness and brightness, is also possible in one's sixties and after; it certainly has been in mine. Perhaps only when we know on our pulses (a phrase of Keats's) that our time is limited do we properly treasure it."   — Carolyn Heilbrun

What a great gift it would be if we were the last generation to carry this invisible, secret legacy of fear and ignorance. We can choose to be the generation that approaches this harvest season of our lives with dignity, curiosity, awe, learning, humor, even celebration. We'll explore our harvest season here in chapter 11.

Time

Many concerns about aging involve time. Consider "Time is money" and "Time is precious; don't waste it." What about "Time flies" and "Time Marches On?" Most of us ignore the homely wisdom, "Take time to smell the roses."

> "Old is wherever you haven't gotten to yet."
> — Anna Quindlen

Our perceptions of time are particular and experience-bound, neither universal, nor conscious. As older adults we feel its urgency. Some of us succumb in despair to the inevitability, but we can grasp the opportunity to make sure we use the time we have left to make a difference, to do what matters most to us.

> "In seed time, learn; in harvest, teach; in winter, enjoy!"
> — William Blake

One of my favorite authors, Eva Hoffman, challenges us: "to become more intimate with time, to ask how it shapes our lives, and what may be our happiest dealings with it; and also to discover-insofar as possible-what philosophical fortification may be gained against its invisible laws and inevitable passage."

> **"Time is at once the most valuable and the most perishable of all our possessions."** — **John Randolph**

As we arrive at a certain age, it's natural to pay more attention to our health, to be anxious when we forget names, words or our keys, when we experience reduced physical energy and slowing down. As in all seasons of our lives, we have choices about what to harvest and be enriched by, what to ignore, and everything in between.

A Time to Grow and Learn

In this chapter we'll explore ways to use aging to continue to grow and learn. We'll learn about Lars Tornstam's theory that aging provides a natural opportunity to blossom into heightened spirituality. And we'll investigate our opportunities to give forward what we've harvested during earlier stages in our lives.

Gerotranscendence, Lars Tornstam's theory, suggests that as we age, our natural tendency is for our spiritual relationship to become more and more important. Our priorities shift, and we are more comfortable hanging out in the spiritual realm than earlier in our lives, when friends, family, and career took most of our energy and our time.

> **"Simply put, gerotranscendence is a shift from a materialistic and rational view of the world to a more cosmic and transcendent one, normally accompanied by an increase in life satisfaction."** — **Lars Tornstam**

What's most important here are his last five words ... "an increase in life satisfaction." He suggests that we move to a new developmental stage, experiencing new values and new priorities. We redefine ourselves, our relationships and ask fundamental questions about time, life, and death. We experience increased affinity with past generations and a decreased interest in casual social interaction and material things, and have an intensified need for solitude and reflection.

Younger family members and professionals often misinterpret and misunderstand, believing they see disengagement, depression, even dementia. Tornstam suggests instead that this shift is a natural progression in aging. He suggests this process can be understood as "actively restoring the soul."

In a 2010 *New York Times* interview "Aging's Misunderstood Virtues," Paula Span, author of *When the Time Comes: Families With Aging Parents Share Their Struggles and Solutions*, wrote about Tornstam's 25-year investigation of aging. Here are excerpts from that interview:

".... In an example of the state he calls gerotranscendence, Tornstam described a hypothetical daughter planning a cocktail party. Her elderly mother usually attends the affairs and enjoys herself, so the daughter invites her as usual — but this time, the mother declines. Naturally, the daughter worries. Is her mother ill? Depressed? This is not like her.

"Dr. Tornstam: 'But perhaps there's nothing wrong. Our values and interests don't usually remain static from the time we're 20 years old until the time we're 45, so why do we expect that sort of consistency in later decades?

"'We develop and change; we mature...It's a process that goes on all our lives, and it doesn't ever end. The mistake we make in middle age is thinking that good aging means continuing to be the way we were at 50. Maybe it's not.'

"An increased need for solitude, and for the company of only a few intimates, is one of the traits Dr. Tornstam attributes to this continuing maturation. So that elderly mother isn't deteriorating, necessarily — she's evolving.

> "Growing old exacts a price. But aging is also a privilege. It is not visible to the eye, for it is a new state of our spirit: changed priorities, reordered values, serenity, and hopefully, a pervasive sense of gratitude." — W. Gunther Plaut

"Dr. Tornstam: 'People tell us they are different people at 80.... They have new interests, and they have left some things behind.'

"Merrill Silverstein, a social gerontologist at USC speaking about Tornstam's theory: 'It turns on its head the current ideas about 'successful aging' — avoiding disease, remaining productive, forming social relationships. This advocates the opposite, a retreat into your own consciousness.'

"The American emphasis on activity and productivity — the vow that we're not going to retreat to a rocking chair on the porch — can make it hard to listen to someone arguing that a rocking chair, and the contemplation and rest that accompany it, might provide a fine way to age.

"Dr. Tornstam: 'What I'd like to tell grown-up children is that your mom or dad might develop into someone different than they were in middle age. Don't automatically label what they're saying, doing or thinking as a symptom of something bad.'"

In 2008, Rachel W. Cozort wrote a dissertation that built on Tornstam's theory. She posited that the developmental tasks for older adults include seeing past life events with new eyes, attaining wisdom, and preparing for death. Tornstam's theory may lead to a more balanced understanding of how older adults continue to mature at the end of life.

Importance of humor

Age like most things has no objective truth; it's more about perspective. It helps us face our truths when we have a sense of humor, and remember we're not alone.

I remember complaining to my therapist that as I've aged, people more than ever before, give me compliments that don't feel accurate: "Oh,

you're so compassionate, so wise, so spiritual, such a good grandmother."
None of these statements ring true or feel like who I really am. She sat
back in her chair, reflected for a moment, and spoke with a perfectly
straight face, " I don't mean to burst your bubble, but this is not an exclu-
sive problem." We both howled with laughter. How fortunate I am to be
with someone who takes me seriously and simultaneously encourages me
to laugh at myself.

Laughing at Ourselves

Being with grandchildren and great-grandchildren help us to enjoy the
humor in their viewpoints, especially about us. Here are third grader's response to the question, "What's a Grandparent" from *Listen to the Children*:

**"Grandmothers don't have to do anything except to be there.
They're so old that they shouldn't play hard or run.**

**A grandfather is a man grandmother. He goes for walks with
the boys, and they talk about fishing and stuff like that.**

**It is enough if they drive us to the market where the pretend
horse is, and have lots of dimes ready. Or if they take us for
walks, they slow down past things like pretty leaves and cat-
erpillars. They never say, 'Hurry up.'**

**Usually, grandmothers are fat, but not too fat to tie your
shoes. They wear glasses and funny underwear. They can
take their teeth and gums off.**

**Grandmothers don't have to be smart, only answer ques-
tions like, 'Why isn't God married?' and 'How come dogs
chase cats?'**

**Grandmothers don't talk baby talk like visitors do. When
they read to us, they don't skip or mind if it is the same story
over again.**

**Everybody should try to have a grandmother, especially if
they don't have a television, because they are the only
grown-ups who have time."**

> "My mother always used to say, 'The older you get, the better you get, unless you're a banana.'" — Betty White

> "My grandmother started walking five miles a day when she was sixty. She's ninety-seven now, and we don't know where the hell she is." — Ellen DeGeneres

> "One of the great things about being the age I am now and having a reliably unreliable memory is that I can reread mystery novels." — Anna Quindlen

Writing About Aging

Before we begin our own reflection and writing about aging, here are three legacy writers who've tackled the topic and generously shared their words with us.

The first is a woman filled with gratitude and love of nature following an experience with breast cancer. Her reflection and gratitude fit so well with Lars Tornstam's theory of what matters to us as we age.

The second, a blessing to grandchildren, is a letter that might model for us all the vitality and achievements possible as we age. The third courageously writes to her adult son about her aging and her fears of its potential effect on their relationship. Her words might have come from your pen or mine.

"My sense of joy and appreciation for the world around me changed radically when I was diagnosed with breast cancer when I was 55. Since then my perception of nature and the world seemed to go from black and white to vivid color. I began to understand at a deeper level than before, that someday I would see my last sunrise and my last sunset.

My bedroom has both east and south facing windows and throughout the year I experience the magical journey of the sun. When lying on my back the sun rises up over my feet straight in front of me in the summer and then rises to shine directly into my eyes if I sleep on my side in the winter. Back and forth each year, welcoming me from alternating locations as the seasons come and go.

The trees outside my windows change, too: from the tight green knots of earliest spring, then summer's shimmering leaves in multi-shades of green, then the fall palette of yellows, reds and browns. Finally, the barren branches of winter, sometimes encased in ice, sometimes sprinkled with snow like a powered sugar donut.

I live on what used to be called a pond and is now referred to as 'the wetlands.' .... From my deck I can watch the turtles climb aboard the fallen willow branch to sun and witness the intensity of the two green herons as they wait patiently for the right moment to dive for their dinner.

The squirrels play tag in the trees and the birds call to each other in a language I can't understand but enjoy hearing.

Flowers that I plant in pots --- growing, filling out from buds to blossoms to drooping and then to dying. Just like my body, aging, and I find myself in the drooping stage.

What makes me laugh, however, isn't that I now notice the details, it's that I care so much and find such inner joy from my discovery of this glorious aspect of life that has been there all along. I was just too 'cool' to notice. As a younger woman I was apparently so busy 'doing' that I really did forget to smell the roses.

The wonderment that I experienced as a young child of holding a frog or watching a caterpillar climb up my arm has returned. I am in awe of the world God has created and grateful that I am learning to simply sit and observe.

> "Age has given me what I was looking for my entire life – it gave me me. It provided the time and experience and failures and triumphs and friends who helped me step into the shape that had been waiting for me all my life."
> — Anne Lamott

Dear Grandchildren,

When your parents were born, I was 20, 21, and 22. Today, that seems very young, but at the time, I felt very mature. Your Grandpa Dick and I divorced in 1968 and Pam, Rick and Roger made many moves with me as I did my best to care for them. Our lives changed when I got sober in 1975. I didn't make good decisions for them because I didn't know how, but I loved them fiercely.

They each have their story that you can ask them to tell. My story is this: When I got sober, I had to learn how to live. I didn't know how to have fun without a drink. I couldn't imagine talking to anyone without a drink and I couldn't imagine my life without a man.

But by the gift of sobriety and God, I matured enough to go to college and finally get a Master's degree in social work at age 66. I was the oldest graduate in my class.

What I learned from this is that it's never too late! I wrote out my goals sometime in the 1980s. When I found them about 2010, I realized I'd achieved every one, except a loving relationship with a man. I'm still not too old, but I'm also okay as I am.

May you have the blessings of determining your goals – first of all. Then accomplishing your goals and celebrating every accomplishment!

I love you, Grandma Evy

> "Life is no brief candle to me. It is a sort of splendid torch that I have got hold of for the moment, and I want to make it burn as brightly as possible before handing it on to future generations." — George Bernard Shaw

Dearest John,

Now in my middle 50's, I have been thinking more and more about aging, about getting older. I am afraid of it, probably more afraid of it than of dying. I am afraid that the inevitable changes that come with aging: less attractiveness, ugly teeth, wrinkled skin, slower mind, anxiety, forgetfulness, repeating myself, less competence, physical agility and strength, will make me less loveable and perhaps you, John, will love and respect me less.

Your grandparents did not model aging well. They fought it mightily. As they grew older they pushed their way into situations, demanding even more forcefully to be seen and heard. They did not model reflection, or sitting back relishing children and grandchildren, or savoring nature's wonders or enjoying quiet time. Sadly I believe they died feeling that their value was based only on their daily accomplishments. I hope I can die feeling all right about my own skin. I hope I can die feeling good about an ordinary day of watching the world around me.

Aging is inevitable. The only fair thing is that it doesn't single out just a certain few. I will do my very best to age gracefully...and to accept this chapter of my life. I will try to be a person who does enjoy listening and watching others and can accept a less central role. I believe I can appreciate simply being included. I will try to respect your life and your need for time apart from me for your family and yourself.

I fear that what you admire and love in me now in my 50's will disappear and that you will love me less. I want to believe we will find new ways to connect over the years. I ask you to accept the inevitable changes in me. I ask that you never make fun of me, especially for some of the early changes, like being less interesting to talk to or more repetitive. I hope you won't become irritated with me. I would love to think that if I live into my 80's and 90's, that you will still be happy that I am around, and that you won't be annoyed that you have to have me for dinner or visit me in a depressing nursing home.

The fear of the loss of your love and respect and that of others makes it harder for me to face the inevitable.

With much love, Mom

> **"I don't miss the rush of being a young revolutionary. People who have those feelings at old age need to get a grip. You need to play your role, which is to carefully observe and listen and see if you have anything to offer."**
> **— Tom Hayden, 1960s radical**

In 2009 I was honored to address 900 older adults at a National Older Adults Conference, named 'Legacies of Wisdom: Weaving Old and New' sponsored by the Church of the Brethren.

Who are these 900 souls I now carry in my heart? Men and women: vital, vibrant, committed, some with physical disabilities. None seemed diminished in energy, spirit, humor, joy, or purpose. All were attending to 're-store their souls.' They welcomed me, a stranger in their midst, as one of them, which I'm not by denomination, but am by age and our common belief in the sacred nature of legacy.

Making my way to the auditorium one morning I found myself behind a woman inching her way across the street, bent over her walker with osteoporosis. Approaching her, I slowed. I greeted her. 'How are you this morning?' She looked up. Her sparkling, lively eyes met mine. 'I'm just great,' she responded. There was no doubt she meant it!

The conference moved at a pace perfect for older adults, median age seventy-seven: relaxed, but neither lethargic, nor resigned, nor depressed. It was full engagement at a pace of respect and patience, peace and acceptance of who we were.

I hope I will retain what I learned from them; that I'll continue to appreciate the qualities they radiated. Their vitality nurtured each of them and their community, keeping them not only young at heart, but fully alive.

Robert Butler, respected spokesperson for life review, memories, retrospection, and reminiscence, studied healthy aging with the master, James Birren, at NIH in the 1950s. Earlier psychologists and gerontologists devalued reminiscence and failed to understand the importance of memories. What Butler and Birren learned from their long-term, longitudinal, comprehensive study of vibrant older adults was that they were engaged in a fascinating inward journey, responding to their need to synthesize and integrate their lives.

> **"If we mean to try to understand this self, it is only in our innermost depths, by endeavoring to reconstruct it there, that the quest can be achieved."** — Marcel Proust

Reflections and Legacy Practice

Of course most of us are neither master novelists nor memoirists, but we can nurture our own sense of who we are, deepen our understanding of ourselves and the meaning of our lives by writing legacy letters to our loved ones.

How fulfilling for us as aging people to combat invisibility and be known at this time in our lives. We may even have wisdom to impart to younger generations that we couldn't have known or learned until we reached a certain age. We should not mistake age for wisdom; not all people who are elders are wise ... perhaps the reflections and writing we'll undertake (pun intended) in this chapter will help transform secret feelings, unspoken thoughts, careful reflection about what it is to be an aging human being – and we can be better known to ourselves and to those who follow us.

These letters fulfill our own need to tell our stories and harvest the learning from our experiences. Then we can happily take responsibility to share what we value in life, and bless future generations with our wisdom.

Here are two ways to harvest your own thoughts and feelings. For now write and store them in your Legacy File. Later you can decide how and what to share in legacy letters with younger family members and friends. For now, allow yourself the courage (and the peace of mind when you've finished) to tackle this still taboo subject.

All of the prompts may not interest you; you may fill in 2 in one category and 5 in another. The prompts that are here are not exhaustive; if you think of other meaningful categories, add them. Use the reflection in a way that makes sense to you.

Exploring Values as I age . . .

3 things I most like to do in my life now
3 things that I most enjoyed twenty (then forty) years ago
3 things I fear as I age
3 things that frustrate me about aging
3 most important relationships in my life today
3 life-changing decisions I've made in my life so far
3 things that matter most to me at this time in my life
3 things I've learned (harvested) from an earlier time in my life
3 things I still want (yearn for) in my life today
3 things or people you've forgiven in your life
3 ways I want to give back/forward at this time in my life
3 wishes for my end-of-life care.

If lists are not your style, try this: With a cup of tea or mug of coffee, your favorite pen and paper, and no deadline, take time to reflect and begin a written exploration about one or more of the following topics. Allow yourself to slow down to a leisurely, thoughtful pace. No conclusions are necessary; no full sentences required...this writing is to explore your thoughts, assumptions, and beliefs.

- Who are you at this time in your life?
- What matters most to you now?
- What are some of the qualities you value most in your relationships with others?
- What are important learnings you've harvested from earlier seasons of your life?
- How are you connected to past generations - ancestors?
- What childhood memories do you recall and want to communicate to others?
- What stories of your life do you want to tell and preserve?
- How do beauty and gratitude inform and enrich your life?
- What did 'time' used to mean to you, and what does it mean now?
- What can you give birth to now to help you age and approach the end your life with a sense of completion?
- What are your present thoughts about aging, dying, and death?

Continue to reflect and journal regularly (or randomly) about any or all of these topics (and those that pop up while you're writing about something else). Seek partners with whom you can share your reflections and listen to theirs: other older adults, friends or family members. When you're ready, choose from your saved reflections those things you want to include in legacy letters.

Good to Go: Advance Directives

Before we move to the next chapter, there is one more thing we need to consider. At a certain age (though I think young people should also be prepared) our medical practitioners encourage us to prepare a legal document, commonly called a living will, also known as an advance health directive. We'll not look at that legal document in detail here, though what follows are resources to help you with the steps to complete and legalize that document.

In order to think through the medical issues, choices, and decisions that either we or our legal representative will have to make when the time comes, we need to ask ourselves and answer questions, like: What will happen to me if I'm ill and unable to speak for myself? How can I make sure my wishes regarding my end-of-life care will be carried out?

An advance directive is a signed, dated, and witnessed legal document in which you state your wishes regarding the use of life-prolonging medical treatment. Just to confuse us, these documents are called by various names: advance directives, healthcare directives, advance care directives, durable powers of attorney for healthcare, living wills.

While the laws governing this document vary from state to state, your directive will likely include the following:

- The person you appoint to make healthcare decisions
  on your behalf, should you become unable to communicate
  your preferences

- The kind of medical treatment you want or don't want at the end of life
- Your concerns and preferences related to comfort and pain
- How you want to be cared for by loved ones (your wishes related to touch, massage, prayer, music, and other simple comfort measures)
- Thoughts and values to help guide decision-makers in your medical care

To prepare an advance directive, you will need the appropriate paperwork in your state. Contact any of the following to obtain the necessary materials:

- Your state government, listed online, supplies both health directive forms and instructions.
- "Five Wishes," legal in most states, in 26 languages and Braille. www.agingwithdignity.org , 888-594-7437 or Aging with Dignity, P.O. Box 1661, Tallahassee, FL 32302.
- Online tools to create a values-driven legal document, www.MyCareDirectives.com. *My Voice, My Choice, A Practical Guide to Writing a Meaningful Healthcare Directive*, a print resource by Anne Denny.
- Medline Plus, www.NIM.NIH.GOV/medlineplus/ advancedirectives.html
- The Community Alliance for Compassionate Care at the End of Life is an additional online resource: www.missouriendoflife.org.
- Physicians Orders for Life Sustaining Treatment. POLST forms, legal in 26 states. Visit www.polst.org.

After you've gathered, read, and absorbed the information, you're ready to write a draft of your directive. When you're finished, put it aside for a day or two, then reread and edit it. Be gentle with yourself; this is emotionally strenuous work. Take your time and feel free to stop and come back to the task again. Continue this process until your words accurately express your choices and preferences. Then simply copy your words onto the form.

Conversations with Our Families

Now you're ready to have a conversation with the person(s) you've chosen to be your legal representative should you be unable to advocate for yourself when the time comes. Once you have their agreement to join you in this sacred relationship, you are ready to complete and sign your document and have it witnessed. (Note that the "Five Wishes" packet includes specific directions for legalizing and filing your directive.)

Give copies to family members, your doctor, and other appropriate professionals. Your treatment preferences may shift over time as your circumstances change. Perhaps one day you may need to select a new representative. It's a good idea to revisit your directive every three to five years or when you experience changes in your health situation.

Making changes requires filling out a new directive and having it witnessed. Be sure that each person who received your old directive gets a copy of the new one, dated of course, and destroy the old copies so there is no question about your preferences.

The advance directive, though necessary, is an impersonal legal form void of feeling. Our legacy perspective supports writing a legacy letter to family and loved ones to clarify the important choices you've made and why you've made them.

This legacy letter has a double function: it can be attached to copies of the advance directive that you provide your family and loved ones. Perhaps more important, once you have written the letter, it will be easier for you to initiate conversation with your loved ones to reduce their apprehension and normalize the situation.

After her mother's death, Ellen Goodman, author and Pulitzer Prize-winning syndicated journalist, created "The Conversation Project" to support people having this most important conversation. Visit the website: www.theconversationproject.org

> **"I realized only after her death how much easier it would have all been if I heard her voice in my ear as these decisions had to be made. If only we had talked about it. And so I never want to leave the people I love that uneasy and bewildered about my own wishes. It's time for us to talk."**
> **— Ellen Goodman**

Here is the introduction of such a letter attached to the advance directive from a 63 year old legacy writer:

I want you to know what is important to me, and to leave you my legacy…in this letter in relation to my dying and death. Each of you will have a copy along with my Advance Health Care Directive. The originals of both will be in the basement safe. Somehow I hear you asking the detail questions of where can we find it and is it complete? ….

You may be wondering why I am doing this at my age of 63. Perhaps you know part of the answer: the chest pain and resulting stent placement in January of this year awakened me to the surprises that life hands out when we least expect it – and how these surprises place the possibility of death at our door. I have considered my age in reality (63) and my age in my mind (35) and decided my real age was calling me to address this for the first time. I shall update it yearly, but in case I forget, always refer to the most recent year as listed above.

So here I am, now considered a "heart patient." I never thought I would have that name replace my name when I received medical care, but it seems that it is only that label that is tattooed on my forehead when I see a medical professional. I ask, then, that you continue to see me as a person, as a loving woman, mother, and grandmother. I am living and aging in good health comprised of physical exercise, nutritious food, blood-work and medications poised to keep me healthy, engaged in those activities that give meaning to my life and to others as well, and a sense of trust and quiet serenity graced to me by the God Who calls me Beloved.

That said, my desire is that there would be no changes in my health. Since that is not possible, there are some items I wish to have you be attentive to as changes occur: ….

Editing Tip

If you write the way you speak, your letter will engender trust in your loved ones. No style is better for your writing than your style. That said, here are some samples:

Sample Excerpts

These introductory paragraphs are a gift to you offered by legacy writers who have preceded you in this work. They vary greatly, and may be useful as you think about what and how you want to begin your legacy letter to accompany your advance directive.

1.   Facing one's own mortality is never easy; it involves so much more than writing wills and health care directives. All of my legal documents are in order; so it is the issues of the heart that matter most to me now. As I think about my death, I envision myself being in my 80's or early 90's. I'd like to have a minimum number of health issues and still be vital and alert. But that may not be the case. And, it is in the spirit of 'not knowing' that I address this letter to you now.

2.   With this letter I have enclosed a notarized copy of my Advance Health Care Directive. It is a legal document outlining, for hospital and health care professionals, my simply stated desires for end-of-life care. It isn't personal, it isn't personalized, and it is hardly a good read, but it is necessary.

At this point in my life (age 51), I write these instructions for use in the event I am in an accident or suffer some other sudden injury or illness. I promise to amend this every few years as I grow nearer the likelihood of Alzheimer's disease, dementia, or long-term health issues. On that note, though, please keep in mind that I do not wish to ever be a burden on my family. If you feel I would be unsafe living alone, please find a nice residential assisted living center near one of you and set me up there. I would prefer a center with lots of activities, friendly staff, and a great view, and I hope someone could visit occasionally.

3.   There's no perfect time to write down one's plan for what might be challenging end-of-life circumstances. In fact, dozens of so-called 'priorities' have ambushed my intentions to do so in the past – busy with work, the garden needs tending, gotta cook dinner. You get the gist.

Today, I'm healthy as could be, and if I'm lucky I'll live a good, long life – physically active and always curious to explore new opportunities. But I also think it's important to have a back-up...to prepare for the universe moving sideways on my best-laid plans.

So I'd like to share a few thoughts to bless your future, along with my Massachusetts Advance Health Care Directive, which I've attached.

4.   This is not an easy letter or set of documents to think about. I hope to be vital for many years, but if this is not the case, I feel the need to leave some instructions for you. I will review these instructions as I go along life's path. But for the moment, should a sudden illness or accident befall me, you will have a plan stating my wishes and wants.

And here are two sample paragraphs to close a letter:

1.   I intend for you to read this letter and my health directive now while I am well, so that if you have concerns, or want more details, we can talk about it. Then I can amend or add to this letter.

2.   This was far less difficult to write than I'd imagined. It actually gives me a sense of relief, of peace, to both acknowledge my own mortality, and the blessing it is to live in a time when one can speak about it, and in a time when there is hope for a pain-free conscious death, and the best blessing of all, to have you two children whom I love more than my life, and who love me enough to take care of my end-of-life needs. Thank you.

Many of you are caring for a partner or are caregivers for aging or aged parents. Discussing aging with those more aged than we provides another view of aging. We can be scribes or assist others with their legacy letters giving them an opportunity to express their perspectives about aging.

The Alzheimer's Association reports that one in three seniors dies not from but having either Alzheimer's or some form of dementia. Such a statistic suggesting that our dying will arrive wrapped in memory loss or dementia of some kind awakens us to the urgency to prepare documents sooner rather than later, and to talk with our children, our partners, and our close friends about how we want to be treated in our dying.

One summer some years ago, my rabbi and I co-facilitated a five week legacy experience for couples over sixty-five. When we issued the invitation, we thought it would be successful if eight or ten people showed up. We were surprised to have thirty-six people sign up, all of them interested, most feeling some trepidation. This was new territory for them and for us. On the third evening a man stood to express his gratitude for the opportunity to tell his grown children what mattered to him. He explained that he had recently been diagnosed with early Alzheimer's. His words hung in the air followed by our audible and embarrassed silence. After a moment we continued, all of us feeling more keenly the significance of what we were doing together.

This excerpt from "Carol's Song" reminds us of our privilege and obligation to bless our children before we no longer can. Hear the yearning and need in Carol's daughter's voice:

**"Through vacant, hollow eyes,
I wonder if you see me.
I am here with you, beside you.
Can my love sustain, remind you
You will always be my mother?
And, I'll always be your child."**

— Anne Elizabeth Denny

Our legacy letters can be offered to family and loved ones while we have our mental faculties and can initiate non-threatening conversation. It gives us the opportunity to express personal desires, like the kind of music we'd like to hear, if we'd like to be read to, if we like to be touched or not.

"Although we have only one life cycle to live ... to do this gracefully and carefully is our greatest vocation."— Henri Nouwen

> **"Aging can be understood, affirmed, and experienced as a process of growth by which the mystery of life is slowly revealed to us."** — Henri Nouwen

> **"Aging is not a reason for despair but a basis for hope, not a slow decaying but a gradual maturing, not a fate to be undergone but a chance to be embraced."** — Henri Nouwen

Of course, all of us handle sensitive topics uniquely and idiosyncratically. One conversation may do it for some; others may need to take small bites over a longer duration of time to integrate these new and changing realities. Here's where we legacy writers are doing groundbreaking work. We're talking about aging and end-of-life as if this were normal and natural in the larger scheme of life. What a revolutionary legacy this leaves future generations!

When I first addressed my aging with my grown son, he was reluctant to have the conversation. I persisted, because I needed to tell him about changes I was aware of in me. I could sense his discomfort, though of course I didn't know what the conversation brought up in him.

No child ever wants to have to think about his Mom not being his Mommy, no matter that he is a man approaching his own middle age. His own mortality might have seemed more present and real than he was comfortable with. Difficult though that first conversation was for both of us, the results were positive. Now I can tell him things that, before that conversation, I wouldn't have felt he would understand. We have a new, deeper level of intimacy between us. We're more honest about the reality of where we both are in the life cycle, appreciating that and each other more deeply.

It seems most appropriate to close this chapter about aging by honoring the legacy of a remarkable woman who lived to be 96, Florida Scott-Maxwell. She died in 1979. Her most celebrated and beloved writing, *The Measure of My Days* is a journal that harvests her wisdom about successful aging among the old-old. It was published when she was 85. Here is some of her wisdom, so consonant with Lars Tornstam's theory that we naturally evolve spiritually and experience changed energy and interests as we age.

"As we age we are more alive than seems likely, convenient, or even bearable."

"Another secret we carry is that though drab on the outside... - inside we flame with a wild life that is almost incommunicable."

"Age is truly a time of heroic helplessness.... I still have the vices that I have known and struggled with - well, it seems like since birth. Many of them are modified, but not much.... This is not the effect of age; age only defines one's boundaries. Life has changed me greatly, it has improved me greatly, but it has also left me practically the same.... I know my faults so well that I pay them small heed. They are stronger than I am. They are me."

"Age puzzles me. I thought it was a quiet time. My seventies were interesting, and fairly serene, but my eighties are passionate. I grow more intense as I age. To my own surprise I burst out with hot conviction. Only a few years ago I enjoyed my tranquility; now I am so disturbed by the outer world and by human quality in general that I want to put things right, as though I still owed a debt to life...."

"Life does not accommodate you; it shatters you. Every seed destroys its container, or else there would be no fruition."

"You need only claim the event of your life to make yourself yours. When you truly possess all you have been and done, which may take some time, you are fierce with reality."

"It is not easy to be sure that being yourself is worth the trouble, but we do know it is our sacred duty."

— Florida Scott-Maxwell

Chapter 12
The Measure of Our Days

When asked if they're interested in writing a legacy document, many people say, "Oh, I don't have time now, maybe after I retire," or "This is perfect for my grandmother or grandfather." Because we don't know how much precious life we have ... we can only be sure we have "today."

With the personal surprise of a disturbing diagnosis or the public surprise of 9-11 or the Boston Marathon bombing, the crisis wakens us to the importance of legacy. No matter our age the time to write is "now." People who are motivated to write legacy are perhaps attracted to the idea of harvesting our life stories and values as an aspect of a life well-lived. Perhaps they feel the gravity about influencing future generations. Or perhaps they want to say their farewells while they still can. It is to this last need, saying farewell, to which we turn in "The Measure of our Days."

As legacy writers, you've already experienced the relief and peace of mind that comes as you sign your advance directive, attach your accompanying legacy letter of explication to it, and present it to your loved ones. Writing about our mortality opens us to the preciousness of our lives and the love we feel for others. Like writing a blessing, writing about mortality adds to wholeness, completeness, and serenity in your life going forward.

Elisabeth Kübler-Ross' 1969 groundbreaking book, *On Death and Dying*, left us a monumental legacy by bringing death and dying out of the closet, and proclaiming death as a normal part of life.

Through my legacy writing, I have come to experience my life as precious. When writing the chapter on dying in my first legacy book, Women's Lives, Women's Legacies, *I realized that the way I approach my own dying process and how I ask to be treated at death is just as important as any other thing I can express to my children and grandchildren. That may sound logical and not at all profound, but it changed everything for me.*

I remember vividly the moment of my son's birth (something I've never spoken of with anyone). I'd been awake throughout labor, declining the nurses' seductive offers to take something to 'take the edge off.' I'd been practicing natural childbirth exercises for months, and wanted to experience every moment.

I recall the sense but not the sensation of the miracle of birth and I remember pushing at the very end. The intensity was beyond words – if my baby didn't come out NOW, I would literally split in half; I would die. Then in a flash he delivered; I heard his first sound. An unforgettably sacred moment! The nurses wrapped my shaking body and trembling legs in a heated blanket that felt wonderfully warm in that cool delivery room, womblike and safe, like I was the one who'd just been born.

Elizabeth Alexander, poet of the 2009 presidential inauguration, is a turner of beautiful phrases. She speaks of, "the proximity of birth and death."

Although birth and death are different phases of life, each is unique and inexpressibly sacred. The experience of birthing my son makes me want to experience my own dying and death as consciously as I can. I am willing to experience some level of physical pain for the opportunity to be awake to experience a once in a lifetime journey. (I hope when my time comes, we've invented drugs that can reduce pain without diminishing consciousness.) I don't look forward to dying, at least not for a couple more decades, nor am I free of fear about it, but my attitude is evolving, and my tongue's been loosened.

I hope that a portion of my legacy to my children and grandchildren will be that they will witness this miracle. I also hope that my family will take time to mourn my passing enriched with the understanding that they participated in something mysterious and sacred. Lastly I hope their period of remembering will flow naturally to experiencing gratitude for our relationship, imperfect certainly, but overflowing with love.

It has become more acceptable to talk directly about dying, and the more we do, the more peaceful we become, and the more able to initiate the conversation. It's like being freed from any secret we've held inside. It offers us the opportunity to explore new ways to think and to hear from others. (Ellen Goodman's "The Conversation Project" referenced in Chapter 11 provides support for conversation about death and dying.)

> **"To be alive is to have a story to tell. To be alive is precisely to be the hero, the center of a life story."**
> **— Daniel Mendelsohn**

Once we've thought about, planned, and written about our desires, we can use that legacy letter to introduce conversation with our families, when they can begin to confront the reality of our deaths without the stress of its nearness. Conversation is still difficult in our culture, but it is happening more and more. Adapted from Swiss sociologist, Bernard Crettaz's "café mortels," Jon Underwood, a Brit, organized the first Death Café. He envisioned it as "a space where people can discuss death, find meaning, reflect on what's important, and ask profound questions." So far there have been meetings in more than 40 cities and towns across the US.

Kim Rice, author of *The Goodbye Party Workbook*, believes a plan is a generous legacy to family and friends, who can spend their time remembering and grieving, instead of being saddled with details that distract them. These plans can include funeral or memorial service wishes, favorite readings and music, burial and cemetery preferences, contact lists, and more. Rice suggests: Make a plan, update and revise it annually, and designate someone outside your inner circle to carry it out.

We were three generations that beautiful spring afternoon, the sun filtering through the lush trees, everything green from the previous night's shower. My son and daughter-in-law and their four children accompanied me to the cemetery where I was going to choose my gravesite. We were the only live people there. It was so peaceful. I thought: "There is no better place for me to rest for eternity."

I'm best known by all seven of my grandchildren as the "Book Granny." I love to read to them, and give books to celebrate not only every birthday but also every holiday I can wring out of the calendar.

My oldest grandson Mitch, who was ten years old at that time, suggested that if I put a bench by my grave, he would come and sit there and read to me as I have read to him. His younger sister, Lily – our eight-year-old artist - overheard our conversation and expressed concern about how she could be with me. I pointed to a square stone planter at a nearby grave, and told her I'd prefer a planter to a tall monument, and that she could be in charge of planting and maintaining its flowers. Lily was delighted.

Some people would consider such an outing and its conversation macabre, but for me it was an opportunity to mix reality with love. It happened spontaneously. I did no lecturing. We did not explicitly discuss death. It seemed perfectly natural and non-threatening.

I don't feel ready to die yet, but I remember that afternoon with pleasure. I enjoy envisioning Mitch sitting on the bench reading to me while Lily refreshes the planter with the vibrant blossoms of spring. The legacy that I hope was implanted that day is this: Dying can be talked about and mortality can be confronted as a normal part of life; it's a reality for all of us that is not limited to the grief of mourning.

It takes a long time to transform a culture, but Kübler-Ross' perspective was a beginning. Her book gave us permission to confront the reality of our mortality, to think about it with more curiosity and less fear, and to have real and intimate conversations with those we love about this mystery.

> **"I still grieve for the words unsaid. Something terrible happens when we stop the mouths of the dying before they are dead. A silence grows up between us, profounder than the grave."**
> **— Faye Moskowitz**

I'm not suggesting that the discussion of death is easy, but it is important. Just as with any other aspect of our lives, how we handle our dying and death leaves a legacy for the future. If we maintain the silence of the cultural taboo, then that's the legacy we'll perpetuate. If we think, write, and talk about dying and death realistically – putting our affairs in order, making sure all our i's are dotted and our t's crossed, our wills signed and our philanthropic gifts made – we'll experience the spiritual gift of peace of mind. By communicating our thoughts and feelings to family and loved ones, we can continue to experience acceptance of who we are and what our journey has been.

Thanks to Kübler-Ross, and those who came after her, consideration of our own deaths and conversation about it with our loved ones is becoming more normal and natural.

Acute and Urgent

Steve Jobs of Apple fame understood the necessity of talking about his cancer after he was diagnosed in 2011:

> "My doctor advised me to go home and get my affairs in order, which is doctor's code for prepare to die. It means to try to tell your kids everything you thought you'd have the next 10 years to tell them in just a few months. It means to make sure everything is buttoned up so that it will be as easy as possible for your family. It means to say your good-byes."   — Steve Jobs

Just before cancer surgery, Bill wrote a letter to his beloved wife, which he thought might be his last words. Bill, who survived and is well at this writing, shared his letter with you and me:

My Dearest,

If you are reading this, it means I'm on the operating table. Since at moments like these, you want to be close to the ones you love, I thought I'd communicate to you via this letter while you wait with me for the outcome. While I know I will be just fine after the surgery, nevertheless this feels like another milestone in our relationship. This feels like we're about to begin writing the 'last chapter' of our lives together, you know...the one that begins with the words "...in sickness and in health..." and ends with the words "...'til death do us part...."

Only God knows how long this Chapter will last. I'm hopeful I'll get up from this table and live another 20-25 years. I know there is a 99.9% chance that this is exactly the outcome we'll experience together. However, if by chance I don't get up from this table today, or my life is prematurely ended because of cancer, I want you to know that I will have left this world a very happy and fulfilled man, and I would want this letter to be the last thing I write.

Do you remember what you wrote in our first chapter together 45 years ago? You wrote in my high school yearbook that "I never want to say goodbye" and "I'll never forget all the wonderful times we've shared together and I hope we will have many more." God heard your (our) prayers at the time and gave us a life together that many couples can only dream of having....

I'm so proud of our family and I know in my heart that our family is proof that our Love while so young those many years ago...was true and right, and meant to be.

I'm sorry for those times in my life when my actions have not lived up to my words, for those times in my life when I took our love for granted. I can only promise you that I plan to emerge from this surgery a 'better' man, husband, and father for as long as God intends for me to be around.

Thank you for sticking with me. All my Love,
Bill

"Death is not the greatest loss in life. The greatest loss is what dies inside us while we live." — Norman Cousins

I visited a friend recently, a man not as fortunate as Bill, who knows he has only weeks, perhaps a couple of months left. His body is being ravaged by cancer. He asked the question most ask when I suggest writing legacy letters to loved ones, "What should I write?" I presented my response to Lenny the day after he asked his question. Though it was personal to him, it is also pertinent beyond him, and so I share my letter here:

Lenny, first write a letter to your unborn grandson (and perhaps to his also unborn siblings and cousins) who you're fighting to stay alive to be able to hold in your arms.

In the letter tell him everything you won't be here to tell him as he grows up (grandfatherly wisdom). Tell him how much you love him, how much you wish you could be here to watch him grow to manhood, to see him graduate from college, to share the joy of him finding purposeful work, and experiencing a loving and meaningful relationship with another. (Never mind that to understand your letter, he'll have to reread it many times as he grows.)

Tell him who you are and tell him about who and what you've loved and appreciated in your life.

Tell him your favorite stories about his Mom and his aunts, but most of all tell him stories about *your* life, the things that have been most important to you, the values you hold to this day, the events that made you the complex man you became. Tell him about your travels, your appreciation of beauty and adventure (your last train ride across the country to Seattle and a favorite train ride...from Jerusalem to Tel Aviv).

Tell him about your love for ... Israel, the Jewish and Italian parts of you, your relish for cooking and your zest for eating (how ironic that when the cancer obstructs your swallowing, your end will be near). Tell him what you read and your love of learning, in particular about history and politics; your pleasure in stimulating conversation in which you are more often than not the devil's advocate to deepen the discussions you delight in. Tell him about your humor and your desire to make people laugh . . . and so much more, so he'll know his grandfather.

And finally tell him what you hope and dream for him and for the world he'll live his life in. Bless him with your very personal words and love.

After all of that, if your energy permits, write a letter to each (or all three together) of your daughters. And finally, write letters to anyone with whom you've unfinished business...let yourself forgive them. Putting that on paper releases you whether you choose to enclose those letters in envelopes to be given to them now or after you're gone or not. Presenting a letter is a different choice than writing for your own peace of mind.

Please know that every word you write will be treasured by your loved ones, and that the very reality of you writing to and for them is a blessing they will treasure. Your words will nourish them, encourage them, inspire them, and will live as a blessing long beyond your years.

Once we ourselves have confronted our dying, we can talk about both aging and dying with younger family members, who, like us, have carried the invisible legacies of taboo: silence, fear, avoidance. If part of your purpose for writing your legacy is "to make a difference," freedom to talk about dying is one important difference you can make for those who come after you.

> **"Without a legacy, every generation starts over."**
> — Edna C. Groves

My Reflections (process notes)

In chapters 4, 5 and 10 I suggested writing reflections or process notes about your legacy writing. Here are my reflections after visiting Lenny and writing him the letter responding to his question, "What should I write?"

Lenny was touched that I'd returned with this letter. He began to read it as I was taking off my jacket, and told me that he was crying. I assured him that was normal. I sat down next to him on the bed, a good idea, because he felt safer with his feelings not having to look directly at me as he absorbed the ideas in the letter.

He got very excited about the idea of telling the next, unborn generation the stories he loved about his mother and aunts. Two stories popped into his mind spontaneously, and after he shared them with me, he was ready to get started.

I'd functioned as a quiet cheerleader, an interested and safe observer, who would occasionally respond, but mostly enjoyed his stories and we laughed together. (I love this wise observation: God gave us two ears but only one mouth.) I feel grateful to have offered Len both a viable, simple path to peace of mind, and something significant to do in the time he has left, that will be treasured gifts for his grandchild and three daughters.

There was more I might have written in that letter, but I wanted it to be simple enough that Len wouldn't be overwhelmed. I could have provided him with a whole box of envelopes for letters to say what he won't be here to express: write to those you love to mark the celebrations of their special life events: confirmations, bar and bat mitzvahs, college graduations, engagements, marriages, birth of their children, their 50th birthdays…I could go on, but enough.

When presented with the concept of legacy writing, many of us want to put it off; we think it's not for us, only for our elderly parents. We want to be the ones receiving the legacy letters. My friend, just 63, was, until five months ago, an active, energetic, healthy man. Now he's just days or weeks from moving from assisted living into hospice. Need I even say the obvious? None of us know when it is our time, so I urge all of us, no matter our age, circumstance, or season of life, to write now.

Helping others write legacy letters

We're capable of supporting our friends in the acute circumstances when they need to write a legacy letter to their loved ones. With Len, I made just two visits, neither for more than an hour: the first to introduce the idea; the second, to return with some paper, envelopes, a pen, and the letter (page 197) answering the universal question, "What should I write?" You can do that for those you care about too.

> **"The only religious way to think of death is as part and parcel of life."**
> — **Thomas Mann**

Suicide

We've come a long way as a culture talking openly about cancer; not too long ago we clandestinely whispered "the C word." We've not spoken about "suicide" as openly. When someone dies from suicide, the family not only suffers the grief of loss, but also endures the endless shame associated with suicide in our culture.

The excerpt below is a eulogy given by a friend of mine for his younger brother who died from suicide. My friend spoke courageously and directly to all of us who had gathered, both family and friends, in a way that respected his brother's choice. Later I learned that he was unaware that his words were a legacy, a legacy that liberated us to think about suicide in a new way, and freed his brother's children from carrying a burden of shame.

Suicide!

There, I've said it. . . . We often react to suicide as a selfish, irrational act. Those of you who knew my brother know he was neither selfish nor irrational. So, what happened?

_____ struggled with depression to one degree or another since he was a child. Recently he also found himself less and less able to do the things he liked due to physical pain. Even more recently he realized that he was losing more and more of his memory.

My brother, along with the rest of our family watched our father go through a slow decline into nothingness. It was very difficult to watch.

_____ decided to take his destiny into his own hands on his own terms. He put his affairs in order in a three ring binder that he left on the dining room table. He wrote letters to those close to him: his children, his siblings and special friends.

His actions were not the actions of a selfish, irrational individual. On the contrary, his planning, his preparation and his action were those of a selfless individual who wanted to save his family from long-term pain. His action was fully rational. The medical examiner told me she had never seen anything like it; he truly loved his family. She gleaned this from the five pages of instructions she found and passed on to me. These instructions, in part, indicated how each member of the family should be told of his passing. As she looked around his home, she saw everything in order including happy family photos. _____ was rational right to the end.

My son _____ sees death and family reactions to it on a regular basis in his professional capacity. He told me last night that those families that celebrate the life of the one who passed regain a sense of normality much more quickly than those who decry the loved one who is gone.

Let us all celebrate the _____ we knew and as he told his children, "Move on with your wonderful lives."

May his memory be for blessing.

> **"The story of Orpheus is not just about the desire of the living to resuscitate the dead but about the ways in which the dead drag us along into their shadowy realm because we cannot let them go."** — **Meaghan O'Rourke**

The Significance of Rituals

We've all attended memorial services that opened our hearts and our tear ducts. That may be as much about the service itself as the loved person we've lost. Whether rooted in tradition or personal, rituals comfort and support mourners while honoring the sacred life of the deceased.

> **"All the flowers of all the tomorrows are in the seeds of today."** — **Indian Proverb**

Ritual is a significant aspect of all our lives: favorite prayers and music, flowers and foods, evoke memory and deep connection with each other and perhaps gratitude and awe for death and life itself.

I still remember with tears when we honored a friend of mine from junior high who died from pancreatic cancer. She had planned her funeral and chosen women friends as pallbearers. As they carried her casket from the sanctuary, we heard Frank Sinatra's recording, "I Did It My Way." We wept that day because we already missed Melanie's style, her love of life, her strength of will, and her iconoclastic humor.

It's normal to want to be remembered; it's one of those universal needs we all carry in our hearts but don't think much about. Some believe that we ensure our mortality by living on in people's memories. Barbara, a legacy writer recovering from breast cancer surgery, expressed it this way, "I intend to survive this disease. Nevertheless, having permission to write about the end of my life has given me a sense of peace." She used her writing reflections to confront her fears about dying, to clarify the values of her life, and to express to her family how she wanted to be remembered after her death. You may want to reflect using the same simple exercise Barbara used to clarify your thoughts and feelings about what you've valued most about life on earth, and how you wish to be remembered.

Reflection on Rituals

Before you write *your* letter to family and loved ones, consider the rituals that have impacted you throughout your life and in the memorials you've attended. Take as much time as you need to determine the rituals you prefer. Choose rituals that reflect who you are and have been. Choose rituals that resonate with you and have touched your soul. Here are some things to consider:

- Do you and your family participate in a religious tradition? If so, does it include particular funeral music or readings? Are there other traditional rituals – bells, incense, prayers, songs, drumming, blessings, candles, flowers?
- Is it customary in your family to hold a wake or viewing? If so, where? Where does the memorial ceremony take place?
- Are special items placed in the casket? How is the body dressed? Does your family prefer burial or cremation? Are there traditional burial rites or the scattering of the ashes?

- Are mourners invited to share a meal to honor the deceased? Are special foods served?
- Does your family observe particular mourning rituals: lighting candles, decorating the grave with flowers, stopping clocks, covering mirrors, cutting off hair, wearing specific colors or symbols, marking a visit to the grave by placing a stone? How do these rituals help you remember the deceased? How does your family mark the anniversary of a death?

Reflection

Find a comfortable place to have quiet and to write without being interrupted. If comfort food helps, bring a glass of milk and your favorite cookies or whatever food or beverage is soothing and quieting. At the top of your paper write "What I'll Miss When I Die" or "What I've Loved About My life." Then begin writing what comes to you as you write those words. Begin each sentence, "I'll miss..." or "I loved...." Write for as long as you think of new things to write.

Set your reflection aside and return to it another day. Reading your list will likely prompt additions to your sentences. As the pattern of your unique values begins to appear, you may also experience gratitude for the abundant blessings in your life, and re-value much that you've taken for granted, or not even noticed. Some of the simplest things you may find most sacred.

When you're finished, consider including this writing as part of your legacy – just as it is, in your own handwriting and from your heart. While most reflections don't appear in your letters without editing and revision, (see the Afterword), this writing may be a gift, spontaneous and uncensored, allowing your loved ones to appreciate your passion for life. Another suggestion is to use this writing as a foundation for a legacy letter that accompanies your advance directive (see chapter 11).

Now that we've reflected about rituals and other things that have mattered in our lives, it's just about time to write. But first two tips: one about changes over time, and the other a reminder that reading others' writings can be helpful. Then enjoy the generosity of legacy writers who have shared their writing with you here.

Tips

You may want to make changes in your letter over time. It's a good idea to look annually at your end of life preferences. You may hear a new piece of music or a poem that suits you better than your original choices. Remember to pass on updates to family and friends when you make them. Such adaptations can be a focal point for a renewed and deepened conversation with your intimates.

If you leave specific instructions, consider that family members may be uncomfortable carrying out your every wish. Use a part of your legacy letter to give them permission to do what feels right to them. After all, our goal is not to "control from the grave" but to free family members from having to decide difficult questions in the first few days when shock and disbelief may color their thinking.

On pages 21 and 100 I mentioned that copying was a way that apprentices learned in the Renaissance. These excerpts are from letters written by generous legacy writers of today's Renaissance. Many of them benefitted from writing in a legacy circle, where they heard others' letters read aloud; these letters now inspire us all.

The first letter, written by a courageous woman, is about things difficult for her to even contemplate. She ably sprinkled personal and internal family humor throughout, to support herself as she wrote, and to enable her family to receive her preferences. Each uniquely personal excerpt expresses care-full thought. As readers we can sense each writer's integrity and deep love for those who will fulfill her wishes.

Dearest Sandy, Jessica, Meghan, and Sanford,

Naturally I am wondering how on earth you will all muddle along without my being there to micro-manage and stick in my oar; who will tell you you're cold or tired and shouldn't you be turning out your light? But you are all loving wonderful extremely competent people and I have full faith and tremendous pride in all of you. You all know how very much I love you. . . .

I do <u>not</u> wish to be kept alive if my brain is permanently damaged or if I am in a coma from which in the estimation of my doctors I am not going to recover. However, I would like to have life support in the case of injuries or illness from which there is a reasonable possibility of recovery.

I know that you will all ensure that I am comfortable if I am in hospital – that I am clean and warm and adequately fed and cared for.

When I die, see if there is anything useful that can be salvaged from my body to be used to ease others' lives.* There is no point in wasting perfectly good corneas, heart, lungs, kidneys, liver, etc. if someone can use them. However, I do not want my body to be donated to medical research or to a medical school. I have always hated the smell of formaldehyde.

[*I mention this because it is a difficult decision to make when someone you love has just died.]

I would prefer to be cremated and my ashes spread . . . .

If it is possible, I would like my memorial service to be held at . . . . I want lots of music, rousing old familiar hymns that everyone can sing. Not ones where the congregation is hunting and pecking for the melody. Here are some suggestions: . . . . NO Onward Christian Soldiers!

. . . .Bring kleenex. Without me there to pass it out, you all may be sniffling. Please don't have any of those ghastly funerary flower arrangements in the church unless they're sent by friends, in which case, of course you must display them. You all know that tulips and peonies and lilacs and spring flowers are my favorites. If it is high summer, have daisies or sunflowers.

At the party after at the house, make sure there are lots of delicious.
. . . . If you display pictures of me, please none where I look like the Witch
of Endor. . . . . I don't want my grandchildren thinking, "What a hedgehog
Grandma was."

D/Mom

"The question is not whether you will die, but how you will live." — **Joan Borysenko**

Dear Chuck, Paige and Charles,

.... I've never before attempted to put in writing what I want done when
I die. Several years ago Dad and I wrote Advance Health Care Directives and
I know these need updating to keep them legal. I may have ignored issuing
specific instructions with the hope that somehow I would be overlooked
when God checks his schedule of who should die each day. (You know we
Presbyterians are supposed to believe in pre-ordained futures!)

The health directive will indicate that, in Dad's absence, Charles will take
the lead – in consultation with Paige – regarding life support systems. I don't
want to live as a vegetable, but do give me a chance at a miraculous recovery.

Having always been claustrophobic, I can't tolerate the thought of
burial; therefore, please have my body cremated. I have thought I would
like to have my ashes scattered at Seal Point in the park south of Carmel.
Being a part of such a spiritual spot might make it easier for you to visit
than a cemetery. I would like invited friends and family to gather with a
few inspiring words and with the song "Morning Has Broken." Otherwise,
anything that makes you feel better is fine. (I intend to keep considering
these requests and revising them as needed.)

Never think that my death could have been postponed by anything you
might have done. I have lived a wonderful life and loved you all tremen-
dously. I've already lived 10 years more than my mother, so it's all a gift.

Love L/Mom

> **"It's not the years in your life that count. It's the life in your years."** — Abraham Lincoln

---

Dear John,

It feels strange at 56 when I still feel young and quite healthy to tackle writing about my funeral, to put down on paper my wishes around the events connected with my death. It is hard merely to ponder the topic, overwhelming to imagine being dead but especially unsettling to think about the conditions of my dying. Will it be quick? Will it be a sudden unexpected accident? Will I experience a long illness? Will my mind give out as well as my body? I guess if I don't express my preferences, no one will ever know how I would have wanted my funeral. . . .

[Included next her wishes regarding the eulogy, readings and psalms ; music, hymns; flowers; the service; picture boards and the obituary]

. . . .Here are a few more thoughts. I wish to be cremated. . . . I wish to have my ashes scattered in. . . . Feel free John to scatter some of my ashes at any special places you would like. I would love to think that some of my ashes might end up mixed up with the dirt at Wrigley Field. . . .

In finishing, I feel good to have put this on paper. Remember I happily relinquish all choices to you. I can live with whatever you work out...How about that for a pun?

The most important thing to me is that you do my eulogy. Let the people know who I am. I wish to be known and seen. May you remember me with love.

A REQUEST: Make a real effort to inform friends and family about my death and the details of any service that will be held.... I want people to know that my life here has ended.

There is another sadness that I feel as I write this. I am sad again about Christopher. I am sad that you must do this funeral without the help and presence of your brother. But we all know that he is forever inside each of us.

With much love, Mom

> **"Those who love deeply never grow old; they may die of old age, but they die young."** — Benjamin Franklin

---

Dear Carlin and Emily,

. . . .

When I started to work with people who were dying, I know that there were periodic murmurs between you about how that was all that I thought about. But what I want you to know is that one of the primary reasons I love this work is that I have learned and have full permission to talk about what is essential with people who know that they don't have time. When people get a life threatening illness, they are forced to culti-vate and strengthen other parts of themselves if they choose to do the work of preparing to die and close their life with healing. While I know when I was your age I couldn't believe this, no matter what you do or what you eat, your body will disease, decay and die. There is no way to ward this off. . . .

What I have learned, which has in large measure helped me to age with some ease, is that I can't take my body with me. The time I have spent on my body over the years would have been better spent learning how to love more fully. That I hadn't done so, might be one of the biggest regrets of my life. . . .

I know that wisdom is hard to pass on. But what I would most wish for you, Carlin and Emily, is that you work with the illusion that you have for-ever and be mindful of how you spend each day. May you find the joy of risking living with an open heart, of trying not to let the needs of your ego dictate your life, to cultivate a presence with whatever is real and true for you, pushing nothing away and not grasping at things, and find the ease of living that comes with being willing to let your heart break open. . . .

With love, Mom

For my dearest Sons,

   . . . .Being your Mother and sharing your lives has surely been the highlight of my life. . . .Know that I rest in peace leaving you as my legacy and my investment in eternity.

> **"A man is not old until regrets take the place of dreams. "**
> **— John Barrymore**

To my loved Ones,

   Do understand as I go that I have looked on my end with the greatest curiosity and desire to get on with it. I have been in no rush getting here, but great urgency lies now in wanting to know "What's it all about?" If there is nothing I am none the worse for wear. I won't know anything. If there is, as I logically assume, life in its nature is so purposeful, then I will be learning the purpose of why I lived. Wish me well in this. Do not grieve my death, grieve my absence.

   . . . .After I have kicked, bury me, burn me or in whatever other way, dispose of me. I see my body, handsome and manly as it was, but a temporal husk for housing that real part of me occupying it during my lifetime. Don't clutter the world or the environment with it. Have whatever vigil and service that is satisfactory to you to wish me farewell and assuage any sense of loss you might have.

> **"Do not grow old, no matter how long you live. Never cease to stand like curious children before the Great Mystery into which we were born. "**
> **— Albert Einstein**

Patti's poem, "Post Humus," epitomizes her realistic attitude about dying and an ability to reflect about her death with humor. At the same time she tells her loved ones in vivid phrases who she is and how she wants to be remembered: as a passionate lover of life.

Post Humus

Scatter my ashes in my garden
  so I can be near my loves.
Say a few honest words,
  sing a gentle song,
  join hands in a circle of flesh.
Please tell some stories
  about me making you laugh.
I love to make you laugh.

When I've had time to settle
  and green gathers into buds,
  remember I love blossoms
  bursting in spring.
As the season ripens
  remember my persistent passion.

And if you come in my garden
  on an August afternoon,
  pluck a bright red globe,
  let juice run down your chin
  and the seeds stick to your cheek.

When I'm dead I want folks to smile
  and say, "That Patti, she sure is
  some tomato!"

— Patti L. Tana

To my children ... Rosanne, Shannon, Matthew, January and Kathryn,

. . . .While I am now at 62, in vigorous good health and come from a genetic pool of wise elders nudging 90 – God may have Her own thoughts about my demise. So whenever the wick in my lamp grows dim, it is my heartfelt wish to stay in my own home to die, as Grandma did. It is my wish to be surrounded by my beloved books stacked on my bedside table, and my family photographs, sharing space on that same table. It is my wish that the windows be open wide, that I may see the blue sky, always changing, always perfect and that I may hear the birdsong by day – and the crickets play their whiskey guitars at night. If you can bring me to hear the loons a last time, I will be grateful – even though I may not be able to tell you so. Please know that for all your tender care I am grateful. I would also love you to bring me flowers. Wild daisies to remind me of the Island in summer, lilies for their exotic fragrance, and roses for the romance I've had with life.

I want you to remember in my days of leaving, that I have always believed Heaven is only a thought away. Like stepping out of old slippers, from one room into the next one evening. . . . and turning on the lights. I want you to know that I leave our beautiful blue planet Earth, and my cherished life here – departing as a good house guest might, saying, "Thank you so much for having me."

It is my wish that my ashes be scattered, some few, on the prairie road by our farmhouse where I played as a young girl. And some greater, on my beloved Kipling Island, about which you have always heard me say, "This is where I park my soul." It is my wish that they be scattered on the night of a full moon down by the lake where we have our summer bonfires. And that banjos be played with abandon. . . .

It is my wish that my grand-daughters – "The Little Ya-Ya's" of Kipling Island will continue our tradition of going to the WISHING CHAIR, on the last day of summer – to make each, one wish until they meet again. It is my hope that they will remember the promises we made ... to be loyal to each other, to never tell lies about each other, and to pray every night for 'Peace on Earth.'

My last wish, and I smile as I write this ... is that my grandchildren search for, and find ... an amazing big boulder rock that reminds them of Mormor. And that this VERY large rock be placed (you may need a crane!) under a white pine tree, near the trampoline where I listened to you all jump for joy, for so many summers. Place it partly in the sun, and partly in the shade --- so the children can sit on it by day with their popsicles. And tell their secrets on it by night.

And my very last wish is that you will find a stone mason who will carve into this precious rock … the words I found carved into a poet's tomb in Rome so very long ago…"QVI SOLAMENTE FELICE" "It is here, that I am truly at peace…"

Your grateful mother

"When it's over, I want to say: all my life I was a bride married to amazement." — **Mary Oliver**

I can't complete this chapter without telling the story of my first powerful experiences about knowing I would die. I've told this story before; it appeared in *Women's Lives, Women's Legacies*, and has been published in newspapers and magazines. Writing it today, twelve years later, as Sophie prepares to leave us all for college, I'm again surprised by its power to bring me to tears.

"Death steals everything except our stories." — **Jim Harrison**

Several years ago I presented my then five-year-old granddaughter, Sophie, a blank book, a granddaughter-grandmother journal. This journal, I explained, was just for us. She wouldn't have to share it with any of the other grandchildren. Each time we were together we'd write or draw in our special journal, then we'd put it away in a secret place in my writing room.

Because Sophie wasn't writing yet, I would be the scribe and she would decide what we would write about. When she was a little older, we would share responsibility for the writing.

Sophie's eyes sparkled as she looked at all the blank pages. She picked out a pink marker, printed her name on the first page, beautifying it with a heart or two. Witnessing the birth of a natural journal writer, I imagined the wonderful events, thoughts, and feelings that would fill this record of our relationship.

Sophie looked up at me with her innocent, dark eyes, and happily exclaimed, "Oh, I get it, Granny! Then when you're dead I'll know everything that we did together."

She got it! My eyes filled with tears, my heart with the bittersweet reality of love and death – the truth she so easily understood and accepted. One day she would have our special journal, and I wouldn't be here to enjoy her anymore.

Here is country singer Tim McGraw's profound song about a father dying and his son's response and reflections about his own mortality. If you can, listen to him sing it; it will touch your heart.

He said I was in my early forties
with a lot of life before me
when a moment came that stopped me on a dime
and I spent most of the next days
looking at the x-rays
Talking bout the options
and talking bout sweet time
I asked him when it sank in
that this might really be the real end
how's it hit you when you get that kinda news
man what'd you do

and he said
I went sky diving
I went Rocky Mountain climbing
I went 2.7 seconds on a bull named FuManchu
and I loved deeper and I spoke sweeter
and I gave forgiveness I'd been denying
and he said someday I hope you get the chance
to live like you were dying.

Like tomorrow was a gift and you got eternity to think about
what'd you do with it what did you do with it
what did I do with it
what would I do with it

Sky diving
I went Rocky Mountain climbing
I went 2.7 seconds on a bull named FuManchu
and then I loved deeper and I spoke sweeter
and I watched an eagle as it was flying
and he said someday I hope you get the chance
to live like you were dying.
To live like you were dying
To live like you were dying
To live like you were dying

> "The most remarkable thing about death is its insistence on harvesting life's meaning, even in those not prone to intro-spection."
> — Joan Borysenko

Now you're ready to write *your* legacy letter about *your* dying. Let yourself mingle the riches of your own reflections and the gifts legacy writers have shared with you. Listen to your inner voice and hold your angel(s) close as you dig deeply and fly high. May you be blessed with self-acceptance and gratitude for the blessings of your life as you write.

Before we are finished, please turn the page to what I've called the "Afterword" to wrap up the loose ends. (My superstitious nature would not let me write the final chapter as chapter 13, but that's really what the Afterword is.)

Afterword
Wrapping Up Loose Ends

Before we can wrap up loose ends and celebrate our rich harvest, there's one more legacy letter that needs to be written. Throughout this book we've written legacy letters that are ethical wills, wills of values, aware that they aren't legal documents. Then in chapter 11, we wrote legacy letters to accompany our advance health directives to personalize that legal document and initiate conversation about end of life care with our loved ones.

To complete our work we need to write a legacy letter to accompany our legal wills, the document that passes on our valuables, assigning property and our material things.

Letters to Accompany our Wills

What makes a will and this letter difficult is that most of us are not at all comfortable with money. There are many print resources and financial experts available to help us, (the best of them in my not-so-humble opinion is *My Financial Legacy*, a monograph I wrote to help women in particular think about their values as they relate to money. It also provides assistance to consider the myriad of questions that need to be answered, including how to find expert and compassionate financial advisors.)

The need for all of us to demystify money, to include money in family conversations is corroborated by Ted Beck, president for the National Endowment for Financial Education (NEFE). Their mission as a nonprofit foundation is to inspire empowered financial decision making for individuals and families.

> **"If I could wave a magic wand and have one wish, it'd be that parents and kids could sit down and have a candid conversation about money."** — Ted Beck

Anticipating our own needs and desires, deciding how much and to which loved ones to leave money, and leaving money or property to charitable causes are the biggest decisions. Once we've decided what we want to do with our money, whether we have lots or only a little, we need to find and build trusting relationships with professional advisors to help us complete the legal document.

Like with our health directives, a legal will is just that. There's no place in it to explain why we've made the decisions we have. There's no place in a will to clarify our hopes that the family not be pulled apart by what might seem inequities to them. There's no place to write about the values that accompany passing forward the family homestead, the farm, the cabin. There's no place to tell the stories of the heirlooms being divided.

These topics are appropriate to write in a legacy letter to accompany our wills. The same purposes for the letters we wrote to accompany our health directives apply here. We want to personalize the legal document and initiate family conversations: this time about the financial decisions we've designated in our legal wills.

Americans are a generous people. We give over eight billion volunteer hours annually. More than ninety percent of us give annually to charity. But only ten to fifteen percent of us make charitable gifts in our wills for perpetuity. Yet this is one more way to leave a legacy that makes a difference, leaving the world a better place because we've been here.

Our tendency to give of ourselves is only a hop, skip, and jump from giving money, so it's no surprise that we want our legacies to include making a difference in our world. Our legacy letters will have an impact and so will our financial gifts.

Reflection

Consider any question here that makes an impression on you: as something to be explored, something that would lead you to financial decisions imprinted from the perspective of your legacy. You can file this writing in your Legacy File for later consideration or for a planning meeting with your attorney or financial advisor.

- How much money do you want to leave to your family: some, most, or all of it? Be as candid and truthful as you can be with yourself.
- Consider how you will distribute your money among your heirs. Take into account: age, a child with special needs, a child more successful than your others. Consider how these factors influence your decisions about inheritance. In this world of blended families, will you differentiate between your own children and your stepchildren?
- If you distribute the money equally, what are your reasons? If you divide the inheritance according to need or other considerations, what issues might this raise among your heirs?
- Are you envisioning gifting a portion of your financial legacy to people other than your children and grandchildren? Nieces, nephews, nonrelatives? On what basis will you make this decision?

- What values do you want to pass on with your money?
  Do you want to influence the use of the inherited money?
  Do you want to ensure that a portion of the inheritance is
  tithed annually to charitable causes?
- Is this money an outright gift? Is it a reward for your loved ones'
  values and achievements? How would you feel if one or more of
  your heirs failed to handle their inheritance in a responsible
  way? Why do you want your heirs to have this money?
- How do you want to distribute this money, in one payment
  or a planned amount over time? Will you designate trustees
  to oversee distribution? Will you set the money aside until
  your heirs reach a certain age? Will you distribute part or all
  of this money before your death?
- How might this inheritance complicate your loved ones' values
  or life challenges?
- Will you leave a portion of your estate to charitable causes?
  Which ones and why? This may be an opportunity to inform
  your family of what matters most to you. It will also inform
  younger generations about your value of helping those less
  fortunate than yourself.

> **"How wonderful it is that nobody need wait a single moment before starting to improve the world."** — **Anne Frank**

Wrapping Up Loose Ends

Now we can wrap up loose ends, answering questions we may have had since we wrote our first blessing letter in chapter 2. Questions to be answered before we celebrate include: What's the best way to edit my legacy letters? How should my letters look? How can I organize my legacy letters – should I think of each individually or gather them to make one document, my ethical will? What are the best ways to preserve my legacy documents? What should I do with all the reflective writing and process notes and letters I've decided not to share with others? When and how should I share my legacy letters?

What's the best way to edit our legacy letters?

We've considered editing throughout this book; here is a summary of earlier editing suggestions from chapters 2, 4, 6, and 11:

Begin by recommitting to the purpose for legacy writing. It's not about perfection or publication. It *is* about preserving and transmitting our learning and love to the next generation. It *is* about finding our voices to express our authentic selves; it *is* about confirming that our words convey our message and the meaning of our blessings.

After writing a legacy letter, set the letter aside overnight or for a few days. After we and our letters have rested (time may offer a fresh perspective or more detailed memories), we can edit with fresh eyes.

These questions may help as we read our letters aloud to ourselves: Is this a blessing, or have I used the words "May you..." to disguise an instruction, a demand, or a command? Have I used words that don't seem quite right, or words that don't sound like me? We can use the dictionary, a thesaurus, a synonym finder or search online to find the word that most clearly and compellingly expresses our message. The last thing we want is for the recipient to believe we copied our legacy letters from some book!

The purpose of all legacy writing is to pass forward our love and our learning. We don't want to mistake love and learning for sugar coating and dishonesty. Many of our legacy letters are serious; their content expresses the truths of our experiences and our learning from them. But (and this is a big but!) we want to discern and accept reality. Expressing your reality speaks love too.

And now to the tone of our legacy letters: Legacy letters may express difficult truths, but should not be vehicles to vent personal resentments, bitterness, or anger. A more appropriate place for these feelings is a personal journal. We can't control how our words will be received or interpreted. We can only do our best to write from our hearts remembering the intention of the Buddhist maxim to "do no harm."

> **"Tell me I'll forget, show me, I may remember, but involve me and I'll understand."**   **— Chinese Proverb**

In short

- Use words that clarify what you want understood and that sound like you. Remember, no style is better for your writing than *your* style.
- Choose vocabulary appropriate to the age of your intended reader.
- * Make sure your tone is consistent with your message.
- Assess how you would feel if you were receiving the letter you'd written by reading the letter aloud. Imagine that you are the recipient of the letter; what's your response to it?
- * Break any rules you've read here to make your letter *your* own!

How should my legacy letters look?

Not only should your legacy letters sound like you, but they should look like you too. We all have unique handwriting. I suggest that at least some of our letters be handwritten on acid-free paper. We highlight the significance when our letters are written in our own hand: This special communication isn't subject to deletion with a casual click. Though many letters may be handwritten, others may be written using newer technology. For preservation purposes, all handwritten letters should be safeguarded with computer copies. It's not unusual for someone having misplaced a letter to approach a legacy letter writer, asking for another copy.

How should I organize and preserve my legacy letters?

There is no one right way to preserve your legacy. Hopefully, you've kept copies of all the legacy letters and documents you've written (anticipating that you will continue to write more for the rest of your life).

For the copies of letters already shared with loved ones, you can keep a paper copy in a folder, file, or binder. A computer folder of those letters is a second copy preserved on a disc, a drive, in the cloud, or technology yet to be invented. Some people choose to publish a small book (easily created and accessible through many online companies) with copies for family and loved ones. With this choice, retrospective photos can add texture to your letters. Others have recorded their legacy writing on audio or video. For one of my daughter's birthday letters, I lined both sides of each page with pictures of her corresponding to the content in each paragraph.

What should I do with the reflective writing, process notes, and letters I've decided not to share?

The writings preserved in your Legacy File (on paper or an electronic device), I suggest you treat as you would a personal journal.

> *I continue to feel conflicted as I de-clutter and clean out my closets about how much and how long to save materials I consider personal. At this time in my life, when I'm continuing to write legacy letters regularly, I'm keeping my reflections and ideas, but I don't necessarily want them read. In case my life ends without time to prepare, I have marked the front of my Legacy File: PERSONAL; Please destroy without reading. I hope this will make things easier for those left with the responsibility of cleaning out the closets I've left behind.*

When and how should I share my legacy letters with my loved ones?

The consideration here is how to prepare your loved ones, and present them with the legacy letters you've written for them. As each of us is unique, so will be each legacy letter written.

You may write with a special purpose in mind that will provide its timetable. There are no rules, except to search your own heart to decide when to offer the letter. When you write to mark a particular occasion or transition in your life or the life of a dear one, the occasion or event will dictate the time to share.

You may write other legacy letters that you want preserved but not given until the end of your life or even after your death. Once you've placed these letters in their carefully addressed envelopes, preserve them in a safety deposit box, a home safe with your other valuable papers, or on your computer (carefully labeled) with a back up. Be sure someone knows of their existence, their whereabouts, and how to access them.

While co-presenting a legacy program with another professional, she asked me if I'd ever had her experience: two legacy writers mailed letters to grown children living in different parts of the country. One set of children didn't respond; they never mentioned that they'd received the letter. The other set of children called immediately, believing the letter was their mother's way of announcing that she was dying.

I've not had that experience in my work, because I caution legacy letter writers that their letters should not arrive as a surprise. It's wise to let loved ones know about the legacy writing you're doing, and to tell them you'll be presenting them with letters. Some legacy writers make the presentation a special moment of celebration: inviting recipients for tea, a glass of wine, or for a special meal.

Celebrating Life

As we come to the end of *Your Legacy Matters*, let's take a moment to review the universal needs we all experience. These include: being connected, being known, being remembered, making a difference, blessing others and being blessed, and celebrating Life. Having these needs addressed is the unexpected gift we receive as we fulfill the purpose of legacy writing: being the link between the generations, as we express our love and learning in legacy letters to loved ones and to the future.

Writing legacy letters to punctuate and commemorate the special occasions in our loved ones' lives is a way to celebrate life. It can be as simple as writing a personal blessing for a nephew, great-aunt, grandchild, friend or colleague to recognize special occasions in their lives: birthday, new job, new baby or marriage. Celebration may take the form of a full legacy letter of reminiscence to honor a parent's 80th birthday, a child's graduation from high school or college.

Remember when we explored "cleaning out our closets" in chapter 10 – we found that young people today are less interested in our 'stuff' than in our values. Legacy letters celebrating loved ones will be treasured long after the 'stuff' has disappeared.

> **"When you move your focus from competition to contribution, life becomes a celebration."**   **— Buddha**

Gratitude

We can explore the idea of Celebrating Life by reflecting on all we have to be grateful for, the abundance of our lives. Gratitude can be a touchstone to keep us focused and fulfilled, aware of the value of a pause to experience the abundance in our lives.

> **"There are two ways to live your life—one is as though nothing is a miracle, the other is as though everything is a miracle."**
> **— Albert Einstein**

Linda Hallen, a legacy writer from Cable, Wisconsin, expressed her gratitude for her "back twenty" on the land her family has farmed for generations:

"You have been there for me, this land, through all the last goodbyes and divorce, death, life-changes. You listen, you don't judge; you nurture and welcome me home with open branches. Yes, like me, you've endured storms, sudden blasts of lightning, the weight of snow, the pelt of rain, the power and sometimes destruction of wind. You've changed your form and so have I. We've aged, died, created new life and new paths. When I come and sit in my vortex spot over the lake in the chair that is always there— you are there with me, the plant and animal spirits, our shared history and a lifetime of love.

"Thank you, precious Cable land, for your consistency and your strength, your ghosts, welcomes, goodbyes, and memories."

Drs. Michael McCullough and Robert Emmons, of Southern Methodist University and UC Davis, conducted research projects on Gratitude, and found that daily gratitude exercises resulted in increased levels of alertness, enthusiasm, determination, optimism and energy. They also noted that people who feel grateful are more likely to feel loved and to do acts of kindness, since one act of gratitude encourages another.

From gratefulness.org come these suggestions to increase our awareness of the blessings of our lives. You might consider choosing one, just one, of these activities to remind you of gratefulness for the next week:

- Say "thank you" for the present moment five times each day.
- Do one random act of kindness for a stranger each day. Have fun doing it!
- Write "thank you" notes to friends, family or co-workers just because.
- Each time you write in your personal journal name five things you're grateful for, focusing on people, events, and the natural world.
- Call someone, send a text or an email, take someone out to lunch or for coffee and express your gratitude.
- Practice "beauty gratitude." Look for the beauty around you when walking or driving. Take time to absorb and connect with that beauty.
- Keep a "gratitude rock" in your pocket to remind you to be grateful when you touch it.

"The miracle of gratitude is that it shifts your perception to such an extent that it changes the world you see."
— Dr. Robert Holden

Reflection

Here are some suggestions for writing about your experience doing one of these exercises: Did it add to your experience of gratitude? Did you see, hear, smell, taste more beauty? Did you feel less isolated or more connected to others, to the human race, to our planet?

After this reflection, take time to write one last legacy letter for now: one that expresses gratitude for our blessings, communicates abundance, celebrates our lives and the Life we've been given, and awakens new dreams for ourselves and future generations.

Looking Toward the Future

As we come to the end of this long, sometimes arduous journey together, every day a journey of purpose and fulfillment, I am grateful for this work that I am privileged to be a messenger of. I am grateful for being able to plant legacy seeds and harvest love and lessons. I am grateful for the generosity of all the legacy thinkers and writers who have contributed to this book in so many ways. I am forever grateful for the blessings of my life, most especially my children and grandchildren, all nine my teachers. I am grateful for my life, filled with purpose, for my learning from relationships with interesting people. I am deeply grateful for the privilege of intimate friendships. I am grateful for my willingness to learn, to grow, and to change. I continue to be grateful daily for my health and the length of my days. I am eternally grateful for the wisdom of my faith and Al-Anon; both sustain me every day. I am grateful for humor and joy, for beauty, and finally for love.

> **"If the only prayer you ever say in your entire life is thank you, it will be enough."**   **— Meister Eckhart**

As we part ways, know that your loved ones will be enriched by your legacies. Your blessings will teach them love. The stories about your ancestors will fill the gaps in their history. Your values, expressed through your stories and learning, will help them know you and will inspire them in joyful and troubled times.

This prayer, written by Judith Z. Abrams, always awakens the gratitude in my heart:

> God of goodness, we give thanks
> for the gift of life, wonder beyond words,
> for the awareness of soul, our light within;
> for the world around us, so filled with beauty;
> for the richness of the earth, which day by day sustains us;
> for all these and more, we offer thanks.

To conclude *Your Legacy Matters* I want all of you legacy writers to know how much I appreciate you: for your legacy work, for your daring thinking and deeply-felt writing, and most of all for your generosity to those who will come after you. Here is my blessing to you:

May your life continue to be blessed with abundance as you share with those who matter most to you. May your legacy be an eternal link between you and those you love, between you and the generations who came before you, and between you and the generations who will come after you.

Appendices

Appendix A: Three Historic Ethical Wills

1. Sholom Aleichem, the pen name of Solomon Rabinowitz, (1859-1916) requires no introduction to readers of Yiddish, or the many languages into which his works have been translated. What is not widely known is that Sholom Aleichem spent his last years in New York, where he died in 1916. Mourned by 150,000 people, young and old lined the streets at his funeral. His will was read into the Congressional Record, and published in *The New York Times*, which called it one of the great ethical wills in history.

To be opened and published on the day of my death: New York, 11 Tishre, 5675 (September 19, 1915)

Today a great misfortune has befallen my family: my elder son, Misha Michael Rabinowitz, has died and taken with him into the grave a part of my own life. It remains for me now to redraw my will ... which consists of ten points:

1. Wherever I may die, let me be buried not among the rich and famous, but among plain Jewish people, the workers, the common folk, so that my tombstone may honor the simple graves around me, and the simple graves honor mine, even as the plain people honored their folk writer in his lifetime.
2. No titles or eulogies are to be engraved on my tombstone, except the name Sholom Aleichem on one side and the Yiddish Inscription, herein enclosed, on the other.
3. Let there be no arguments or debates among my colleagues who may wish to memorialize me by erecting a monument in New York. I shall not be able to rest peacefully in my grave if my friends engage in such nonsense. The best monument for me will be if my books are read, and if there should be among our affluent people a patron of literature who will publish and distribute my works in Yiddish or in other languages, thus enabling the public to read me and my family

to live in dignity. If I haven't earned this in my lifetime, perhaps I may earn it after my death. I depart from the world with complete confidence that the public will not abandon my orphans.

4. At my grave, and throughout the whole year, and then every year on the anniversary of my death, my remaining son and my sons-in-law, if they are so inclined, should say *kaddish* for me. And if they do not wish to do this, or if it is against their religious convictions, they may fulfill their obligation to me by assembling together with my daughters and grandchildren and good friends to read this testament and also to select one of my stories, one of the really merry ones, and read it aloud in whatever language they understand best, and let my name rather be remembered by them with laughter than not at all.

5. My children and children's children can have whatever beliefs or convictions they will. But I beg of them to guard their Jewish heritage. If any of them reject their origins to join a different faith, then that is a sign they have detached themselves from my will "and they shall have no portion and inheritance among their brethren."

6. (Here Sholom Aleichem apportions the royalties from his books and plays among his family, and for his two grand-daughters' marriage dowries.)

7. From the incomes mentioned in the above paragraph, a sum shall be set aside for a foundation for Jewish authors (writing in Yiddish and Hebrew) of: 5% up to 5000 rubles a year; 10% if more than 5000 rubles. Should such a foundation exist at that time in the United States or in Europe, let this contribution be given annually to it...But if such a foundation should not exist, or if one should be established that would not meet my wishes as set forth in this paragraph, then the money shall be distributed to needy writers by my heirs directly, as they may agree among themselves.

8. (He speaks here of a stone to be placed over Misha's grave in Copenhagen, where he died, *kaddish* said for him, and money given to the poor).

9. (He asks that his works be not sold in perpetuity and arranges for his family to have a permanent income from them).

10. My last wish for my successors and my prayer to my children: Take good care of your mother, beautify her old age, sweeten her bitter life, heal her broken heart; do not weep for me—on the contrary,

remember me with joy; and the main thing—live together in peace, bear no hatred for each other, help one another in bad times, think on occasion of other members of the family; pity the poor, and when circumstances permit, pay my debts, if there be any. Children, bear with honor my hard-earned Jewish name and may God in Heaven sustain you ever. Amen.

Sholom Ben Menahem Nahum Rabinowitz,

Sholom Aleichem

Appended to the will is his Epitaph, like the text of the will written by him in Yiddish, and engraved on his tombstone in the Workmen's Circle plot in Mt. Carmel Cemetery in Brooklyn, NY.

> Here lies a plain and simple Jew
> Who wrote in plain and simple prose;
> Wrote humor for the common folk
> To help them to forget their woes.
>
> He scoffed at life and mocked the world,
> At all its foibles he poked fun,
> Forgetting troubles of their own,
> The world went on its merry way,
> And left him stricken and undone.
>
> And while his grateful readers laughed,
> Forgetting troubles of their own,
> Midst their applause—God only knows—
> He wept in secret and alone.

Source for Judah ibn Tibbon and Eleazar ben Samuel HaLevi's ethical wills: Medieval Sourcebook: www.fordham.edu Jewish Ethical Wills, 12th to 14th centuries

2. Judah ibn Tibbon, born in Granada, migrated to Lunel, in southern France. He was a cultured and wealthy man (at least in ownership of many books, prior to the printing press). He lived from approximately 1160 C.E. His Ethical Will to his son (Samuel ibn Tibbon, a student of medicine and Torah) is a strong admonition, expressing disappointment in Samuel, and a hope that he will "repent" of his "youthful indolence."

But most of Judah's attention focused on books, providing his son an "extensive library" relieving him of "the necessity to borrow books." Judah wrote of their care, in more detail than his instruction about Samuel's wife, calling them his son's "treasure." He spent much time discussing to whom they should be lent, how to check them in and out on a list when borrowed, how to catalogue them so as not to waste time looking for a reference, honoring the notes that Judah had put within the pages, and how to keep them clean and safe from moisture and animals.

He concluded his will with the following:

"I enjoin on you, my son, to read this, my testament, once daily at morn or at eve. Apply your heart to the fulfillment of its behests, and to the performance of all therein written. Then wilt you make your ways prosperous, then shall you have good success."

3. Eleazar ben Samuel HaLevi of Mainz, Germany, died 1357, was unusual in his time; he wrote to both his sons and daughters. He stressed most of all silence ... as a way to be saved from slander, falsehood, scandal and frivolity, warning them also not to listen to gossip. He stressed honesty in all dealings, tithing and never turning away a poor person. He suggested that they should live in communities, not isolated from other Jews, so that their sons and daughters may learn the ways of Judaism. The most amazing thing is that he says that "the young of both sexes [should not] go without instruction in the Torah," even if they would have to borrow money to pay for a teacher!

Most amazing are the details of what he wants after his death: no funeral oration, carry his body not on a bier, but in a coach, wash him and prepare his body to be clean as how he went clean to synagogue every Sabbath. About his burial, he writes:

"At a distance of thirty cubits from the grave, they shall set my coffin on the ground, and drag me to the grave by a rope attached to the coffin. Every four cubits they shall stand and wait awhile, doing this in all seven times, so that I may find atonement for my sins. [hibbut ha-keber ... symbolic punishment to atone for sins committed during a life time.] Put me in the ground at the right hand of my father...."

Appendix B:
Template for Writing a One-Page Legacy Blessing Letter

No matter the content a template provides a structure to make writing legacy letters easier. A letter written in one page, writing for no more than fifteen minutes can be accomplished in four paragraphs. Here is the template:

Context:
Paragraph 1: Provide history and context. One of my mentors once said, "All texts have a context." We are seldom aware that the context beyond our personal lives affects us. The time when family history was contained in a family Bible and passed down from generation to generation is long gone. An opening paragraph providing a context for what follows gives the reader a snippet of family history and a snapshot of the historical times and enriches what follows.

Story:
Paragraph 2: Tell the story. All of us have a sacred story, and all of us want to tell our stories. It is by writing our stories that we feel known and have a sense of belonging. The "story" may be about most anything that you want to preserve and pass on: a memory of an ancestor (remember Dora Klayman's memory of her grandfather in chapter 4, page 48). It might be a story that illustrates a value that you want to pass forward to the future. It could be the story including why it is precious of something material that you want to give someone (remember Aunt Ginny's letter about the diamond ring in chapter 10, page 153). It could be an apology (remember the mother's amend to her son and daughter in chapter 9, page 136).

Learning:
Paragraph 3: The story is not as meaningful as it can be unless you write what you learned from your experience. State the lesson learned. Learning from our experience is often defined as wisdom. It's this learning with the story that we want to preserve and pass forward to future generations along with our love.

Blessing:

Paragraph 4: Offer a blessing. Your blessing flows naturally to your loved ones from your story and your learning. We experience being blessed as we bless future generations. We're not always aware of the importance of being blessed, but we all need blessings from our elders. The ancient ethical will was extracted from the story of Jacob blessing his twelve sons as he lay dying at the end of the book of Genesis (49). That same Jacob earlier had stolen his father Isaac's blessing from his older brother Esau. Esau's response was a plea to his father, in my opinion the most poignant words in Genesis: (27:38) "'Have you but one blessing, my father? Bless me, even me also' .... And Esau lifted up his voice and wept."

We never outgrow our need for blessings!

Appendix C:
Template for Writing a One-Page Legacy Love Letter to Our Children

**for parents whose children
are celebrating a major life event**

Reflect about and write one paragraph corresponding to the five topics. Craft a legacy letter that includes some or all of the exploratory information you've written to honor your child and mark and celebrate this moment in their lives.

The range of experiences includes confirmations, graduations, new jobs, marriages, momentous birthdays from 18 to 50, and more. [Note the blessing letter I wrote to my daughter marking her 40th birthday in Appendix D]

An example of an occasion when you likely have much to say and it might be better heard after reflection and writing is when your child passes the driver's test, and experiences the freedom and responsibility of "wheels".

1. Remember yourself at the age of your child: your thrills and disappointments, your challenges – excitement and fears, your interests and priorities, how you spent your days, what your personal space and neighborhood were like, your school experience, your friends, mentors and angels and what you learned from them. Write a paragraph about what meant most *to you* at that time in your life.

2. Reflect about moments, events, times when you were most proud of your child in the last year or two: describe it, articulate the quality in them that you were proud to see - write a paragraph that includes your appreciation of the effort and preparation they made to arrive at this historic moment in their life.

3. Recall and write an anecdote or story that highlights a positive quality that is a gift your child possesses and is developing, refining, using well. Indicate how you imagine that quality will be of use to your child as he takes the next steps in life.

4. Use a story or a quotation to illustrate a challenge facing your child in their life. With compassion, support, and understanding, but not judgment, write a paragraph that acknowledges the struggle and how you see them meeting the challenge. (This may seem difficult, but we need to be real and acknowledge their challenges as well as their gifts if our children are to trust us and our words.)

5. Finally craft a blessing to your child marking this moment or life event and expressing your love (as the child moves forward).

Using all or some of the exploratory information you've written, craft a legacy letter (to be sent and/or read aloud) for your child.

Appendix D:
Letter to My Daughter on Her 40th Birthday

April 7, 2010

Dear Debbie, my beloved daughter,

On this auspicious occasion, your 40th birthday, I celebrate you with this illustrated letter: to reflect on the part of your life that includes me and our relationship, to indulge in memory and appreciation and to express my feelings and thoughts about all I so love about you.

First some snapshots etched literally and photographically in my mind forever.

Beginning at the moment of your birth -- seeing your head emerge into Dr. Meeker's hands (holding my breath with hope that you were a girl) asking him if you were a girl. Before he could see for sure, he assured me by saying you had long delicate fingers, a sure sign that you were a girl. I was ecstatic, even though I joked at your low weight, suggesting that if you were a chicken on sale at Lunds you'd be left at the meat counter because you had -- besides a beautiful head, hands and proportions -- little meat on your thighs. But from that beginning, you were my much wanted girl, the moon maiden.

You were always on the go, like a whirlwind and then I'd find you fast asleep in a doll bed, on the living room floor, or in your tiger toy box. One day when you were about four I sent you to clean up your room and a half hour later I found you there, sitting in the midst of the mess, paralyzed and in tears. You said you didn't know what to do; it was just too much. I sat down with you, and we made four piles: one to throw away, one to give away, one to keep, and one to decide about later. Soon we were done; you were all smiles again and ready to play. We could see your bright yellow carpet, and you had room to cartwheel again. Today you are a superb organizer, whether the challenge is a closet, a house, or a corporation, and you do it with that "cartwheeling" spirit with which you face all the challenges in your life.

My next memories of you are more diffuse as to place, because it was everywhere -- our front yards, the empty of furniture living room on Hilloway, the SF ocean beach, or anywhere there was a space and a moment for you to express joy in your body and in life -- you, cartwheeling -- everywhere and anywhere. It still makes me smile to see you moving simultaneously with such discipline and abandon.

It's interesting that my memories are few between the cartwheeling girl and you going to college, excepting always being so proud of you and your work ethic and hard-won achievements, whether in academics or gymnastics (and you continue to give 110% in everything you do.) Snapshot memories include: you sitting sadly and solemnly on the stairs at the Institute and my not having the courage to stand up for you; you coming downstairs crying because one of the two tops I bought you had to stay home from school; your sense of justice and worrying about having two pairs of mittens when there were kids with none; being cured of your nightmares after we visualized you protected by your "pajarmor"; calling for me in the voice that pierced my heart when Sid was torturing you; your pleasure when we got you a balance beam for your room on Vincent; your courage after being attacked and me putting you into the bathtub that late afternoon and worrying about your sexuality and men and more than anything, I didn't want that damaged in you; laying on the floor in the front hall all night during the rain that flooded our house on Cedar Lake Pkwy because I was afraid the house might implode and you couldn't get comfortable because of the cast on your arm.

Looking back, I know that those young years were particularly painful in your life and mine. Often I focused not on you or my parenting, but on things outside family, like work, where I was respected and felt appreciated and accomplished. I have often told you how sorry I am for having neglected you. I know you've forgiven me as much as you can, and for that I'm grateful. I so regret that I wasn't available to you in the ways you needed then. I know I can't change the past or its hurts, but I do my best to be present to you in your life today.

Beyond my memories and admiration for your beauty, grace, and fierce competitiveness in gymnastics is your persistence and courage through pain, working to return to the gym after your knee surgery. I remember our healing week together in your dorm room before you returned to class on crutches -- you, me, the foam block, pain pills, and me racing to get the Heartmates 10 Healthy Hints written -- which even today remind me of that sweet time with you.

I so appreciate being your teacher, but even more you being mine: the best lesson when you called me crying from Missou and had to stop my suggestions when you explained straight-out that you'd called not for advice, but so that I'd listen to you cry. Sometimes I still get to do that, and feel blessed every time you give me the opportunity to love you in that way. You've taught me other significant things as well: about graciousness, about controlling contempt and being tolerant of others, and about not saying every opinion that flies through my head without considering how it might affect someone else. Of you being brave enough to confront me when I hurt your feelings or do something thoughtless, so I have the chance to apologize, learn about you and how we're different, and that our love is deepened and not threatened because of my imperfections.

Thinking of intimate times, our trips -- first to NY where we shopped til we dropped. And now I'm overwhelmed with the myriad of memories of your post-college trip. The moments I see first involve water. The first: us standing shivering in the rain in Warsaw seeing Chana and Minna and Deborah together on the wall at the Umshlagplatz (regretting I'd not been wiser when you'd come in from playing on Hilloway and mentioned playing with Chana and Minna. I wish I'd asked more detail about them when they were more present to you). Then leaving Sefat that cold rainy afternoon and "temporarily" staying at the Crusader castle -- your tears about being a good sport, but wanting a hot bath and a warm hotel room in Haifa. Being taught how to float in the Dead Sea by the man who looked like God. Watching you swim with dolphins at Eilat.

I loved every minute being with you, sharing discoveries, having adventures and misadventures (ah, the misadventures -- waiting for a taxi in a deserted Arab town at dusk, the wild dawn taxi ride to catch our missed train out of Krakow, our experience of sitting over what may have been a bomb in the Jerusalem bus station). Sharing the pain of experiencing Auschwitz and Yad Vashem. Experiencing the history of our people: feeling the pride in our people and our awe in all Israel had accomplished in such a few short years -- and doing all that emotional experience together.

Those weeks remain a highlight of my life, and I thank you for sharing them with me: the beauty of the Dead Sea Scrolls and the museums, the learning at the Diaspora Museum and everywhere we visited. We can't forget the falafel sandwiches and the Israeli breakfasts. The surprise of coming upon the woman in the Krakow cemetery we thought was the Virgin Mary when we were doing rubbings of the stones.

Returning home to begin collecting sheep for your engagement celebration, and spending time together planning your wedding (all the more thrilling to me because I'd not had a beautiful wedding or a relationship with my mother that would have allowed that). The day we went to the hotel sale and found your beautiful wedding dress -- the rose petals, sampling the food at the top of the IDS, every detail of the wedding so impeccably you.

That transition in both our lives - you becoming a woman, a writer and professional, a wife and mother, over these past 15 or so years and me becoming too -- building a new life for myself post-marriage, and always feeling supported by you. Our intimacy keeps evolving - from mother-child, to mother-mother, companion and friend. I appreciate that in your busy life you make time for us to be together. It's a weekly highlight for me. And I think I've finally learned what you tried to teach me in college -- that you know what to do, you'll ask for my advice when you want it, but that you want me to listen to you. And you listen to me too. What a gift both hearing you and being heard is. Thank you for that. I so treasure our relationship as it is, has been, and who knows what it will yet become.

And you continue to amaze me in so many ways with your astounding and ever-developing talents: as an artist (you should sell it), your home decoration and hostess creativity, your party ideas, your ability to negotiate a full-time job and three active kids, finding time to help them, drive them, read to them, and be a wonderful partner/helpmate with your Jed. (I'm sure I'm leaving something out -- forgive me quick and please don't be hurt by my omissions.)

Sweet daughter, who teaches me today and supports me today in equal measure as I teach and support you. I feel so blessed, and know that we've worked hard on our relationship for a long time, and we're harvesting the benefits of our effort.

I think you know, but I want to tell you in writing how proud I am of you. You are a thoughtful, sensitive, and courageous woman, a superb mother, wife, professional, and server in the Jewish community and beyond. I have only one complaint - that you've not yet read *The Source* - maybe you'll have time and inclination in the next forty years; I sure hope so!

So, my dear peapod, it's your 40th birthday, may it be a happy one... gather all of who you've been and what you've done, and tuck it into the pocket of your heart as you begin a new decade. I pray for you a long fulfilling life, gratitude for your blessings, intimate reciprocal relationships, meaningful work, joy in all that you do, great dignity in who you are, and awe for the miracles in and around you.

I love you more deeply than I ever imagined forty years ago when I first held you, and I will hold you in my heart forever.

Mom

Bibliography

Angelou, Maya. *Letter to My Daughter*. NY: Random House, 2008.

Antin, Mary. *The Promised Land*. NY: Penguin Classics, Centennial Edition, 2012.

Arrien, Angeles. *The Second Half of Life: Opening the Eight Gates of Wisdom*. Boulder, CO: Sounds True, Inc. 2005.

Baines, Barry K., MD. *Ethical Wills: Putting Your Values on Paper*. Cambridge, MA: De Capo Press, 2006.

Bastian, Edward W. and Tina L. Staley. *Living Fully, Dying Well: Reflecting on Death to Find Your Life's Meaning*. Boulder, CO: Sounds True, Inc. 2009.

Bergoglio, Jorge Mario and Abraham Skorka. *On Heaven and Earth: Pope Francis on Faith, Family, and the Church in the 21st Century*. NY: Image/Knopf Doubleday, 2013.

Brin, Ruth F. *Harvest: Collected Poems and Prayers*. Duluth, MN: Holy Cow Press, 1999.

Cohen, Norman J. *Self, Struggle & Change: Family Conflict: Stories in Genesis and Their Healing Insights for Our Lives*. Woodstock, VT: Jewish Lights, 1995.

Cowan, Lyn. *Tracking the White Rabbit*. NY: Routledge, Taylor & Francis Group, 2002.

Denny, Anne Elizabeth. *My Voice, My Choice: A Practical Guide to Writing a Meaningful Healthcare Directive*. Minneapolis, MN: Directives By Design, 2012.

Edelman, Marion Wright. *The Measure of Our Success: A Letter to My Children and Yours*. NY: William Morrow, 1993.

Eve, Nomi. *The Family Orchard*. NY: Alfred A. Knopf, 2000.

Geller, Laura. "Encountering the Divine Presence." From *Four Centuries of Jewish Women's Spirituality: A Sourcebook*. Boston: Beacon Press, 1992.

Glaser, Agathe Maier. *Agathe's Stories, A Child's Journey from Germany to America*. <saraglaser.com/agathes-stories.html>, 2011.

Glückel of Hameln. *The Memoirs of Glückel of Hameln*. Marvin Lowenthal, translator. NY: Schocken Books, 1977.

Griffin, Susan. *A Chorus of Stones*. NY: Anchor Books, 1993.

Grumbach, Doris. *Coming into the End* Zone. NY: W.W. Norton & Co., 1991.

Haley, Alex. *Roots: The Saga of an American Family*. NY: Doubleday, 1976.

Heilbrun, Carolyn G. *Writing a Woman's Life*. NY: Ballantine Books, 1988.

Herman, Judith, MD. *Trauma and Recovery*. NY: BasicBooks/Perseus, 1997.

Hoffman, Eva. *Lost in Translation: Life in a New Language.* NY: Penguin Books, 2001.

Kushner, Lawrence. *Honey From the Rock*. Woodstock, VT: Jewish Lights, 1990.

L'Engle, Madeleine. *Herself: Reflections on a Writing Life*. Compiled by Carole F. Chase. Colorado Springs, CO: Shaw Books (WaterBrook Press), 2001.

____. *Mothers and Daughters*. NY: Random House, Gramercy Books, 1997.

Laurence, Margaret. *The Stone Angel*. NY: Alfred A. Knopf, 1964.

Leider, Richard and David Shapiro. *Something to Live For*. San Francisco, CA: Berrett-Koehler, 2008.

Lessing, Doris. *The Summer before the Dark*. NY: Vintage Books, 1973.

Linn, Denise. *Sacred Legacies: Healing Your Past and Creating a Positive Future*. NY: Random House, Ballantine Publishing Group, 1998.

Janos Maté, "The Making of a Greenpeace Activist," *Reform Judaism,* Summer, 2013.

Mendelsohn, Daniel. *The Lost, A Search for Six of Six Million*. NY: HarperCollins, 2006.

Nouwen, Henri. *Life of the Beloved: Spiritual Living in a Secular World*. NY: The Crossroad Publishing Company, 1992.

Piercy, Marge. *The Art of Blessing the Day*. NY: Alfred A. Knopf, 1999.

Pipher, Mary, PhD. *Another Country: Navigating the Emotional Terrain of Our Elders*. NY: Riverhead Books, 1999.

____. *Writing to Change the World*. NY: Riverhead Books, 2006.

Plaskow, Judith, *Standing Again at Sinai: Judaism from a Feminist Perspective*. NY: Harper & Row, 1990.

Quindlen, Anna. *Lots of Candles, Plenty of* Cake. NY: Random House, 2012.

Reimer, Jack, and Nathaniel Stampfer, editors and annotaters. *So That Your Values Live On: Ethical Wills and How to Prepare Them*. Woodstock, VT: Jewish Lights, 1991.

Roiphe, Anne. *Generation without Memory*. NY: The Linden Press/Simon & Schuster, 1981.

Schneider, Pat. *How the Light Gets In, Writing as a Spiritual Practice*. NY: Oxford University Press, 2013.

_____. *Writing Alone and With Others*. NY: Oxford University Press, 2003.

Scott-Maxwell, Florida. *The Measure of My Days*. NY: Penguin Books, 1979.

Spangler, David. *Blessing: The Art and the Practice*. NY: Riverhead Books, 2001.

Strassfeld, Susan. *Everything I Know: Basic Life Rules from a Jewish Mother*. NY: Scribner, 1998.

Tan, Amy. *The Bonesetter's* Daughter. NY: G.P. Putnam, 2001.

Tana, Patti L. *Ask the Dreamer Where Night Begins*. Dubuque, Iowa: Kendall/Hunt Publishing, 1986.

Taylor, Daniel. *Creating a Spiritual Legacy: How to Share Your Stories, Values,* and *Wisdom*. Grand Rapids, MI: Brazos Press, 2011.

_____. *Letters to My Children: A Father Passes on His Values*. Downers Grove, Ill.: InterVarsity Press, 1989.

Tornstam, Lars, Ph.D. *Gerotranscendence*. New York: Springer Publishing Company, 2005.

_____. "Maturing Into Gerotranscendence," *The Journal of Transpersonal Psychology*. Vol. 43, No. 2, pp. 166-180, 2011.

Tuchscherer, Mary. *Ndu Ku Ona I See You With My Heart*. Oakland, CA: Azalea Art Press, 2012.

Turnbull, Susan B. *The Wealth of Your Life: A Step-by-Step Guide for Creating Your Ethical Will*. Wenham, MA: Benedict Press, 2005, Third Edition, 2012.

Tyrrell, Mary. *Become a Memoirist for Elders*. St. Paul, MN: Memoirs, Inc., 2012.

Weil, Andrew, MD. *Healthy* Aging. New York: Knopf, 2005.

_____. *Spontaneous Happiness*. New York: Little, Brown & Company, 2011.

Wiesel, Elie. *All Rivers Run to the Sea*. New York: Schocken Books, 1995.

Williamson, Marianne. *Everyday Grace: Having Hope, Finding Forgiveness, and Making Miracles*. New York: Riverhead Books, 2002.

_____. *A Woman's Worth*. New York: Ballantine Books, 1994.

Willis, Claire. *Lasting Words: A Guide to Finding Meaning Toward the Close of Life*. Brattleboro, VT: Green Writers Press, 2014.

Wright, Gretchen Brown. *The Chalk Circle: Intercultural Prizewinning Essays*. "Triptych: Paradise." pp. 121-135. Deadwood, Oregon: Wyatt-MacKenzie Publishing, 2012.

Index

How to pass down core beliefs, life lessons, personal stories, and hopes for the future - which truly define who women are - is a key area of planning missing in most financial plans. In order for financial advisors to be successful working with women investors, this work needs to precede the financial planning process, as does the conversation of understanding their relationship with money, which Rachael Freed's work informs so well.

—Kristan N. Wojnar, Third Quarter Advisers, Chicago, Illinois

Women's lives are too rarely the stuff of history, and even less of legacy. Freed gives us simple yet powerful tools to intentionally shape the inheritance we want to leave behind. She gives us a new rendering of history to reclaim the lineage and consequence of women's lives. Like every good sub-version of history, women's legacies will initiate and gain power in our living rooms and kitchens, our community centers and places of worship – anywhere that women gather.

—Bonnie Bazata, Executive Director, St. Joseph County Bridges Out of Poverty, South Bend, Indiana

The ethical will is a wonderful gift to leave to your family at the end of your life, but I think its main importance is what it can give you in the midst of your life. *Women's Lives, Women's Legacies* is invaluable: an inspiring and practical guide for crafting your own spiritual-ethical will to link you to your history, give purpose to your daily life, and communicate your legacies to those you love.

—Andrew Weil, M.D. author of *Healthy Aging: A Lifelong Guide to Your Physical and Spiritual Well-Being*

Using a deft combination of biblical theory, feminist analysis, moving quotations, and personal experience, Rachael Freed has produced a work that is both inspiring and practical. Writing exercises throughout the book allow Freed to accompany her readers in absentia, urging us onward as we consider what our spiritual legacies might be, pointing our thinking as we begin to formulate commentary designed to make our deepest wishes known to those most important in our lives. This is a thoroughly successful mapping for anyone remotely interested in shaping the values of a lifetime into "gifts" for the future.

—Toni A. H. McNaron, Distinguished Teaching Professor Emerita, University of Minnesota, and author of *I Dwell in Possibility: A Memoir*

Discovering the 'Heart of Philanthropy:' The term vocation was once defined as 'where your deep gladness meets a world's deep need.' Rachael Freed's vocation is to help people get in touch with their wisdom and values, then transfer these gifts to future generations. As a development officer who helps people shape their charitable giving, I have found Rachael's writing and teaching a valuable road map to help guide people on this very special journey in their lives.

—William K. Marsella, Director of Partner Relations, Catholic Community Foundation, St. Paul Minnesota

Provides women with all the tools they need to harvest the bounty of their lives for future generations. An invaluable resource for all women, no matter where in their life's journey they find themselves.

—Dr. Ellen Frankel, author of
The Five Books of Miriam: A Woman's Commentary on the Torah

Rachael Freed asks whether our beliefs, values, and family traditions will live on in the hearts of our loved ones, friends, and communities after our death. She invites us to create a spiritual-ethical will to do just that. Her book can help us, in a creative way, to do it today instead of waiting until it's too late.

—Fr. Dean V. Marek, Director, Chaplain Services, Mayo Clinic

This is a beautiful book with a soul. Rachael Freed has taken the concept of ethical wills and enhanced it, enlarged it, and made it accessible to women of all faiths. Her book is a tremendous legacy to others and provides a rich and most useful set of practical instructions for anyone who wants to pass on their values to future generations.

—Larry Raphael, senior rabbi at Sherith Israel, San Francisco, and former director of the Department of Adult Jewish Growth at the Union for Reform Judaism

I felt an urgent need to pass to my daughters not only my dreams for them and my values, but also the idea that these are the most important legacies I have. And it is crucial that this legacy be in writing, for writing is itself an act of faith.

—Wendy Schornstein Good, estate planning attorney

Women's Lives, Women's Legacies is a significant and meaningful contribution to the literature on spiritual legacies. This book will instill confidence in anyone wishing to undertake the creation of her spiritual-ethical will.

—Barry K. Baines, MD author of
Ethical Wills: Putting Your Values on Paper

Thank you on behalf of the Women of Beth Israel and the Jewish Community Women's Foundation for your stellar presentation about *Women's Lives, Women's Legacies*. Your wisdom, warmth, and spirituality touched each one of our seventy participants.

—Bonnie Graff
Program Director, Beth Israel Synagogue, San Diego

What a beautiful concept this is! And written so wisely, so softly, so beautifully. Creating a legacy of the thoughts, values and principles you have learned and live by, and then passing them on to loved ones is a truly significant way to understand and appreciate individual identities, to cement relationships, to inspire righteous living, and to leave a lasting legacy!

—Dr. Stephen R. Covey, author of
The 7 Habits of Highly Effective People **and**
The 8th Habit: From Effectiveness to Greatness

Women's Lives,Women's Legacies is a shining contribution to individuals and institutions concerned with the matter of cultural continuity. It is a thoughtful, well-written, caring book, a delight to read, a delight to follow. In detail and in form, it is friendly and accessible. It possesses a kind of 'god mother's' loving touch. In an intimate, lively, and learned way, Rachael Freed shows us how the use of a spiritual-ethical will may become the instrument of self-reflection and personal narrative. You do not have to think of yourself as a writer in order to be fruitfully guided by her exercises and examples into fashioning a kind of testament to your life. But beware: by the time you are done, you may realize you are more of a writer than you thought.

—Peter Pitzele author of
Our Fathers' Wells **and** *Scripture Windows*

About the Author

Rachael Freed, founder of Life Legacies, is a Senior Fellow at the University of Minnesota's Center for Spirituality and Healing, a Licensed Clinical Social Worker, and emeritus Marriage and Family Therapist.

She is the legacy consultant for LifeSprk (previously AgeWell), a Life-Care company in Minneapolis, and the legacy expert for Dr.Weil.com. Her writing about Legacy appears regularly on The Huffington Post Living - GPS for the Soul, DrWeil.com and LegacyConnect.com. She writes a monthly column (free email) Legacy Tips&Tools that can be subscribed to on <www.life-legacies.com>

A lecturer and workshop designer / facilitator, she consults to and delivers legacy programs for religious, philanthropic, and healthcare organizations. She has designed legacy programs specifically for succession planning and generally for wealth advisors / development officers in public and non-profit organizations. She leads legacy writing retreats and workshops for diverse individuals experiencing life transitions and questing for life purpose at every age.

She is the proud mother of two, Sid Levin, and Debbie Stillman, and a prouder grandmother of seven: Sophie, Mitch, Sam, Lily, Harry, Aidan, and Gigi.

Also by the Author . . .

*Women's Lives, Women's Legacies, Passing Your Beliefs
and Blessings to Future Generations*

*The Legacy Workbook for the Busy Woman:
A Step-by-Step Guide ...*

*Heartmates: A Guide for the Partner and Family of
the Heart Patient* (25th Anniversary Edition, 2012)

*The Heartmates Journal:
A Companion for Partners of People with Heart Disease*

Monthly Legacy Tips&Tools
Subscribe free (http://www.life-legacies.com/tips/index.html)

Contact for Programs, Presentations, Consultation

MinervaPress1@gmail.com
612-558-3331
Facebook: Life Legacies
(www.facebook.com/LifeLegacies)
LinkedIn: Rachael A. Freed
Twitter @legacy writing

XII - Legacy: Passing our blessings, values & love to future generations

14 - Blessing for a "messy house"
15 For a grandchild
16 For a birthday
18 4 paragraph template
38 - Tante Toby
* 48 - Tzedakah box memory "Be as generous as you can be"
* 49 - How to: Memory of Mom & me at the airport
How she let me "fly". Dad always cheerful
* 50 - Editing

CPSIA information can be obtained at www.ICGtesting.com
Printed in the USA
LVOW13s1243291213

367300LV00005B/542/P

9 780981 745053